MW01097735

Missionaries,
Converts,
and Rabbis

JEWISH CULTURE AND CONTEXTS

Published in association with the
Herbert D. Katz Center for Advanced Judaic Studies
of the University of Pennsylvania

Series Editors:
Shaul Magid, Francesca Trivellato, Steven Weitzman

A complete list of books in the series
is available from the publisher.

MISSIONARIES, CONVERTS, *AND* RABBIS

The Evangelical Alexander McCaul
and Jewish-Christian Debate
in the Nineteenth Century

DAVID B. RUDERMAN

PENN

UNIVERSITY OF PENNSYLVANIA PRESS

PHILADELPHIA

Publication of this volume was aided by a generous gift from the family
of Eleanor Meyerhoff Katz and Herbert D. Katz

Published by
University of Pennsylvania Press
Philadelphia, Pennsylvania 19104-4112
www.upenn.edu/pennpress

Printed in the United States of America on acid-free paper
1 3 5 7 9 10 8 6 4 2

Library of Congress Cataloging-in-Publication Data
ISBN 978-0-8122-5214-9

For Jonah, Gabriel, Sydney, Ella, and Caleb

CONTENTS

Introduction   1

Chapter 1. Portrait of an Evangelical Missionary to the Jews:
Alexander McCaul and His Assault on Rabbinic Judaism   13

Chapter 2. Sketches of Modern Judaism in McCaul's Other Writings   32

Chapter 3. From Missionizing the Jews to Defending
Biblical Inerrancy: The Last Years of McCaul's Life   47

Chapter 4. The Intellectual and Spiritual Journey of Stanislaus Hoga:
From Judaism to Christianity to Hebrew Christianity   67

Chapter 5. The Christian Opponents of McCaul and
the London Society: John Oxlee and Charlotte Elizabeth Tonna   81

Chapter 6. Moses Margoliouth: The Precarious Life
of a Scholarly Convert   110

Chapter 7. The Jewish Response to McCaul: Isaac Baer Levinsohn   142

Chapter 8. From Vilna to Aleppo: Two Additional Responses
to McCaul's Assault   165

Afterword   197

Appendix: A Sampling of Contemporary Christian Authors
Cited in Isaac Baer Levinsohn's Polemical Writings   205

Notes   209

Index   243

Acknowledgments   249

Introduction

This book examines a chapter in the history of Jewish-Christian relations in nineteenth- century Europe, focusing on one prominent cleric and several of his associates, both allies and opponents, engaged in a broad conversation about the nature of Christianity, Judaism, and their intertwined destinies in the past and present. The central figure, the Reverend Alexander McCaul (1799–1863), was one of the leaders of the Protestant evangelical organization the London Society for Promoting Christianity Amongst the Jews, and a prolific author and scholar on Judaism. Educated at Trinity College, Dublin, he became absorbed in the subject of Jews and Judaism and was sent as a missionary to Warsaw in 1821, where he studied Hebrew and rabbinic literature in depth. Over the next nine years, living at the epicenter of rabbinic culture in eastern Europe, he deepened his knowledge of rabbinic texts and of living and practicing Jews. Upon his return to London, he became the principal of the Hebrew College in East London, the primary educational institution of the London Society, and eventually became professor of Hebrew and rabbinic studies at King's College.

While McCaul and his fellow missionaries never succeeded in converting large numbers of Jews, they could always point to individuals who had come under their sway. Two Polish Jews who were deeply inspired by McCaul and considered him their spiritual mentor, at least initially, were Stanislaus Hoga (1791–1860) and Moses Margoliouth (1818–81). Hoga was converted by McCaul while still in Poland, accompanied him to London, and assumed a critical role in translating his major work against rabbinic Judaism into Hebrew. Only later in life did he sever his relationship with McCaul, openly criticize him and his missionary organization in print, and espouse a faith in Jesus still rooted in rabbinical law and practice. Margoliouth was not converted directly by McCaul but proudly acknowledged him as his primary teacher, even dedicating his first book against modern Judaism to the missionary. Despite his long career as an Anglican minister in various small parishes, Margoliouth openly displayed his cultural loyalty and personal affection for Jews and Judaism. Both converts were prolific scholars who thought deeply about Judaism and Christianity and attempted to explain and justify their own life choices in electing the Christian faith without fully relinquishing their Jewish one.

McCaul's highly conspicuous role as a leading missionary to the Jews elicited both admiration and disapproval from some of his Protestant contemporaries. Two of his detractors were the evangelicals John Oxlee (1779–1854) and Charlotte Elizabeth Tonna (1790–1846). Oxlee, the so-called rector of Molesworth, was a highly accomplished Hebraic scholar who devoted much of his scholarly life to revealing the intimate connections between Jewish and Christian doctrine. While he hoped, like McCaul, for the ultimate conversion of the Jews, he strongly protested the aggressive proselytizing tactics of the London Society. Intimately involved in conversations with Jewish intellectuals, he was perceived by some as a friend and ally, especially in defending their right to live as Jews and to follow rabbinic norms. Tonna, although not a close associate of Oxlee, adopted similar positions regarding the fate of Jews living in English society. Social reformer and editor of the *Christian Lady's Magazine*, she was a strong advocate of the restoration of the Jews to the Holy Land. And she objected strongly to the missionary tactics of the London Society and its denigration of the sanctity and integrity of Jewish religious life.

Even more defiant were McCaul's Jewish detractors. Among the not insignificant number of Jewish intellectuals who noticed and reacted to McCaul's missionary pursuits and his assault on the rabbis were three prominent Jewish figures who penned elaborate responses to him: Isaac Baer Levinsohn (1788–1860), Samuel Joseph Fuenn (1818–90), and Raphael Kassin (1818–71). The first two were major figures of the eastern European Haskalah, advocates of social and educational reform among their coreligionists, and highly learned Hebraic scholars. Levinsohn of Kremenetz, Ukraine, composed two books against McCaul, both published posthumously, defending rabbinic Judaism while attempting to undermine each of McCaul's arguments. Fuenn of Vilna completed his own substantial composition against McCaul but was unsuccessful in publishing it. Kassin, rabbi in Aleppo and Baghdad, published two books against McCaul, based on a still larger work that remained in manuscript, reacting to the impact of Protestant missionary activity that had reached as far as the Middle East.

These seven individuals then—two evangelical Christians, two proselytes, and three Jews—constitute the primary focus of my narrative. Their intellectual and religious itineraries all share one common feature: their profound interaction with Alexander McCaul. Each of their reactions to and encounters with the missionary and his colleagues helped shape their own attitudes to Christianity and Judaism and the relationship between the two. The network McCaul unconsciously forged with this unusual assembly of intellectuals provides a window through which to view the dynamics of a larger relationship between these two faith communities at a significant moment in the modern history of the Jewish-Christian encounter. This book accordingly is neither a history of a missionary organization from the perspective of its acolytes or critics nor a collective biography of a cluster of religious leaders. It instead seeks to capture the original reflections of several intellectuals remarkably dissimilar from each other but, nevertheless, in dialogue with one another, attempting to make sense of the past from which their respective faiths emerged and the meaning of their religious affiliation in their own era.

The story the book attempts to tell is transnational in scope. While it begins in Great Britain, it reverberates across the continent to eastern Europe and beyond to the Ottoman Empire and the Middle East. McCaul was Irish by birth, and Oxlee and Tonna were English. Hoga and Margoliouth were both Polish Jewish converts who had migrated to England and Ireland; despite their most valiant efforts, the two men were not fully recognized as English by their contemporaries, nor did they fully identify themselves with their adopted countries. Levinsohn and Fuenn, of course, were eastern European Jews at their core, and Kassin was a Syrian Jew, having wandered in Europe for several years, but who ultimately returned to the Middle East. The conversations of this book's protagonists were directly stimulated by the efforts of a missionary organization originating in Great Britain but ultimately international in scope, related but clearly not identical with the political aspirations of the British Empire at a time it was enjoying the heyday of its colonizing efforts. A central part of the discussion between McCaul and his interlocutors was fixated as well on the land of Israel and its central role in the ultimate restoration of the Jews and the eschatological visions of Protestant evangelicalism.

In highlighting the reflections of thinkers from England, eastern Europe, and the Ottoman Empire, this book departs from the conventional narrative of modern Jewish thought with its heavy emphasis on Germany. In focusing on thinkers on the margins, those usually excluded from the canon of modern Jewish thought from Moses Mendelssohn to Martin Buber and Franz Rosenzweig, it modestly seeks to enlarge the parameters of modern Jewish self-reflection. And by simultaneously considering the writings of Jewish intellectuals with those of a missionary to the Jews, two converts, and two Christian "friends" of the Jews, it also seeks to broaden the context in which thinking about modern Judaism emerged.

The triggering event of this intense conversation between McCaul and his associates was the 1839 publication of McCaul's magnum opus, *The Old Paths*, in its Hebrew translation, attributed to Stanislaus Hoga and entitled *Netivot olam*. McCaul's arguments against the Talmud were hardly novel; from the Middle Ages on, Christian missionaries had insisted that the Jews' reliance on the Talmud was their ultimate "heresy" and primary obstacle in adopting the authentic Jewish religion, which for them was Christianity. What was new about McCaul's assault was the author's impressive command of rabbinic literature, history, and thought, his powerful rhetoric, and his intimate understanding of contemporary Jewish life. McCaul was also dangerous because, as a Protestant evangelical, he professed to love Jews and their culture with great intensity. He composed numerous books, sermons, and addresses displaying his vast Jewish erudition and his genuine appreciation for Jewish culture. His treatise against the Talmud was a continuation of the medieval Christian polemic with rabbinic Judaism yet reformulated and updated in the context of nineteenth-century Jewish life and Jewish-Christian relations. And most important, it represented a new and bold invasion into the relatively insulated centers of traditional Jewish life in eastern Europe, the Ottoman Empire, and the Middle East. Disseminated widely through the offices of the London Society, McCaul's book, particularly in its Hebrew and later Yiddish and Judeo-Persian versions, caused something of a sensation among educated Jews who had considered the old Jewish-Christian disputation a relic of the remote past.[1]

There were several other works composed by Christians against the Talmud and rabbinic Judaism in the nineteenth century, but none were published in so many editions and so widely circulated throughout the world.[2] Although it would be hazardous to overstate the connection, one can hardly miss the irony of the near simultaneity of the Hebrew publication date of McCaul's work in 1839 with the worldwide reaction on the part of Jews and Christians alike to the notorious blood libel of Damascus the following year. The organized international response to this latter accusation, so brilliantly documented by the late Jonathan Frankel, ironically included a publication written by McCaul himself defending the Jews against this slander and garnering the support of an entire community of "Jewish Christians" that he had identified and solicited.[3] That this same author had just published his stinging rebuke of rabbinic Judaism while defending the helpless Jews of Syria underscored the danger such a "friend" of the Jews posed to the Jewish community. While the international Jewish response to the Damascus affair was considerably more noteworthy than that generated by the Hebrew publication of McCaul's book, both events reveal how Jews were beginning to organize themselves and others in defending their communal interests and their reputation as a "civilized" people in Europe. If the Damascus affair was a cause célèbre for the transregional display of Jewish antidefamational activity in the nineteenth century, the response to McCaul's offensive publication, though more muted, was still worthy of notice.

Jews and Christians in the Nineteenth Century

This book joins a significant body of scholarship emerging in the last several decades on the history of Jewish-Christian entanglements from antiquity to the present. Especially relevant is the notion argued by Israel Yuval among others that Judaism, throughout its formative periods, was considerably shaped by its polemic against and dialogue with the majority Christian culture, either appropriating the latter's conceptual discourse or defining itself against the other through a hidden or subtle polemic with its rival faith.[4] At first appearance, however, one might not immediately consider the nineteenth century as a prominent period for the revival of the Jewish-Christian debate. In an era during which Jews had already experienced the mixed results of enlightenment and emancipation, and where secularizing tendencies and the decline of religious institutions in Europe had eroded the very foundations of religious faith, a rehearsal of the tired arguments of past centuries might have seemed out of place.

In fact, during the nineteenth century, the importance accorded to the formative place of Christianity in the self-definition of Judaism did not diminish at all. Given the new scholarly tools and perspectives in studying the history of ancient Judaism and Christianity, some Christian scholars discovered new and compelling arguments to demonstrate the superiority of their own faith over that of the Jews. Jewish thinkers, particularly non-Orthodox ones, felt obliged to engage directly with this new Christian scholarship, to counter its arguments, and to champion the vital place of Judaism in Western civilization. They vigorously demonstrated the intimate connections between the two religious traditions, the Jewish roots of Christian teachings, and the immoral behavior characterizing the long history of Christian oppression of its Jewish minority. Liberal thinkers from Abraham Geiger to Leo Baeck constructed their own counternarratives of Judaism against the background of Christian supersessionist theology. More traditional thinkers such as Heinrich Graetz and Naḥman Krochmal defended the integrity of Jewish history and thought before an increasing number of Christian cultural critics impatient with the pace of Jewish integration and resistant to allowing Jewish full citizenship in the West or more improved minority rights in the East.[5] The subjects treated in this book should accordingly be situated within this wider context of the history of Jewish thought and scholarship, linked to the formidable debates over the fitness of Jews to be accepted and tolerated as equal citizens within increasingly intolerant European societies.

Although the intellectuals this book closely examines were part of these larger cultural and political debates raging throughout the century, the particular character of their background and beliefs and their dialogue with each other was distinct in other respects. All of the eight took their religious backgrounds quite seriously and were deeply committed to their respective faiths. All of them also cared deeply about the study of Jewish texts and Jewish history and fully appreciated the Jewish contribution to European society. At the same time, all displayed a degree of inconsistency and ambivalence, each in his or her own way, in their convictions. McCaul, but also Oxlee, Tonna, Hoga, and Margoliouth, professed a faith in the teachings of Jesus and in his imminent second coming to the earth, criticized certain aspects of contemporary Jewish attitudes and practices while displaying an obvious kinship to Jews and Judaism. A similar ambivalence might be detected among the Jewish critics of McCaul. Levinsohn, Fuenn, and even Kassin identified with a cultural camp critical of traditional Judaism, articulating sincere misgivings about its narrowness and parochialism. Yet these same individuals, in the wake of McCaul's assault, felt obliged to defend their ancestral faith and, in particular, the authority of the rabbis and the sacred legal and homiletical literature they had created over the centuries.

Acknowledging the unique character of this special group of interlocutors need not imply, however, that their reflections were merely idiosyncratic and unrepresentative of larger intellectual and cultural trends. The participants in this conversation exemplified the ambiguity and equivocality of confessional borders in the modern era. Missionaries could be proponents of

Hebrew and Jewish culture, while converts, even those who became clerics, could express their loyalty to their Jewish pasts in profound and intimate ways. Moreover, evangelicals could profess their love of Christianity while preaching Jewish restoration, a love of Zion, and a sincere admiration for Jewish practice and faith, while Jewish thinkers and leaders could offer an internal critique of their own tradition while defending it from Christian attacks with all the intellectual tools at their disposal. There was no one Jewish-Christian debate between two clearly defined adversaries; the boundaries were remarkably porous and the meaning of being a Jew or a Christian was hardly obvious anymore. Murky entanglements rather than clearly defined adversarial positions often marked the history of the Jewish-Christian encounter in this era. All of this was further complicated by the fervor of the Catholic-Protestant divide, particularly as it was articulated by English Protestant clerics,[6] as well as by the internal divisions and heated debates within Jewish culture between the Reform and Orthodox, or the enlightened and the traditional. In responding to the other, each individual was compelled to examine the conflicting loyalties that informed his or her own religious identity.

Perhaps the greatest anomaly in this period was the founding by Joseph Frey in 1809 of what would become the largest and most heavily financed missionary society in the history of Jewish-Christian relations. Of course, both Catholics and Protestants had sought to proselytize Jews for centuries and continued their efforts throughout the modern era. But the London Society's range of activities, its army of missionaries, its incredible publication program of translated Bibles and other works of Christian apologetics and polemics, its extensive campus of schools for missionary training at Bethnal Green, London, called Palestine Place, and the support it garnered from political and clerical elites was without precedent.[7]

The era in which the London Society became prominent was, of course, the very age of missions across the globe, fueled by the expansive reach of European colonialism in general and British imperialism in particular. For all its size, the London Society was a relatively small part of the rapid growth of missionary societies across Europe, the Americas, Africa, the Middle East, and Asia throughout the nineteenth century. As the century progressed, the focus of missionary activity significantly shifted away from Jews and Muslims to the indigenous populations of Africa and Asia. Undoubtedly this was due in part to the lack of success in converting the former while the latter groups gradually embraced the Christian faith in remarkably large numbers.

Yet McCaul during his lifetime gave priority to the Jewish mission and insisted that the conversion of the Jews was the determining factor in precipitating Christ's return. In reaching out to Jews in both western and eastern Europe, he approached his subjects in a manner not unlike those missionaries assigned to convert members of other ethnic groups and religions around the world. Like his other colleagues, McCaul was not ultimately driven by political calculations but rather by his sincere faith as a Christian inflected, however, with European notions of cultural superiority. In identifying with the values of his "civilizing mission" to the Jews, he learned to love his subjects and identified with them, extolled their virtues, mastered their languages and literatures, and sincerely admired some of their customs and traditions. But he also sought to transform them into Protestant Christians of Jewish descent who shared his same values and beliefs and were shaped in his very image of what constituted a true Christian. And at times, he also revealed his own prejudices as a European and an Englishman, particularly enamored of his Protestant upbringing, which he deemed superior to that of Catholics and Jews alike. Interspersed among his appreciative comments about the Jews he met in Warsaw and elsewhere were more derogatory remarks about the "primitive" behavior of other Jews, some in Poland, but especially those living in Africa or the Middle East.

Moses Margoliouth also shared some of these same assumptions of English cultural superiority, despite his mixed upbringing in Poland and Great Britain, and displayed them especially in his journal documenting his travels throughout the Middle East. John Oxlee and Charlotte Elizabeth Tonna held more romantic notions of Jews and Judaism, reflecting their own theological and eschatological beliefs nurtured in Protestant England more than by any actual encounters with Jews in other countries.[8] Kassin, in contrast, responded in indignation to the "civilizing" posture of the Protestant missionary. McCaul's treatise elicited by him a tirade of social criticisms of Christianity—its harsh stands on celibacy and divorce and its lack of social norms. The true barbarians for this proud Sephardic Jew were those Christian clerics themselves.

Was the Missionary a Cultural Imperialist?

In referencing McCaul's mixed feelings of cultural identification with and superiority toward at least some Jews he encountered, might we think more broadly about his own self-image as a missionary and the extent to which his religious goals coincided with the political goals of English colonialism, imperialism, and globalism? Prior to the 1990s, it was a commonplace of scholarship, in part under the influence of Edward Said's influential *Orientalism* (1978), to posit a direct link between the Christian mission and the construction of European colonialism. Missionaries like McCaul were often perceived as agents of cultural imperialism. Evangelical Christianity's teachings were explicitly associated with commerce and civilization, or in the words of Andrew Porter, "While missionary boards saw in wealth, stability, and expansion a divinely ordained, providential role for Britain, commercial money flowed through subscriptions to missionary societies."[9] Such a description might aptly fit the profile of the London Society in particular and the apparent collusion between its religious mission and the remarkable political and economic benefits it received, far beyond the record of its actual accomplishments. Was McCaul, one of its primary leaders and spokesmen, a cultural imperialist?

Scholarship since the 1990s has offered a more nuanced and balanced account of the complicated connections between Christian missionaries and the expansion of the British Empire. No doubt missionaries contributed to English perceptions of Great Britain as a superior Protestant nation. In publicizing their international efforts to disseminate Christian teaching throughout the world, they popularized as well the idea of a civilizing empire among the English public. Nevertheless, in Porter's careful formulation:

> There is no simple causal connection in this period between religious expansion and Britain's imperial outreach. It is difficult not to be struck by the insignificance of Empire in many evangelical minds, whose thinking was dominated by the concept of an all-embracing, superintending Providence unfolding a Divine plan for the world. Although there was a certain mystery about the operations of Providence, the French and American revolutions, European wars and economic disruption provided abundant scope for millenarian speculations, based on their supposed congruence with eschatological signs in the Bible's prophetic books. . . . In such a world national developments might have their place, Empire might provide an arena for providential fireworks, but no necessary priority was to be attached to either. . . . Empire held limited potential when set within the global perspective of evangelical Christianity.[10]

What seems especially relevant in understanding the meaning of McCaul's mission in the recent work of Porter and others is the need of the historian to take the missionary's theology most seriously.[11] Surely Christian missionaries always operated within a political framework of European colonialism and inevitably imbibed the cultural values associated with imperialism. But that did not necessarily imply, especially in the case of the English missionaries, an explicit or even tacit identification with the political aspirations of the British government. Missionaries often saw themselves as anti-imperialist and their relationship to politics often ambiguous if not emphatically negative. Missionaries cared more about the millennium, biblical interpretation, and the practical means of "educating" the indigenous populations they served. In encountering the latter, many realized that the only way to communicate their message was through translation, through a rigorous exposure to vernacular languages and cultures.[12] They were, of course, in some fundamental sense agents of hegemonic Western culture but, at the same time, were also facilitators of intercultural communication. In the final analysis, their gaze was always through the lens of faith; they acted under the conviction that the world's salvation depended on their religious activity.

Such a perspective helps us to understand the ultimate values of Alexander McCaul as well as the strong reactions his activity evoked on the part of friend and foe alike. No doubt McCaul, along with his other colleagues in the London Society, acted and reacted politically and diplomatically in dealing with foreign governments such as Russia or the Ottoman Empire. The survival of his missionary organization depended on it. He also vigorously protested the victimization of Jews around the world even as he refrained conspicuously, along with his fellow missionaries in the London Society, from promoting the cause of civil and political emancipation for British Jews. Reducing these actions to mere political calculations on his part, however, would misconstrue his ultimate concerns.

McCaul was first and foremost a Protestant evangelical, a fundamentalist and literalist, and a premillennial. He believed in the ultimate authority of the literal word of the Bible; he aspired to convert the Jew so as to reorientate his or her life to accept Christ's teaching; he held to the belief that Jesus would physically return to the earth before the millennium; and he was firmly committed to establishing a Jewish presence in the Holy Land to facilitate this transformative event. Granting the Jews civic equality in Great Britain was clearly at odds with such eschatological aspirations. Within the evangelical tent that he shared with others, there were certainly disagreements and a variety of doctrinal approaches. But all Protestant evangelicals ultimately valued the Jews because of their central role in the divine plan of salvation. It was the Catholics, not them, so they claimed, who treated the Jews with contempt. And McCaul prided himself on the special affection he displayed toward his Jewish subjects. This was his ultimate priority as a Christian missionary.[13]

Scholarly Foundations

Like any historical work, this book builds on the foundation of previous scholarship on a variety of specific subjects. With one exception, however, this is no comprehensive treatment of McCaul and his Christian and Jewish associates in the context of modern Jewish-Christian entanglements as outlined above. That exception is the master's thesis written by Yaakov Shaḥak at Bar Ilan University in 1999. It is indeed a pioneering work on McCaul's attack on the Talmud and the response of three maskilim to his polemic, two of whom are treated here. I acknowledge its importance and hope I have added to Shaḥak's preliminary findings with my own.[14]

There is hardly any recent scholarship on McCaul other than the celebratory tributes published by the London Society in the nineteenth century. The activities of the London Society were documented primarily in the official 1908 history of the organization by the Reverend W. T. Gidney and in the much later overview of Mel Scult, published in 1978.[15] In recent years, however, Agnieszka Jagodzińska has published a whole series of articles and now an entire book on the London Society's activities in Poland based on extensive archival research in Poland and in Oxford; and Israel Bartal had written on the relationship between the Hasidim of Ḥabad and the London Society.[16]

A number of important studies on converts to Christianity in modern Jewish history have appeared recently, including books by Todd Endelman and Ellie Schainker.[17] These writings help contextualize my own efforts to study Hoga and Margoliouth. McCaul's Christian critic John Oxlee has hardly been studied at all, while the activities of Charlotte Elizabeth Tonna as editor and social activist and her strong Jewish connections have been noticed by several scholars.[18] There has been much recent work on the Haskalah and particularly the Haskalah in eastern Europe by Shmuel Feiner, Immanuel Etkes, Mordechai Zalkin, and others, and I have relied heavily on their scholarship.[19] Finally, I mention two essays by Eliyahu Stern on the

Jewish responses to McCaul, which I discuss later in the book.[20] The many other works I consulted are referred to in the notes to each individual chapter.

The book that follows is a story about an old religious debate recast in a nineteenth-century setting and propelled into the public sphere through the engine of a powerful missionary organization and its publication network, disseminating its message widely and loudly among Jews and Christians alike. In the Middle Ages and throughout the early modern period, Jewish-Christian debates in either oral or written form were generally elite affairs restricted to small groups interested in hearing or reading them, often initiated by and restricted to a small circle of expert debaters or apologists. They were also primarily one-sided. The power relations between Jews and Christians usually dictated the outcome of the debate from the start: a victory for the Christian side. In the era of McCaul's polemic, the power of print in multiple languages and the economic resources and energy of the missionaries transformed this esoteric work into a publication accessible to a much larger readership over time and space. It became a stimulant or an irritant to both faith communities and their leadership whether its detailed arguments were read fully or not. And it clearly motivated some Jewish readers to respond forcefully and openly in kind, defending their own interests and demonstrating the flaws in McCaul's arguments and the virtues of their own. In the debate over McCaul and his publication, accordingly, we find a novel and fresh perspective for examining both continuities and discontinuities in the long and complex history of Jewish-Christian engagements.

CHAPTER I

Portrait of an Evangelical Missionary to the Jews

Alexander McCaul and His Assault on Rabbinic Judaism

Alexander McCaul was not only a key clerical and political leader of the London Society for Promoting Christianity Amongst the Jews but one of its most profound intellectuals, deeply learned in Jewish literature and intimately familiar with contemporary Jews and Judaism. Educated in Dublin and London, living for a long period in Warsaw in the heart of a vast traditional Jewish society, conversant in Hebrew and Yiddish, McCaul was deeply committed to Jewish learning while openly critical of the Talmud, Jewish law, and the rabbis. His long career and writings present a remarkable case study of a dialectical relationship with Jews and Judaism, one of sincere affection but also bitter criticism, and of intense devotion to his subjects paired with contempt for the very core of their beliefs, especially in his repudiation of their rabbinic leadership. He demonstrates profoundly the rich complexity of a Christian missionary mind-set seeking to identify with and fully appreciate his subjects while simultaneously trying to undermine their religion and core beliefs so that they might accept his own.[1]

I begin with three snapshots to introduce the man, each revealing a distinct and different aspect of his character and calling. The first is from one of two eulogistic essays penned in 1863 by the Reverend William Ayerst, a colleague of McCaul's at the London Society who also dedicated a book to him.[2] The essay entitled "The Rev. Dr. McCaul and the Jewish Mission"

PREBENDARY A. MCCAUL, D.D.

FIGURE 1. Alexander McCaul. Reproduced from W. T. Gidney, *The History of the London Society for the Promotion of Christianity Amongst the Jews* (London: London Society for Promoting Christianity Amongst the Jews, 1908), opposite p. 330. By permission of the British Library.

opened with an acknowledgment of some of the early and later luminaries of the London Society in this era of mission to the Jews. He then turned to McCaul and described his special outreach to the Jews of Poland and his high regard for them and their literature. In Ayerst's estimation, McCaul was unique in comparison with other Christian scholars and missionaries who had come before him: "We do not speak of scholars like [John] Lightfoot [1601–1700], [John] Gill [1697–1771], Bishop [John] Pearson [1613–86] and others who carefully studied the writings of the rabbies [*sic*], in order that they might better understand the sacred text; or of those who, like Bishop [Richard] Kidder [1633–1703] and [Philipp van] Limborch [1633–1712], have detailed the arguments which can be adduced in reply to Jewish objections to Christianity; these criticisms and discussions were carried on in a fair and just manner, not unworthy of the cause which led to their use. But these writers seem to have had little actual intercourse with the Jews now actually living among us. They treat the matter as a question of literary and sacred interest."[3]

Ayerst then extended his comparison of McCaul with other Christian scholars of Judaism to include Johann Christoph Wagenseil (1633–1705) and Johann Andreas Eisenmenger (1654–1704) who shared McCaul's objective to demonstrate that the doctrines of modern Judaism were radically different from those of Moses and the prophets. McCaul distinguished himself from the other two, however, in introducing a new style of writing. Wagenseil's fifteen-hundred-page work entitled *Tela Ignea Satanae* (Fiery darts of Satan) did little good for the cause of Christianity, claimed Ayerst, since it called upon faithful Christians "to unite in attacking, beating, smiting, wounding, and routing the Jews." Similarly Eisenmenger produced in his "2000 closely printed pages of quotations from all classes of Jewish writers, good, bad, and indifferent" a mere demonstration of how the Jews had departed from the truth. While Ayerst acknowledged the worth of such a massive undertaking, he wondered what good it ultimately produced and added parenthetically: "It is scarcely necessary to observe, that if anyone would take the trouble to collect passages from many writers who have been a disgrace to the name of Englishman, it would be easy to fill ten times as many volumes with matter ten times as objectionable as that which Eisenmenger has collected in his too notorious work."

But McCaul was unlike these two writers in his sincere wish to contribute to the welfare of Israel: "He does not spare error but he speaks the truth with love. He was raised up by a Divine Providence to counteract the baleful influence of the spirit which was manifested by those who had preceded him." Ayerst concluded by citing no less a contemporary Jewish authority than Dr. Isaak Markus Jost (1793–1860), who praised McCaul's *The Old Paths* for presenting its arguments "in language intelligible to everyone, and that not as formerly in a spirit of hatred and division, which irritate and embitter the mind, but with a love and good will which gain the hearts of all."[4]

My second snapshot is remarkably different from that of Ayerst's affectionate tribute to his teacher. It is a negative portrait of McCaul and the London Society written by one of his closest associates, the convert named Stanislaus Hoga (1791–1860). Hoga was born in Lublin to a rabbinic and Hasidic family, given a serious rabbinic education while also learning several foreign languages that allowed him to work as a translator. He eventually moved to Warsaw, was employed as a Hebrew censor, and converted to Christianity apparently under McCaul's patronage. He followed his Christian mentor to London where he actively participated in the translation of the New Testament into Hebrew and translated several other works. Most important, he was the alleged Hebrew translator of McCaul's *The Old Paths*. But his relationship with the London Society eventually soured, and he criticized the mindless efforts of the society to pressure naive converts into abandoning rabbinic law. In several works written in the 1840s, he ultimately articulated his claim that Christian faith could go hand in hand with performance of the ritual law of Judaism as prescribed by the rabbis.[5] In the first, and apparently only, issue of a periodical he had inaugurated entitled *Zir Ne'eman: The Faithful Missionary; A Monthly Periodical, Illustrating the Value of Judaism, with a View to Opening the Eyes of Some Deluded Christians in England to the Doings of the (So-Called) "London Society" for Promoting Christianity Among the Jews* (London, 1847), Hoga lashed out at McCaul directly. After a long diatribe against what he called the "glaring imposition and wickedness covered with the cloak of piety and religion" of the London missionaries and their futile attempts to convert any Jews except for the most destitute and vulnerable, he turned to his former mentor "the famous author of the 'Old Paths,'" citing from the preface to the second edition of the book, where McCaul took credit for the emergence of Reform Judaism in England.[6] Hoga found this claim ludicrous; moreover, he proceeded to attack the very work he had translated, even implying that the Hebrew version was hardly identical with the original work of the Christian cleric in the first place:

I say he [McCaul] deserves the thanks of the British Jews; yes I repeat it; if one who, with a design to curse the Jews, involuntarily does bless them [an allusion to the biblical Balaam], deserves their thanks, then none is more deserving the gratitude of the whole Jewish nation than the author of the "Old Paths." The Hebrew book adapted to, and which he unjustly calls a translation of his English, will I am sure do the Jews nothing but good. They are too sensible to be seduced by his ridiculous arguments in favour of apostasy. On the contrary, that book will undoubtedly awaken many Jews in distant countries to reflection and to the defence of the faith of Judaism.[7]

My final snapshot is taken from a manuscript letter penned by McCaul during the time he was living in Warsaw in 1826. Addressed to the Reverend C. S. Hawtrey in London, it regards the details of his involvement in the London Society's project of preparing a new translation of the Old Testament, in this case, the Pentateuch alone. What is interesting is a comment he made unrelated to the primary purpose of the letter, describing the purchase of certain Jewish books:

> You shall see by Mr. Berhers' [another official of the London Society] last amount that I bought some books for the society. One of these I shall send by the first best opportunity as an important acquisition to the Library of the Seminary. Its title is *Kabbala Denudata* [compiled by the Christian Hebraist Christian Knorr von Rosenroth (1636–89)] [which] is a very rare book and has been sold in Germany at a very high price—one copy in Vienna was sold for 100 ducats. I bought it from a collector of rare books who does not understand Hebrew for four ducats. It contains a lexicon to the difficult book Sohar, translations of several cabbalistic texts and the texts of several tracts of Sohar, pointed for the use of the student, with a Latin translation accompanied by Rabbi Isaac Luria's commentary. The whole was compiled by the editor of the celebrated Sulzbach edition of Sohar, assisted by three Jewish rabbies [*sic*]. Another book which I bought from the same person is a Latin translation of *Shebet Jehudah* [of Solomon Ibn Verga (ca. 1460–1554)] by means of which the Committee may see what the book contains. But a book which is of more immediate importance to the Polish

mission is a Jewish edition of *Chizzuk Emunah* [by the Karaite writer
Isaac of Troki (ca. 1533–94)], which I wished to possess, and which
I have seen almost everywhere in Poland where I have been, but
which no Jew would sell to me. This I bought from a poor Jew in
Warsaw who had no money to keep the feast of Tabernacles, and
therefore brought it to me. It is the grand book of Jewish Polemics
against Xianity. It would be well of the Committee to have the
whole reprinted in Hebrew and Jewish with an answer following
each objection. I hope to be able to send you an English translation,
with such an answer as my experience in the subject may dictate
before I begin [to translate] the prophets.[8]

Here is yet another face of McCaul, astute and enthusiastic collector of
Jewish books, specifically works well known and utilized by Christian Hebraists. One might argue that the third book directly related to his work as a
missionary in countering Jewish arguments against Christianity. But the first
two dealing with the Jewish mystical tradition, especially the Lurianic texts,
and Jewish historiography are of broader significance and suggest McCaul's
keen interest in the Jewish library as a whole.

In seeing these three images of McCaul written respectively by a devoted
acolyte, a former Jewish convert, initially an associate and later an adversary,
and by McCaul himself, we might ask who the real Alexander McCaul was.
Was he a unique Christian pastor with a genuine love for Jews and Judaism?
A deceiver and ineffectual missionary who denigrated the rabbis and their
writings unfairly and wrongheadedly? Or was he a sincere Hebraist who
greatly valued and admired the learning of Jews for its own sake? Perhaps he
was simultaneously all three.

McCaul's Life and Career

The basic outline of McCaul's career is easily constructed from the standard
history of the London Society of W. T. Gidney;[9] from the numerous references to McCaul in the annual minutes of the London Society extant in its
archives at the Bodleian Library at Oxford;[10] from the annual proceedings of
the London Society for Promoting Christianity Amongst the Jews called the
Jewish Intelligence;[11] from the warm reminiscences of his daughter Mrs. Elizabeth Finn;[12] from McCaul's numerous books, sermons, and other addresses

over the course of a long and illustrious career;[13] and from references to him on the part of many other contemporaries, particularly those associated with the society during and after his lifetime, including several eloquent eulogies written at the time of his death.[14] During his lifetime, McCaul was a figure of enormous stature within the missionary world he inhabited, holding many important clerical and educational offices, and eventually a distinguished professorship at King's College. I will touch only some of the highlights of this career in this and the next chapter, focusing primarily on the variegated strands of McCaul's complex attitude to Jews and Judaism.

Alexander McCaul was born at Dublin on May 16, 1799. He was educated at Trinity College, Dublin. At the young age of twenty-two he was sent as a missionary to Warsaw, Poland, in 1821, where he studied Hebrew, Yiddish, and especially rabbinics. While serving as a missionary in Poland, he gained the attention of such public figures as the grand duke Constantine, the crown prince of Prussia, and Sir Henry Rose, his benefactor. After briefly returning to London to receive his ordination, he resumed his Warsaw post accompanied by his new wife, Mary Clarke Crosthwaite, in 1823 and they remained in Poland until 1830. They had at least eleven children, several of whom became clergymen, and one daughter, Elizabeth Anne, became the wife of James Finn, the British consul for Jerusalem and Palestine.

In 1836 McCaul began publishing the weekly installments of his elaborate attack upon the Talmud under the title *The Old Paths*, which would appear in book form the following year.[15] This elicited considerable interest among the leadership of the London Society as a critical tool in its mission to the Jews. It was translated into several languages, including German, French, and Italian, and especially into Hebrew (*Netivot olam*) by the aforementioned Hoga (who apparently claimed to have contributed more to the book than its mere translation, as we have seen). When the Hebrew edition appeared in 1839, Jews quickly took notice as multiple copies of the book were circulated throughout Europe and the Middle East. Despite some fifty other publications and numerous homilies that appeared in printed form, McCaul was known especially for his anti-Talmudic diatribe, which laid out a powerful case to Jews to abandon rabbinic Judaism and to embrace the Christian faith. Soon after, McCaul wrote vigorously against the notorious Damascus blood libel of 1840, demonstrating his profound respect for the high moral standards of Jews and profoundly displaying his self-described image as a friend of the Jewish people.[16] After serving as the head of the London Society's seminary for training missionaries like himself as well as other church offices, he was eventually invited to serve as professor of Hebrew and rabbinical literature at King's College, London, which he accepted, and served in that post until his death in 1863.

Elizabeth Anne Finn, his aforementioned daughter and wife of James Finn, devoted several touching pages to her beloved father in her memoirs of England and Palestine, which provide a more intimate glimpse of the man than the public image emerging from the London Society's official publications.

Finn recounted her father's early educational background and the event that particularly stimulated his interest in missionary work, his meeting with the Reverend Lewis Way, one of the original founders of the London Society. This charismatic cleric altered the whole course of McCaul's life, inviting him to forgo his scientific studies to join several other young men in London to study Hebrew literature: "He [McCaul] devoted his life to what he considered to be the highest good of the Jewish people, and through them the whole world." His mission to the heartland of eastern European Jewry soon followed, and he was engrossed in the study of Judaism from firsthand sources, which left a lasting impact upon his life: "My father took very great pains to become thoroughly acquainted with the Jewish character and mode of life. He found that among them [the Jews] learning was everything and wealth nothing. . . . It was thought an honour to be the wife of a learned man. I remember well the Yiddish phrase I so often heard in my childhood: 'Er ist sehr a gelernten Mann,' as the highest praise."[17]

In such learned surroundings, where he witnessed daily the mastery of Talmudic tomes by young rabbinical students, McCaul was eager to immerse himself in Hebraic studies as well and even to instruct his daughter in Hebrew and Yiddish: "My father was resolved to become proficient in the Hebrew language and learning; in order to become familiar with the Law of Moses and the cursive writing of Hebrew, which is different from the square characters that we see in printed books or in Rolls of the Law, he wrote out the whole of the five Books eight times with his own hand. He also taught me that cursive writing, and I continually get letters written in it, the language being either pure Hebrew or Yiddish."[18] From Warsaw, McCaul visited the principal Polish Jewish communities, interacted with Jews wherever he traveled, received them in his home in Warsaw, often leading to heated conversations with them, and even succeeded in converting a handful of them.

Upon his return to London, McCaul devoted his life to encouraging Jewish students to study with him in his home and later in the seminary he directed. The McCaul home was filled with visitors, constant lectures, and prayer services. He also worked in his spare time on translations of the English liturgy and New Testament into Hebrew. He was aided by Stanislaus Hoga, Mrs. Finn interjected, "an accomplished Hebraist, who was a Roman Catholic converted from Judaism in Poland and who came to London. He was an interesting man with considerable scientific attainments." When the translated liturgy was ready for regular usage, McCaul conducted Friday evening services in the library in Hebrew: "This my brother and I were privileged to attend, and we joined with delight in singing 'The God of Abraham Praise' in Hebrew; this was a fine old hymn of which the melody was written by Leoni."[19]

Mrs. Finn singled out the publication of *The Old Paths* as the greatest accomplishment of her father's life:

Father began writing a series of papers to show how the rabbis had departed from the Mosaic law . . . and that the Christian religion was the proper outcome of that of Moses and the Prophets. . . . These subjects had been deeply impressed upon him while in Poland. He had learnt to love and admire the Jewish people there, and to deplore the manner in which their fine intellects were enslaved by Rabbinical teaching, and he longed to set them free, and now at last he had the opportunity of attempting to do so. These papers he called "The Old Paths" and used as a motto the words of the prophet Jeremiah, exhorting his people to look back to "the old paths." The papers took the form of a double page, in English, with Hebrew quotations from the Talmud and the Bible. They were widely distributed and excited much attention for about a year. One result was the founding of Reformed Judaism [a claim ridiculed by Hoga, as we have seen]. A Jewish gentleman was sent to my father to verify his Hebrew quotations from the books in the library. It was in that way that Mr. [David Woolf] Marks' congregation was begun.[20]

One final glimpse of the special connection between father and daughter was her adventure of sleeping one night in her father's study: "There I found on the bookshelves volumes of Schlegel's Shakespeare, in German, and in the early morning I read *Romeo and Juliet*, *A Midsummer Night's Dream*, and others, in German. This was my first acquaintance with Shakespeare."[21]

Finn's special relationship with her father emerges quite distinctly in these short passages; she identified with his profound quest for Jewish learning and the deep conviction that he was serving the Jewish people through his missionary efforts. He was portrayed as an avid student of Judaism who also loved his Shakespeare, especially in German, a committed teacher, and loving father. She confirmed Stanislaus Hoga's presence among McCaul's close associates and her father's claim that he had exerted a major influence on English Reform Jews.

The Old Paths

In *The Old Paths* McCaul was especially clever in making his case that Jews must abandon the rabbis and their rulings and adopt a purified version of biblical Judaism shaped in the image of evangelical Protestant Christianity. He knew well how Christians had improperly manipulated rabbinic aggadic (homiletic) passages found in the Talmud and Midrashim during centuries of Jewish-Christian debates. These were taken out of context and misconstrued as confirming the Christian faith. He also knew how Jews had emphatically rejected such unreliable readings. He declared instead that he would prove his case by only utilizing sources that no contemporary Jew could reject: the standard halachic codes that outlined normative Jewish behavior and the standard liturgy that reflected the beliefs of those Jews who faithfully recited their prayers on a daily basis. And, indeed, McCaul remained consistent throughout, relying on these two bodies of sources, even utilizing the well-known and accepted English translations of David Levi of the Ashkenazic and Sephardic prayer books that he knew traditional Jews living in Great Britain could not easily dismiss.[22]

McCaul's other means of attempting to win over his Jewish readers was his constant praise of their remarkable legacy, a distinctive approach later mentioned by Reverend Ayerst and Mrs. Finn. In addition to his well-known defense of the Jews against the infamous Damascus blood libel, he published an apology for the study of rabbinic literature by Christians;[23] wrote empathetic sketches of Judaism and Jewish cultural figures;[24] translated one of the biblical commentaries of the medieval Jewish exegete David Kimḥi;[25] and composed numerous sermons and addresses displaying his impressive erudition in Jewish sources and his genuine appreciation for Jewish culture. A typical example illustrative of his knowledge of Jewish literature and his sincere admiration for the latter may be taken from his *Sketches of Judaism and the Jews*, a collection of essays previously published in the *British Magazine* and appearing only a year after the printing of *The Old Paths* in 1838. He first listed the various genres of Jewish literature including the Talmud, kabbalah, biblical commentaries, and philosophical works, especially those of Maimonides. He then mentioned the Jewish printing presses at "Slawuta, Wilna, Lublin, Warsaw, and Cracow" and finally concluded with the following encomium:

> Indeed, whether we look at the Rabbinic Jews of ancient or modern times, we must admit that they are a people of no mean intellectual power. Let anyone reflect on the Jewish history, and let him remember that, for nearly 1,800 years, they have been an outcast, wandering, persecuted, and oppressed people, and he will find it little short of a miracle that the Jews should have any literature at all. But, when he looks at the extent of that literature, its variety, and the noble monuments of industry, genius, and intellect which it comprises, he must admit that there is, in the conformation of the Jewish mind, an innate love of learning, a native nobility, an irresistible elasticity of intellect, which has enabled them to bear up against the pressure of calamity and contempt which threatened to overwhelm them. . . . The history of the Jews proves incontrovertibly, that, as long as a nation retains a love for its religion, even though that religion have a considerable admixture of error, it can never sink into barbarism. The body may be led into captivity, but the power of religion will still preserve the mind unconquered and free.[26]

Yet accompanying this high acclaim for Jews and Judaism was also a consistent critique of the rabbis and their unbearable legislation, which McCaul viewed as inhumane with respect to both Jews and non-Jews and contradictory to the original intent of the Mosaic law. This theme, of course, was hardly novel, having been part of the standard repertoire of Christian polemicists from late antiquity until his own time. But there was clearly a nineteenth-century flavor to McCaul's unrelenting criticisms of the rabbis regarding their treatment of three specific groups: the non-Jews, especially those like enlightened Protestants who profess a monotheistic faith; the poor and indigent Jews whose horrendous economic conditions were exacerbated by an uncompassionate and uncompromising rabbinate; and Jewish women whose nobility and dignity were diminished by their inferior status under rabbinic law.

So, for example, following a long tradition of critical Christian comment, McCaul addressed the prominent place the rabbis assigned to the following passage at the Passover home ritual: "Pour out thy wrath on the heathen that have not known you, and upon the kingdoms that have not called upon thy name" (Psalm 79:6–7). Adding other similar biblical passages, McCaul had no doubt that the subject of these verses was not merely ancient pagans but Christians as well. He was even ready to concede that such verbal outbursts of violence were understandable when referring to the ancient Romans who destroyed the Temple or when speaking of crusaders who massacred many innocent Jews, but how justify such vituperative language in the present enlightened day and age?

> During the persecutions of the Crusaders or the Inquisition it might be excusable, but in the present time and circumstances it is indefensible. Who are the heathen and the kingdoms, whom the offerers of these perditions wish to be pursued with God's wrath, and to be destroyed from under the heavens? Are they the Christians, or the heathen idolaters of Africa and India? The Mahometans profess a faith in the Unity very similar to that of the later rabbies; they, therefore, cannot be intended. If it be said that the idolatrous heathen are here intended, we must still protest against the intolerance of this imprecation; why should the Jews wish for their destruction? What evil did these poor ignorant people ever do to the Jews in England that they should pray for their destruction rather than their conversion? If it be said, that nobody at all is intended in the present day, why, would we ask, is it still made a part of the Passover ceremonial? We have before us several copies of the Haggadah, some printed very lately, and it occurs in them all.[27]

McCaul was also critical of the observance of the Jewish holiday of Purim, particularly its encouragement of drunkenness and violence. He could not fathom why the rabbis appreciated the book of Esther where God's name is never mentioned. On the contrary, the book "furnishes more gratification to the spirit of revenge so natural to all the children of Adam, whether they be Jew or Gentile." The book represents an account of revenge that the Jews took upon their enemies and this is reproachable: "But to curse a dead enemy, to pursue with unrelenting hatred those who have already fallen into the hands of the living God, is certainly not a divine ordinance, and cannot be an acceptable act of worship in poor sinners."[28]

The odious behavior of Jews in cursing Edom, commonly associated by the Middle Ages with Christianity as the archenemy of the Jews, was copiously documented by McCaul in citing Maimonides, Kimḥi, and Abravanel among others. To an enlightened Christian like McCaul, such expressions appeared totally inappropriate: "Above all, are they suitable in an English synagogue, and in the present day? You may say that Kimchi and those other commentators lived in the times of Popery, and Edom only means the Roman Catholic Christians. But what will those Jews say who live in Rome itself, and France, and Bavaria, and other Roman Catholic countries? You may think them in error, so do we, but we cannot for that pray that God 'would satiate the clods with their blood, manure the earth with their fat, and cause the stench of their carcasses to ascend.'" Clearly there was no excuse for Jews to utter such horrible things.[29]

McCaul's economic argument against the rabbis highlighted especially the burden that adherence to the rabbinic dietary laws placed upon the indigent. From the vantage point of London with its large population of poor and needy Jews, McCaul viewed the laws of kashrut as an intolerable imposition on needy members of the community who were in no position to reject any sustenance offered them. There is no doubt that he had in mind the material support offered by the London Society in encouraging needy Jews to embrace Christianity. After describing the prohibitions of the rabbis to consume the bread of Christians or drink their wine, McCaul professed his indignation over the rigid inhumanity of such laws that, in some instances, might force some of the needy to starve. He continues:

> They [the rabbis] must know that these laws about milk and butter, and the art of slaughtering, cut off many a poor Jew from the last refuge of the destitute—the poorhouse. Many a one who is now starving with his family, would be glad to have the relief which the parish provides, but he dare not accept of it. . . . If a Gentile government should seize on a number of unfortunate Israelites guilty of no crime, and shut them up in a prison, and then leave them to die of starvation, what just indignation would be excited? Every man would protest against such wanton cruelty, and yet this is just what

modern Judaism has done. By forbidding Gentile meat, milk, cheese, and bread, it has consigned hundreds to starvation. There are at this moment numbers of individuals, if not families, pining away in want, whose wants could be relieved, if the oral law did not interpose its iron front, and pronounce starvation lawful, and help from Gentiles unlawful; and yet their brethren, who pride themselves upon their benevolence and humanity, leave them to perish, and suffer the system to remain that it may be a curse to coming generations.[30]

Elsewhere McCaul explicitly highlighted the specific conditions of poverty among the Jews of London, which, he alleged, were exacerbated by these rabbinic stringencies:

Let any one visit the haunts of the poor Jews in this city, or enter their abodes, and he will find many a wretched family pining away for want of proper food; and yet it is too dear to procure a sufficiency; and if any benevolent Christian should wish to assist them, offer them some of their own, or give them a ticket to some of those institutions which distribute meat to the poor, the starving family would not dare to accept it, even if their conscience allowed them. . . . What can be more pernicious than to teach the ignorant that the food which their neighbors eat is carrion, so unfit for the nourishment of a rabbinist that he ought to die of want, rather than eat it?[31]

The laws of kashrut accordingly were doubly obnoxious: they both engendered economic stress and misery and also maligned those Christians whose food was considered unclean and who were thus considered unworthy human beings incapable of nourishing the unfortunate Jews in their neighborhoods.

The third group who suffered under the yoke of rabbinic law, according to McCaul, were Jewish women. This is a subject that preoccupied him in other works to which I will return in Chapter 2. It is sufficient here to focus on his long discussion on women in *The Old Paths*. There, he compared the rabbis' "utter contempt upon the female portion of mankind" to that of the Muslims who allegedly treated their women like slaves. McCaul surmised that because Maimonides had lived among "the Mahometans," he had apparently adopted their position. This is in sharp contrast to the way Christians treat women, regarding them as rational and responsible beings.

McCaul offered a comparative perspective on the treatment of women in countries less "civilized" than his own, in which his feelings of European cultural superiority were evident: "On the Barbary Coast they hardly ever go [to synagogue], and in Poland how common it is, whilst the men are in synagogue in prayer, to see their wives outside loitering and chatting, as if the public worship of God was no concern of theirs. Even in this country the attendance of females is not at all equal to that of men." After citing the standard liturgy recited by men thanking God for not making them female, McCaul concluded with a question: "Now we may ask every Jew and Jewess, into whose hands this paper may fall, whether a religion which teaches one-half of the human race to despise and degrade the other half, can possibly come from God?"[32]

McCaul continued to challenge the status of women in rabbinic Judaism through a cross-cultural lens. Commenting on the alleged role of women who are expected to teach their children, he asked: "But how is it possible for those Jewish mothers, in Poland and Africa for instance, who cannot even read themselves, to teach their sons?" In Muslim countries, these women remained illiterate; in Christian lands, they got some education since "wherever the light of Christianity shines, however feeble, it ameliorates the condition of the female portion of the Jewish nation, and compels even the disciples of Rabbinism to take a little more care of their souls and their intellects."[33]

From the perspective of this Christian European, women's degradation was clearly a product of Muslim and Jewish cultural inferiority. In the East, McCaul contended, women were men's slaves, the object of contempt even to their own sons. The European—meaning the Christian—state of things, was more agreeable to God's intentions: "Here the intellectual and moral powers of mankind have far advanced towards perfection, but there [in the East] the human race is still debased and barbarous." The most obvious example of this depravity was the common practice of polygamy, tolerated not only by Muslims but by Jews living among them, despite Rabbenu Gershom's famous tenth-century ban for Jews living in northern Europe. Monogamous relations in Europe prevailed, according to the missionary, because of the pervasive influence of Christian values: "Is not the moral, the intellectual, and scientific progress of mankind greatly superior in Christian countries, where men have only one wife? This has been a blessing to Jews."[34]

The Impact of *The Old Paths*

It would not be an exaggeration to say that *The Old Paths* was the most widely read book of its kind in the nineteenth century. This was due to the extraordinary efforts of the London Society to promote the book, to publish it numerous times in large print runs, and to translate it into German, Hebrew, Yiddish, Italian, Polish, Judeo-Persian, and French. The book became the standard manual of missionizing among the Jews for decades. Despite a growing library of similar works published by the London Society and other missionary groups, it was considered the classical statement by appreciative Christian clerics on the subject of the Talmud and the threatening assault on the integrity of Judaism by a disapproving community of rabbinic leaders. As we shall see, the multiple Jewish responses, especially to the Hebrew version of the text, from Poland to Syria, testified to the pervasive impact of McCaul's words on the Jewish community and the sense of vulnerability some Jews felt in the wake of his learned polemical assault.

Most of the information on print runs and approved translations of McCaul's work is found in the London Society's major periodical the *Jewish Intelligence and Monthly Account* or in the society's minute books. For example, in 1839, the London Society announced that two thousand copies of the first ten numbers of *The Old Paths* were printed in Judeo-Polish (Yiddish), while five thousand copies of the entire work were printed in German in Frankfurt am Main, under the supervision of Rev. W. Ayerst. In the following year, one thousand copies of the recently completed Hebrew translation were printed, while another notice mentioned the circulation of 1,130 copies of the book in English, Hebrew, and German in one year alone. Other sources mention still more thousands published.[35]

In 1846, a longer discussion of the circulation of McCaul's book appeared at about the same time as the publication of the second English edition. Writing from the German town of Creuznach, the Reverend J. Stockfeld reported the following: "One Jewish teacher, after expressing the great value put by him upon the 'Old Paths' declared to your missionary his conviction that that work had produced the present great movement among the Jews; and that, although there was as yet much that is objectionable in that movement, yet by means of the 'Old Paths' which had already paved the way so far, the knowledge of the truth will increase more and more." Stockfeld added that "one Jewish teacher informed your missionary that he could not yet openly circulate the work among his congregation, but by introducing passages from it in the lectures delivered by him every Sabbath, he instructs his hearers in conformity with it. Another teacher stated, that his copy of the 'Old Paths' had circulated among so many, and been so diligently studied, that he was obliged to have it re-bound; adding, 'such an instructive and valuable book must not be spoilt.' "[36]

Later in the same volume, the editors paused to congratulate themselves on the new second edition, mentioning with pride an earlier remark of the aforementioned learned Jewish authority Isaak Markus Jost: "It may well be said that the remark of the learned Dr. Jost concerning this book has been fully verified. Speaking, in 1839, of the effect to be anticipated from the writings of Dr. McCaul, and especially of this work, he said: 'His words will make an impression.' An impression has been made—the work has been extensively read by the Jews in Hebrew, German, and French, as well as in English. . . . Christian students have also learnt its value as a compendium of useful information concerning the system of Rabbinism, which cannot be found in any other book in our language."[37]

Of course, such statements of self-promotion were apt to be exaggerated, yet there remains no doubt that the London Society viewed *The Old Paths* as a major publishing success of the organization, especially in the first decade of its existence. Even some fifty years later, in a precious document preserved in the archives of the society, McCaul's tome is revealed to have retained an honorable place among the missionaries themselves. In the summary of a questionnaire prepared by a subcommittee of the London Society on July 29, 1892, and sent to various missionaries to evaluate the usefulness of existing missionary publications of the society, *The Old Paths* continued to be mentioned favorably even if some questioned its viability. So, for example, the Reverend S. J. Bachert still considered McCaul's work "a standard book and much liked and read. It gives the Jew an insight into his own religion." On the other hand, the Reverend W. Becker claimed that "The Old Paths should be corrected with respect to the Jewish defenses, esp. Zorubabel," a reference to the well-known Jewish response to the work by Isaac Baer Levinsohn, discussed in Chapter 7. Similarly, the Reverend G. H. Dalman voiced the need for a new edition of the work that could forcefully respond to McCaul's Jewish critics.[38]

The most interesting response came from a Mr. R. S. Spiegel, obviously a former Jew, who had thought long and hard about the contemporary Jewish community at the turn of the century:

> Most of our tracts have been written for Jews of one mind and religious thought, losing sight of the manifold and various characters (and education) of the Jews we have to deal with. To have to reckon with the orthodox Talmudicals, the Reformed or rather De-formed, the educated, the illiterate, the Chasidic-superstitious, the Socialistic, the Atheistic, the Infidel, the merely National Jew; we have to provide missionary literature for Jews who think that Judaism is more a misfortune than a religion. We have not to forget Jews who with incision think that the different religions are the same wine in glasses, differently coloured; we have to remember Jews who use certain phrases and ceremonies in an emotional way without any sanctifying influence on their lives; we have by no means to overlook the many real and interesting Jewish characters presented to the world by Disraeli, Kingsley, Boccaccio and other writers. We want tracts for each and all of the enumerated classes and we have to meet them on their own fulcrum which we have to lead up to Scripture.

Spiegel finally argued that modern Jewish thought was virtually nonexistent since it borrowed heavily from secular thought in Germany; many Jews harked back to Orthodoxy or semi-Orthodoxy; while others fully emancipated themselves from some shades of Orthodoxy, so that all that remains is belief and faith in the revelation of the word of God. In this new context, he was able to deem *The Old Paths* as still worthy especially in jargon and in parts: "This is and will remain a standard work in Jewish work, not only when dealing with the orthodox, but also when dealing with a neologian Jew. A Jew, even without the least knowledge of Talmudic tenets, is and has been in some instances made ashamed of silently though unknowingly acquiescing in Rabbinic Judaism. Old Paths is a book written sympathetically, helps to destroy Jewish fallacies, and leads on to the building up of the Christian faith."[39]

These illustrations of the continued impact of McCaul's polemical tract throughout the course of the century, despite the changing needs of the missionaries themselves and despite their realization that the Jewish community they had attempted to proselytize had significantly evolved in novel ways, underscore the significance of this publication for the missionary project well after McCaul's death in 1863. Its impact on the Jewish intellectual leadership will also be addressed in subsequent chapters. What remains to consider are other aspects of McCaul's Jewish connections as evidenced in some of his other writings. His profile and passionate interest in Jews and Judaism cannot be reduced to his authorship of a polemical treatise against the Talmud alone. This is the subject of Chapter 2.

CHAPTER 2

Sketches of Modern Judaism
in McCaul's Other Writings

Soon after McCaul had published his first edition of *The Old Paths*, he became aware of a recent English translation of a polemical work against Christianity originally published in Spanish by the seventeenth-century Catholic turned Jewish apologist Isaac Orobio de Castro. Isaac Orobio de Castro was a towering figure in the intellectual world of the Amsterdam Jewish community made up primarily of former conversos who had escaped their native Catholic Spain and Portugal for the freedom Protestant Amsterdam offered in order to reclaim their original Jewish roots. He was known for his scholarly tomes, particularly against Christianity and atheism, and his anti-Christian writing was also known among anticlerical writers of the early Enlightenment. It is a testament to McCaul's vast knowledge of Jewish polemical literature and his detective prowess to have located this relatively obscure publication.[1]

The English translator of Orobio's work was none other than the writer Grace Aguilar (1816–47), called by her biographer Michael Galchinsky "a poet, historical romance writer, domestic novelist, Jewish emancipator, religious reformer, educator, social historian, theologian, and liturgist." Aguilar was an accomplished literary figure and public role model for Jewish women in England during her brief life of thirty-one years. In her novels, poems, and sermons, she articulated a highly spiritual, biblically based, and proto-feminist ideology of Judaism, quite attractive to a large number of readers both in Europe and the United States, where she was published as well.[2]

It is indeed in many ways a fascinating irony that Grace Aguilar would translate an anti-Christian work of a seventeenth-century Portuguese Jew "rendering more clear the rudiments of the Jewish faith to the youthful mind," as she put it, and should herself subsequently become the target of abuse by one of England's leading evangelical preachers and scholars of Judaism.[3] If one accepts the convincing reconstruction of Nadia Valman, and Rachel Beth-Zion Lask Abrahams before her, that Aguilar herself was a kind of Jewish evangelical, echoing the Protestant critique of rabbinism as a metaphor for priestcraft, evoking an earnest bibliocentrism and a Judaism as the religion of the heart, and aligning Jews with Protestant values, it is a strange twist of fate, then, that she would be maligned by none other than a leading evangelical missionary such as Alexander McCaul. Other evangelicals, including Charlotte Elizabeth Tonna, had praised her as she attempted to articulate a Jewish identity in the language of evangelical and feminine Christianity, but McCaul held a different attitude toward her work.[4]

According to Galchinsky, Aguilar had translated Orobio at the request of her father, Emanuel (1787–1845).[5] The elder Aguilar and his wife Sarah (1787–1854) were Portuguese Jews who had immigrated to England in search of religious and economic security, settling in the northeast London suburb of Hackney where Grace was born. Emanuel served as a parnas of London's Bevis Marks Spanish and Portuguese Synagogue, and members of the family were active participants in the Sephardic community. No doubt her father was proud of his converso ancestry and considered Orobio a hero of sorts. But why the need to translate him into English at that moment? By taking on the assignment Grace not only entered directly into public polemics with Christianity, but did so by relying on a kind of born-again Jew of Catholic ancestry. If she believed Protestants were essentially different from Catholics, why stir the pot, so to speak, using arguments against Christianity that would be misconstrued by English Protestants, since they apply more directly to popery, to a Catholic understanding of Christianity? McCaul caught her in a trap, arguing instead that it was Judaism that was closer to popery. He chose to retranslate Orobio more literally to show his true colors and, indirectly, hers. He succeeded brilliantly in pointing out her hypocrisy in attacking Christianity in general on the one hand, while espousing a universal spirit of piety shared by Jews and Christians on the other.

Aguilar's *Israel Defended* was published in 1838 for the use of young persons of the Jewish faith.[6] Based on the French translation of Henriques, but not a literal translation, she believed she was creating an original English

book. Quite aware of the wide difference between the kindly charity of Protestants and the bigoted cruelty of Catholicism, as she saw it, she consciously
adopted a milder tone. She wrote: "We shall pray for the light of our holy
faith to beam on them [the Christians], and not condemn them for their
belief, though we may consider it erroneous." McCaul picked up this line
and saw it as insulting Christianity. She apologetically claimed that the work
was composed not to evoke controversy against other creeds or make converts. Her sole aim was to enlighten Jews in their own faith, but it was hardly
convincing.[7]

McCaul's *Israel Avenged* was published in three parts in 1839–40. He
noted that Aguilar's work was printed for private circulation "owing to the
zeal and talent of a Jewish lady" (he never mentioned her by name, suggesting
he did not know her personally). A Christian response was called for, he
argued, since she wished for the conversion of Christians, but she was guilty
of ignoring Jewish principles of not seeking converts. He accused her of being
a rabbinist: she should have withdrawn the book or protested the principles
of rabbinism, and she should have been aware how it doomed all Jewish
females to contempt. Perhaps cognizant of her image among Jewish women,
or simply responding to her as a Jewish woman, a subject he had treated in
his earlier writing as we have already seen, he undermined her personal image
as well. He purposefully retranslated the first two chapters of the text from
the French, recognizing that Aguilar's rendering was not faithful and hoping
to restore the polemical thrust of Orobio's pointed argument.[8]

McCaul opened the first part by attacking the character of Isaac Orobio
de Castro. On the one hand, it was remarkable, he noted, that Aguilar had
chosen his work as an alleged book of instruction for Jewish youth, thereby
preferring a man who had received a Christian education. This perhaps was
a tacit compliment to Christianity, an admission that Christian training
brought one closer to the truth. On the other hand, Orobio was hardly a
model to young people, as his work was that of a hypocrite who had hidden
his real identity for so long and had later become thirsty for revenge. He
was equivalent to Johann Andreas Eisenmenger, McCaul suggested, whose
personal bitterness to his subject warped his judgment.[9] As a Protestant missionary, McCaul would not accept the responsibility for the Christian persecution to which Orobio had been exposed; indeed, persecuting Christians
were not true Christians at all, though persecuting Jews were true rabbinical
Jews. To prove his point, McCaul juxtaposed the biography of Orobio with
that of his contemporary Uriel da Costa (1585–1640) based on the latter's

autobiography. Drawing from the lurid testimony of da Costa, it is clear, or so he contended, that atrocities practiced upon Jews of Spain were not worse than those prescribed by the Oral Law in Amsterdam. Modern Judaism was just as intolerant as the tribunal of the Inquisition. In addition to da Costa, he evoked the memory of yet another formidable though less well-known converso whom he admired in contrast to Orobio, Thomas de Pinedo (1614–79). McCaul saw his Hebrew attainments superior to those of Orobio. He was a significant classical scholar who never attacked Christianity other than the Inquisition and said positive things about Amsterdam's Christian community. McCaul thus held up two good conversos in the light of history in contradistinction to the one bad one he was attacking, as he saw it. In so doing, he displayed his thorough knowledge and awareness of the cultural ambiance of seventeenth-century Amsterdam.[10]

In the rest of the first part, McCaul focused on Isaiah 53 and challenged Orobio's claim that it was the only proof of Christianity. He also demonstrated, based on a vast array of Jewish sources, that Jews associated this chapter with their own messianic ideology. As he had done in his anti-Talmudic work, his proof came especially from Jewish liturgy. In this case, he illustrated his point from the Yozer prayer recited on the first day of Passover, since liturgy for him reflected the views of the masses of Jews, not merely the views of individuals.[11]

In the second part, McCaul took up Orobio's arguments on biblical prophecies. Christianity never opposed the Mosaic law, and its allegorical interpretations could be compared favorably with those of Jewish exegetes such as Isaac Abravanel. What is clear is how Orobio consciously misrepresented Christianity, according to McCaul; this might have been expected from illiterate Jews of Turkey or Morocco but not one educated in the superior cultural surroundings of western Europe, a clear reflection again of McCaul's European, and particularly English, sense of cultural superiority.

The most obvious fact for McCaul was the evolving nature of Jewish law. In this he relied heavily on premodern Jewish thinkers such as Joseph Albo, who claimed that the only immutable laws were the Ten Commandments and only the first two came directly from God without Moses's mediation. Similarly, David Kimḥi, Abraham Ibn Ezra, and others all acknowledged that changes in the law had existed since the time of Ezra. In the final analysis, the rabbinic code was ten times the size of the Mosaic, testifying to it numerous accretions. Albo is mentioned to refute Moses Maimonides by asserting that the law indeed changed, a stance McCaul compares favorably with that of Tertullian. McCaul constantly enlisted Albo to make his argument regarding the mutability of law; the Hebrew *le-olam* always meant for him a limited amount of time and not eternity. Orobio was thus totally ignorant of the very essence of Judaism, as McCaul proclaimed: "If the Mosaic Law be utterly immutable [as Orobio had claimed], then Judaism, which has made so many and such enormous changes in that law, is necessarily an imposter."[12]

McCaul proceeded to discuss the doctrine of the Trinity at length. It was not irrational, he claimed, citing contemporary grammarians and medieval exegetes' explanations of plurality of the Hebrew *Elohim*. In evoking both the testimony of Isaac Abravanel of the fifteenth century and Wilhelm Gesenius, his contemporary, he demonstrated that a plurality was not inconsistent with unity.[13]

McCaul ultimately returned to pronouncing how rabbinism presented only a faint resemblance to Mosaic law. As articulated by the former Catholic Orobio, its worst feature was its intolerance of non-Jews, a nursling of inquisitorial cruelty, he called it. McCaul asked how the circulators of this book would want to teach these cruel sentiments to modern Jewish youth. Reform Jews saw Christians as non-idolaters but Orobio's opinions seemed to belong to the old-fashioned and intolerant class of Jews. Why disseminate his work if one aspired to be a liberal? he asked.[14]

In the third part, McCaul emphasized that the prophecies of the Old Testament described not merely corporeal redemption but spiritual as well. He pointed out that common Jews living today both in eastern Europe and Turkey focused more on material than spiritual redemption, again casting aspersions on non–western Europeans and their cultural inferiority. Orobio, on the other hand, held both the corporeal and the spiritual to be important: "Orobio's purer idea of a spiritual redemption seems to have been the effect of his education amongst Christians, and his assertion, that such is the hope of Judaism, to be ascribed simply to the ignorance of the religion which he embraced."[15]

McCaul also found something to praise in Orobio's discussion of prophecies, since some enlightened Jews in his day had even removed them from the prayer book altogether. They sought only integration into the body politic. Here McCaul explicitly offered a political message against emancipation and integration. Although he admitted it was harsh to call for the destruction of gentiles in the end of days, yet faith in the divine word remained unbroken in these prophecies. Christians believed in Jesus but also in the national restoration of the Jewish people and the rebuilding of the Temple. Orobio was wrong again, McCaul contended, in arguing that Christians object to Jewish restoration, citing a string of ancient and more recent English Protestant Christian authorities who favored it, including Joseph Butler, Thomas Newton, Samuel Horsley, and Benjamin Blayney.[16]

McCaul concluded that it was Orobio's education in the Catholic Church that led him to misrepresent Christianity. His narrow and vindictive spirit never acknowledged the happiness of gentiles: "We fearlessly ask every Jewish reader, whether he is not ashamed of a champion so bloodthirsty and so vindictive, and whether he does not regard the republication of such doctrine, at present, not only as unseasonable, but as a libel upon the Jewish population of Great Britain?"[17] So he asked: How can modern English Jews look forward to a redemption where their fellow countrymen are excluded and exterminated?

It is hard to gauge the impact of Grace Aguilar's book on the Jewish youth of England whom she hoped to educate through her semipublic translation. It certainly did not win the popularity of some of her other books. McCaul's translation and commentary, on the other hand, seems to have attracted a certain amount of attention. The translation was described in the annual volume of the London Society, the *Jewish Intelligence* of 1839. In the next issue, the Jewish historian Isaak Marcus (Markus) Jost (1793–1860) was quoted on the work: "Here, the same as in his former works, we find him calm, collected, free from every spirit of persecution, and his field of battle, only learning." But Jost rejected the notion that the republication of Orobio's work signaled a new Jewish messianic passion to replace the Jewish passion for emancipation. Similarly, in the same issue, the Jewish editor Julius Fürst's (1805–73) review of McCaul was cited from his journal *Der Orient*, of October 24, 1840, expressing the same sentiment but objecting to the notion of a narrow messianism of Jews and seeking instead their amalgamation into European society. It is indeed fascinating to note how both Jewish intellectuals did not see McCaul's work as offensive and even praised it while disagreeing with it in part.[18]

The new Jewish-Christian debate of the nineteenth century stood in contrast to that of the seventeenth. The terms of the conflict had changed and the players were different. Evangelical Protestantism had disassociated itself completely from the history of Catholic intolerance of Jews; English Christians believed that they were more tolerant and appreciative of their Jewish citizenry and the evangelicals in particular had elevated the status of the Jews as key actors in the hopes of national restoration and the Second

Coming. The other obvious change was that the Christian missionary, despite his passionate criticisms of rabbinic Judaism, perhaps knew as much or more about rabbinic literature than Orobio himself, could cite passages from the Talmud, midrashim, targumim, medieval and modern exegetes alike, as well as from ancient and modern historians. He could offer learned responses to Orobio's pointed arguments and could overwhelm Aguilar with his knowledge of rabbinic Judaism in a way to which she was incapable of responding. The philosophes of the eighteenth century had been intrigued with the novelty of Orobio's assault on Catholicism; in McCaul's time, the attack on popery was commonplace and relatively unoriginal, and Orobio's insight into Judaism could easily be countered by a new generation of erudite Christian scholars who themselves knew more about Judaism than most contemporary Jews, certainly in England. The Jewish-Christian debate continued, but with new philological and especially historical tools, a new scholarship Orobio and his contemporaries could not have anticipated. To answer McCaul, a generation of learned maskilim in eastern Europe was prompted to respond with its own intimate knowledge of rabbinic sources and the latest methodologies of *Wissenschaft* and historicism. But that is the story told later in this book.[19]

On Reform Judaism

In the brief testimony of Stanislaus Hoga mentioned in Chapter 1, the convert had singled out for ridicule McCaul's remarks about his personal impact on the birth of Reform Judaism in England. Here are McCaul's words, taken from the introduction to the second edition of his *The Old Paths* published in 1846:

> Nine years have now elapsed since "The Old Paths" appeared as a volume. They have been translated in the meantime into Hebrew, German, and French; and their merits discussed by the learned and the unlearned of the Jewish people, in all the countries of their dispersion. The reception has in general been favourable, and the effect upon the Jewish mind perceptible. Since their first appearance, the West London Synagogue and the Liturgies of the British Jews, both renouncing that which "The Old Paths" pronounced objectionable, have started into existence. The assembled rabbies at Brunswick and

Frankfort have discussed topics similar to some treated in "The Old Paths," and in some cases come to similar conclusions respecting the value of Rabbinic Traditions. The Reform Societies of Germany have commenced a formidable attack upon the Oral Law, and a free discussion is now carried on in the numerous Jewish periodicals of that country, of which the results are easily foretold.

McCaul emphasized again that his discussion was an attack on rabbinism, not on the Jewish people, on the authors of the tradition and not on its victims. His comment about the close connection between the birth of Reform Judaism in England and his attack on the rabbis appeared to claim less than Hoga had angrily implied.[20]

Nevertheless, for McCaul the foundation of the West London Synagogue, his personal contact with its first rabbi David Woolf Marks, and the parallel developments of the reform movement in Germany were all encouraging signs that the message of anti-rabbinism as articulated in *The Old Paths* were having a positive effect on a segment of Jews dissenting from orthodox belief and praxis when he wrote these remarks in the mid-1840s. McCaul may have been deluding himself into thinking these reforms would lead to conversion to his own brand of Christianity, but he seemed to hold out real hope this would take place, and his daughter, as we have seen, certainly believed it was actually happening.[21]

In *Sketches of Judaism and the Jews*, as we have already noted, McCaul offered a series of essays sometimes quite different in tone and even content from those in his polemical book. It is as if he preferred to emphasize in the later book his genuine positive feelings toward Judaism and to the Jews he actually met, especially those in Poland. He, of course, could and did display his displeasure and impatience with the subjects he described and their reluctance to embrace the pure Christian faith he espoused, but, at the same time, his occasional appreciation and identification with them are easily perceptible.

His portrait of Moses Mendelssohn and early Reform Judaism in *Sketches* is a case in point. For the missionary McCaul, Mendelssohn was a figure of heroic proportions. Here is a part of his lengthy profile:

He [Mendelssohn] shewed them that there was other knowledge besides that of the Talmud well worthy of their acquisition, and that a Jew, notwithstanding all the unjust prejudices against the nation, could attain and maintain high literary fame in the Christian learned world. . . . This one circumstance—the introduction of German, and a taste for general literature—was sufficient to produce a mighty change amongst the Jews. In fact it was itself a revolution. An old-fashioned Rabbinical Jew in Poland still looks with horror upon the acquisition of *Galchas Taitsch* [priest's German]. And a Jew who reads epikorsische Bücher [Epicurean books], as Christian books are called, runs a risk of losing his character. The fact that Moses Mendelsohn [*sic*] broke down this one prejudice, shews incontrovertibly the weight of his character, and the powerful influence which he exercised over the Jewish mind. The Jews read German, loved German literature, and learned to esteem German authors. From that moment the Rabbinic spell was broken. Parents wished to see their children little Mendelsohns; for this German was necessary. . . . Rashi and Kimchi, the Shulchan Aruch and Tosaphoth, were laid on the shelf. Schiller and Wieland, Wolf and Kant, were the favourite books of the holy nation, the kingdom of priests, the sons of Abraham.[22]

McCaul concluded accordingly that Mendelssohn was only outwardly a rabbinical Jew, while inwardly he was "a Gentile philosopher." For a Christian, he added, it was reminiscent of the fight against popery in attaining, as he claimed Mendelssohn did, "free and full possession of the word of God," a kind of Luther for modern Jews. Similarly, Mendelssohn's disciple Naphtali Wessely was also "a restorer of science amongst the Jews."[23]

When it came to describing the first manifestations of Jewish reform in Germany, McCaul was anything but consistent. On the one hand, reform was the inevitable process by which the generations after Mendelssohn would liberate themselves from the yoke of rabbinic law and move ultimately to embracing Protestant Christianity. On the other hand, Reform Judaism had "unjudaized" all its disciples; old Jewish manners had passed away; and Jewish education had vanished: "The reform school will never produce a Kimchi nor a Joseph Karo. . . . Their national language has been deposed from its place. . . . They have renounced the land of their forefathers. . . . In short, reform, wherever it has prevailed, has robbed the Jews of their holy nationality, and sunk them to the level of a common-place religious sect. I rejoice to think that the Jewish books, the writings of Moses and the prophets, cannot be reformed, that they still remain the same. . . . Reformers may say, 'We will be as the heathen,' but still 'the people shall dwell alone, and shall not be numbered amongst the nations.' "[24]

How remarkable an observation from a Christian missionary to lament that Reform Judaism was nothing more than a religious sect that had abdicated its legacy of learning, its national language, and its claim to a national homeland. McCaul, the Hebraist and author of a commentary on Kimḥi, as well as the literalist and restorationist, could not help but express disappointment with the final results of Jewish reform. The endearing authenticity he described elsewhere in the *Sketches* prevalent among yeshiva students and Hasidim in Poland had vanished in the trade-off for Jewish emancipation in Germany.

In a later essay McCaul returned to the theme of reform, asking the simple question whether it had ultimately made any difference in contributing to the positive development of modern Judaism. His answer was unequivocal: "Jewish reform has just done as much for real improvement as the Council of Trent did for reformation. It has talked a great deal—it has done nothing."[25]

McCaul's initial high hopes that Reform Jews would ultimately enter the Christian fold seem to have been dashed as time went on and the reformers failed to take the next step of conversion. In a long description of three catechisms recently composed by liberal Jews in Germany and France, McCaul exhibited an obvious frustration and cynicism in pointing out the alleged hypocrisy of these religious leaders who sharply criticized the rabbinic tradition on the one hand but were unwilling to repudiate completely its hold on all Jews on the other. In the first instance, McCaul examined the *Lehrbuch der Mosaischen Religion* published in Munich in 1826 compiled by Dr. Alexander Behr, under the supervision and guidance of the modern Orthodox rabbi Abraham Bing on behalf of the rabbinate of Fürth.[26] He also reviewed the third edition of *Die Lehren der Mosaischen Religion* of Joseph Johlson, teacher of religion at the Jewish Congregational School at Frankfurt am Main, published in that city in 1829.[27] Regarding both works, McCaul could only conclude:

> A stranger jumble of palpable inconsistency was, perhaps, never presented to the public, and the approbation of such works by public authority does not lead us to form a very high estimate of the state of rabbinic learning amongst the Rationalist divines of Germany.
> . . . Even a dull child—and such the Jewish are not—can see that

the authors [of these two catechisms] are guilty of double dealing; that they meant to deceive one party; that either they did not believe in the Talmud, but found it necessary to cajole the old orthodox Jews, or that they did believe in all the anti-social and intolerant doctrines of the Talmud, but found it necessary to throw dust in the eyes of the Christian public.[28]

McCaul considered one other catechism, this time a French one: *Précis élémentaire d'instruction religieuse et morale pour les jeunes Français Israélites*, published by Samuel Cahen in 1820.[29] For McCaul, this text was as deficient as the other two, speaking about Judaism's embrace of all humankind while never challenging the old rabbinic notions that Christians were idolaters. Writing eight years before the establishment of the first Reform synagogue in London, McCaul, in this instance, refrained from criticizing the English Jews. At the time he wrote these lines, they remained, in his words, "respectable old-fashioned Rabbinical Jews" and "to their honour, be it said, they have never attempted to pass off on the ignorance of Christians a fictitious picture of Talmudism, decked out in the robes of Liberalism."[30]

In the end, McCaul remained unimpressed by the superficial declarations of the new liberal catechisms and the hypocrisy of the reformers in presenting Judaism as more universal and liberal than it really was while clinging to a thoughtless attachment to traditional modes of worship. Whatever the echoes of McCaul's powerful anti-rabbinic arguments within Jewish Reform circles, he ultimately proved incapable of unshackling these supposedly enlightened Jews from the hold of a deep-seated rabbinic tradition. Despite their strong criticisms of the latter, they were unprepared to break from it completely.

On Women in Judaism

One of the most prominent features of *The Old Paths*, as we have already seen, was McCaul's intense critique of the degradation of women in rabbinic Judaism. In the *Sketches*, he also devoted a fascinating essay to "the social and religious condition of the Rabbinic Jewess." He first acknowledged that Jewish reformers had made some progress in creating schools for Jewish female students, "both free schools for the poor and establishments of a higher order for the wealthy." He asked sarcastically: "But whoever heard of a female school amongst old-fashioned Rabbinical Jews? Or whoever saw a Rabbinical schoolmistress, or a Rabbinical Jewess who gained a livelihood from teaching? The female schools in London, in Germany, in Warsaw have all emanated from the power of Christian example, or the direct influence of the government."[31]

The rabbis and their law were the ultimate agents responsible for female Jewish inferiority and illiteracy for McCaul. First, the rabbis undermined the education of women: "Rabbinism lays it down as an axiom, that to study the law of God is no part of a woman's duty, and that to teach his daughters the Word of God is no part of paternal obligation." Second, the rabbis discounted their legal testimony: "Rabbinism teaches that a woman is unfit to give legal evidence, and classes her amongst those who are incapacitated either by mental or moral deficiencies." Third, they were not considered worthy of making up a quorum for public prayer: "Rabbinism excludes women from being counted as part of the Synagogue congregation. Unless there be a minian, that is, a congregation of ten, there can be no public worship of God, but the Rabbies have decided, 'that these ten must all be men, free, and adult'; so that if all the Jewesses in the world could be gathered into one synagogue, they would all count as nothing, and unless there were ten men present, the minister of the synagogue would not read prayers for them."

The ultimate conclusion of these restrictions was clear to McCaul: "Rabbinism teaches, that to be a woman is as great a degradation as to be a heathen or a slave, and provides the same form of thanksgiving for deliverance from womanhood as from heathenism and slavery. The Jew says every day in his prayers, 'Blessed art thou, O Lord, our God! King of the universe, who hath not made me a heathen. Blessed are thou, O Lord our God! King of the universe, who hath not made me a slave. Blessed art thou, O Lord our God, King of the universe, who hath not made me a woman."[32]

Yet despite this harsh denunciation of the status of traditional Jewish women, McCaul was able to present a positive dimension of Jewish womanhood as well. The official rabbinic attitude to women notwithstanding, in his own experience he had met Jewish women in whom he detected an innate spirituality. He offered evidence of this trait by describing a small book of devotion he had perused that had been compiled by a Polish Jewish woman for the use of other Jewish women. He described in scholarly fashion the sixteen-page book lacking a title page that he had seen. On its first page was a text called "The Three Gates." This prayer known as a tehinah was composed by a pious woman named Sarah, the daughter of a doctor and rabbi known as Mordecai of the holy congregation of Brisk. The three gates refer to the three commandments performed by women: knitting the challah bread for the Sabbath; going to the ritual bath for ceremonial cleanliness; and lighting the Sabbath lights. McCaul proceeded to describe other prayers in the small compendium and concluded that this liturgy revealed a deep sense of guilt on the part of Jewish women, a fearful expectation of punishment, and a firm conviction that atonement is necessary to gain divine forgiveness. McCaul readily compared these convictions to those of Catholics: "Like the Romanist," he added, "the Rabbinic Jewess looks to the merits of the saints, and trusts in the efficacy of purgatorial suffering." Nevertheless, in discovering a spiritual world inhabited only by women and translating some of their prayers into English, McCaul surely accentuated the nobility of these subjects, making their subjugation at the hands of an insensitive and indifferent rabbinic leadership appear even more intolerable.[33]

Besides his sensitive discovery, translation, and interpretation of several of these poems written for and by women, McCaul also noted "the chief reading of all Jewesses in Germany, Holland and Poland," the *Ze'enah u-Re'enah*, in his words, "a complete encyclopaedia of Rabbinism, legendary, doctrinal, and judicial; [it] may be read with ease by anyone who understands German and a little Hebrew, and will take the trouble of learning the Jewish-German character."[34] Elsewhere, McCaul characterized this massive compilation for Jewish women as his favorite book and remarked that the " 'Tsennorenna,' or the Weiber Chumash, the women's Pentateuch . . . is a compilation of all that is absurd and marvelous in Rabbinical lore, furnishes the Sabbath reading for the female Jewish population; and shews, on every page, the low state of religious knowledge amongst the Rabbinical Jewesses. If the Biblical citations were taken away, it might be classed with 'Tom Thumb' or 'Jack the Giant-Killer.' "[35]

It is that striking mixture of "the absurd and the marvelous" that informed McCaul's immersion in rabbinic literature in general and Jewish women's writing in particular. There is no doubt that his focus on women in both *The Old Paths* and *Sketches* was intended to underscore the inhumanity of rabbinic law in treating women as subordinate and unequal and to juxtapose this condition with that allegedly found in Christianity, especially among the ranks of the evangelicals. But McCaul could not help himself in appreciating the inspired literature he carefully perused. For him the Jewish "Tom Thumb" was indeed primitive but still charming. The women's poems he translated revealed a degree of religious inspiration he had not anticipated.

There was an authentic piety among traditional Jewish women that was discernable to this Christian cleric even when mired in the filth of rabbinic popery.

While McCaul's focus on the plight of Jewish females, both their victimization at the hands of the rabbis and their distinctive spirituality visible in their feminine liturgy, was relatively new in the long history of Jewish-Christian polemics, it appears less unique and original in the context of evangelical writing in Britain in the first half of the nineteenth century. Thanks to the insightful reading of women's conversionary texts, especially novels, by Nadia Valman, Kathryn Gleadle, Miriam Elizabeth Burstein, and others, it is not difficult to contextualize McCaul's dual positions within the culture of evangelicalism of his day.[36] As Valman has persuasively argued, the culture of conversion at the time McCaul's books were published held "a distinct female accent" regarding not only potential converts but also slaves, Indians, and working-class women.[37] Jewish women were also to be pitied for their suffering at the hands of husbands, fathers, and especially rabbis. Of course, the masculine world of the Anglican Church had hardly liberated its own domesticated and generally subservient female practitioners. But clearly evangelical Christianity in the 1830s and 1840s and beyond offered novel opportunities for feminine leadership within the church. Women were increasingly serving as missionaries both in England and throughout the world; women were preachers, editors of journals, authors of novels, champions of moral causes, all legitimate and praiseworthy expressions of their Christian piety. What was unique about these new outlets of feminine rebellion was that they were cast "in a safely orthodox conservative framework."[38] Christian women were not challenging male clerical or political leadership; they were simply submitting to the will of a higher authority in carrying out the divine imperative as they understood it. With these evangelical women in mind, McCaul was not necessarily acting hypocritically in denigrating the status of the Jewish woman in comparison with her Christian counterpart. On the contrary, he recognized how his own brand of Christianity had liberated and empowered women in a manner far superior to that of either rabbinic Judaism or Catholicism.[39] McCaul must have been fully aware that the majority of subscribers to the London Society for the Promotion of Christianity Amongst the Jews were in fact women.[40]

McCaul's seeming reversal from castigating the rabbinic treatment of women, their ritualistic and educational subordination, to appreciating their emotional and spiritual lives can also be fully understood by comparison to the popular novels written by evangelical authors of his era. As Nadia Valman has noted: "In these texts, Judaism is represented as ritualistic, legalistic, materialistic, archaic, and crucially masculine. At the same time, however, the distinctive philosemitism of Evangelical theology embedded in English culture a particular attachment to Jews. In Evangelical women's writing, this was expressed in the idealised figure of the Jewess. Their texts constructed an intense, emotive intimacy between the reader and the Jewish woman."[41]

Whether knowingly or not, McCaul was articulating in his own writings the same dichotomy Valman elsewhere called "Bad Jew/Good Jewess."[42] This was, of course, a further expression of the complexity of his love-hate relationship to Jews and Judaism that we have already seen throughout his writings and missionary activity. Nevertheless, in this instance, his elevation of the Jewish female over her male counterpart mirrored the dominant way in which evangelical women authors writing to a wide Christian readership effectively deployed the rhetoric of gender in differentiating Judaism from Christianity.

CHAPTER 3

From Missionizing the Jews to Defending Biblical Inerrancy

The Last Years of McCaul's Life

During the last eight years of his life and imposing career McCaul faced an intensely traumatic period brought on by failing health and by two highly publicized series of events that disrupted considerably his lifelong preoccupations and hopes for evangelical Christianity and its mission to the Jews. Both series reshaped his ultimate concerns and self-image as an evangelical Christian and significantly defined his legacy. While he appeared to have withdrawn considerably from his proselytizing activities regarding the Jews to focus during this time on defending the literal integrity of the Pentateuch against a new generation of biblical critics, the two preoccupations were not unrelated, as I hope to argue. McCaul's assault on the rabbis and his assault on the new biblical criticism emerging among certain Anglican clergy both stemmed from his fundamental belief that the foundation of pure Judaism as well as pure Christianity rested on the infallible truth of the biblical text.

Jerusalem Controversies

McCaul was deeply affected by a string of ugly controversies that broke out in Jerusalem around 1858 over the treatment of some recent converts by the Anglican bishop and several missionaries associated with the London Society. But even earlier, in 1855, McCaul's disenchantment with the leadership of the

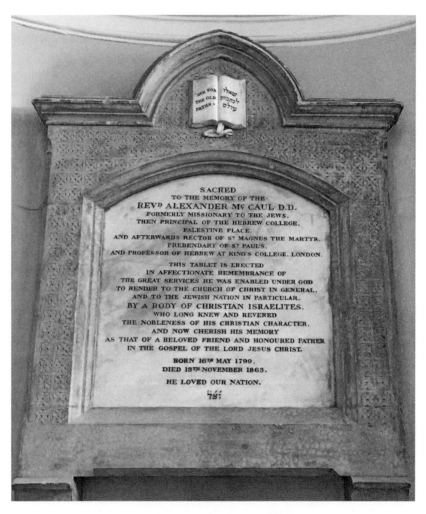

SACRED
TO THE MEMORY OF THE
REV.D ALEXANDER M.C CAUL D.D.
FORMERLY MISSIONARY TO THE JEWS,
THEN PRINCIPAL OF THE HEBREW COLLEGE,
PALESTINE PLACE,
AND AFTERWARDS RECTOR OF S.T MAGNUS THE MARTYR,
PREBENDARY OF S.T PAUL'S,
AND PROFESSOR OF HEBREW AT KING'S COLLEGE, LONDON.

THIS TABLET IS ERECTED
IN AFFECTIONATE REMEMBRANCE OF
THE GREAT SERVICES HE WAS ENABLED UNDER GOD
TO RENDER TO THE CHURCH OF CHRIST IN GENERAL,
AND TO THE JEWISH NATION IN PARTICULAR,
BY A BODY OF CHRISTIAN ISRAELITES,
WHO LONG KNEW AND REVERED
THE NOBLENESS OF HIS CHRISTIAN CHARACTER,
AND NOW CHERISH HIS MEMORY
AS THAT OF A BELOVED FRIEND AND HONOURED FATHER
IN THE GOSPEL OF THE LORD JESUS CHRIST.

BORN 16.TH MAY 1799,
DIED 13.TH NOVEMBER 1863.

HE LOVED OUR NATION.

FIGURE 2. Stone memorial in Christ Church, Spitalfields, London, dedicated to Alexander McCaul. Photo supplied by the Rector of Christ Church, Spitalfields.

London Society, an organization in which he had played such a leading and conspicuous role over the years, was already quite apparent. This had nothing to do with the affairs of running the society in the Holy Land but with fiscal responsibility. On October 4, 1866, three years after McCaul had died, his son Joseph published a letter to the editor in the *Morning Post* entitled provocatively "A Voice from the Tomb," in which he made public a long letter his father had written in April 1855:

> Sir: My father, the late Dr. M'Caul, spent the last thirty years of his life in laboring for the conversion of the Jews, and in connection with the London Society for Promoting Christianity amongst the Jews. During the few years that preceded his death cogent reasons compelled him to sever his connection with that society. The annual income of that corporation amounts to no less a sum between 30,000 and 40,000 British pounds. A variety of unworthy motives have been recently assigned in the public prints, by the official disbursers of this princely charity, as to the causes of Dr. M'Caul's having withdrawn himself from the responsibilities of so weighty a stewardship. In justice to my father's memory I beg you to give publicity to the accompanying letter. It was addressed by Dr. M'Caul to the Jews' Society's Committee 11 years ago. The topics of which it treats, I venture to submit, deserve the serious consideration of all subscribers to religious societies. The subjoined is a verbatim copy of a draft in my father's handwriting and was found amongst his papers after his decease.[1]

Alexander McCaul's long letter offered considerable details regarding the financial improprieties of the London Society, ending emphatically with the following declaration: "For more than a quarter of a century the glory of the London Society was that it every year published particulars of payments. That glory you have removed—these particulars you have suppressed in the last report. That suppression, and the weight it lends to my view of the expenditure, induces me to retire."[2] By the time he wrote this letter, McCaul held only "the honourable position of member of the Correspondence Committee" of the London Society, and it was this role he was abdicating. Nevertheless, the symbolism of so prominent a leader severing his ties from the society could not have been missed by the remaining members of the committee. Joseph's decision to publish the letter eleven years later was obviously meant to document publicly this official break. As he put it, there were cogent reasons several years before his father's death for completely severing his connection with the London Society. This was no longer a mere mis-understanding among colleagues; it was a final break.

Perhaps not coincidently in the same year that Joseph had published his father's resignation letter to the London Society, his brother Samuel pub-lished in London another pamphlet with the following title: *Jerusalem: Its Bishop, Its Missionaries, and Its Converts; Being a Series of Letters Addressed to the Editor of the "Daily News" in the Year 1858, by the Late Rev. Alexander McCaul, D.D., with Other Letters, &c., Illustrative Thereof, Collected and Edited by His Son, Samuel McCaul, B.C.L., of St. John's College, Oxford.*[3] This likely coordination between the two brothers appeared to be a collective effort on their part to defend the integrity of their father against any and all critics, to give voice to his still relevant criticisms of the functioning of the London Society both in England and in Palestine, and to fully document his transfor-mation from public leader to outspoken critic of the society.

The events of 1858 that precipitated McCaul's letters to the *Daily News* were surely ideological but also highly personal. They involved two strong personalities, Samuel Gobat, the Jerusalem bishop, and James Finn, the Brit-ish consul in Jerusalem and the son-in-law of Alexander McCaul. A Protes-tant bishopric had been established in Jerusalem in 1841, a joint endeavor of Anglican and Prussian Protestants. Alexander McCaul had first been offered the position, but he declined, arguing for the need to fill the post with a Christian of Jewish ancestry. Michael Solomon Alexander was thus conse-crated on November 7, 1841, as the first bishop of the Anglo-Prussian Church of St. James in Jerusalem. McCaul wholeheartedly approved of the appoint-ment, waxing eloquently that the bishopric was "a most powerful instrument for the spread of the Gospel amongst the Jews, and for the reformation of the Eastern Churches. . . . A providential opportunity, such as presents itself only once in the course of centuries." For McCaul the appointment of a former Jew with German and English roots not only solidified the partner-ship between British evangelicals and Prussian Pietists; it symbolized the beginning of the process of restoring a Jewish population to Jerusalem and their ultimate conversion to Christianity. The Jerusalem bishopric, with its active proselytizing activities, would be the agent for Christ's imminent return. Thus individual Jews who would be embraced by the bishop and the pious consul in Jerusalem would inaugurate a conversionary process of cosmic proportions.[4]

Michael Alexander unexpectedly died in 1845 and was replaced a year later by the French Swiss Gobat, a choice satisfying neither to the British Anglicans nor the German Lutherans. Among the conspicuous critics of the new bishop was James Finn, who considered the bishop "too German to be allowed to enjoy English protection," a strange allegation regarding an actual non-German. His discomfort, however, arose from more than ethnic differences. Gobat displayed little enthusiasm for the agenda that McCaul and Finn had embraced: the obsessive desire to convert the Jews and facilitate their return to Jerusalem. His alternative focus on engaging with Christian and Muslim populations in Palestine while de-emphasizing the primary mission to a fledgling population of Jewish converts was surely noticed and resented by Finn and his allies.[5]

All of this provides the backdrop for understanding the immediate circumstances that elicited a confrontation between Gobat and Finn during the 1850s and ultimately provoked McCaul's strong reactions. The bishop and consul locked horns over a baptized Jew named Simeon Rosenthal. Born in Brody, Rosenthal traveled to Smyrna and Constantinople. There he met missionaries from the London Society, especially McCaul's close associate John Nicolayson, a conspicuous missionary presence in Jerusalem, one with strong ties to the German-speaking world. Nicolayson eventually baptized him in 1839 with his entire family, and he became the first new convert to join the Jerusalem Protestant community.[6] When his daughter married the son of a prominent moneylender, Bishop Alexander and his wife were in attendance, signaling, no doubt, the hope that the Hebrew Christian community in Jerusalem would ultimately flourish.

In Jerusalem, Rosenthal was employed as the dragoman to the British consul James Finn. In 1849, a feud broke out between Bishop Gobat, who had clashed with several Jewish converts before, his associates, and Rosenthal. Rosenthal had also been appointed an inspector of the London Society's construction projects in Jerusalem, but Dr. Edward Macgowan, the director of the society's hospital in the city, accused him of embezzling funds earmarked for building materials and other expenses. The matter wore on and boiled up in 1857 when Finn appointed Rosenthal to serve as his representative during a brief absence from the city. Gobat strongly protested and received the support of three other members of the London Society, including Macgowan. Rosenthal turned for protection to Finn who briefly arrested Gobat and his three associates, asserting his authority as British consul in claiming that Rosenthal had been unjustly imprisoned and that his sickly son Albert had been denied proper care from the bishop and eventually died.

The officials of the London Society attempted to quiet the embarrassing incident of their bishop fighting with the British consul by refusing to take a stand in favor of either party. Nevertheless, both sides engaged in public controversy over the so-called Rosenthal case. The detractors of the bishop and his party were accused of carrying out a "system of persecution against Rosenthal and his family." Family members added their own testimonies about the horrible treatment of the "pious Albert." In the meantime, despite numerous investigations of the matter, the London Society's officials could not determine whether he had stolen the money or not. The bishop and his representatives also wrote formal responses to two of Finn's associates, James Graham and Holman Hunt, and to Finn himself, denying the truthfulness of the claims against them and claiming their complete innocence in the matter; on the contrary, they claimed that they were dishonored by Finn's aggressive behavior toward them.[7]

Samuel McCaul's pamphlet, based on letters his father had originally published in 1858 and now reissued as a collection eight years later and three years after their author's death, testified to the festering controversy the Rosenthal case had initiated and the bitter resentment the son still harbored against the London Society. As Samuel wrote:

> The prospect of a real and impartial investigation into the manner in which the Jerusalem Missions of the London Society for Promoting Christianity amongst the Jews have for many years conducted, has induced me to publish, in a collected form, the letters addressed by my late father to the Editor of the *Daily News*, in the year 1858, upon the subject.
>
> The testimony of one who had sacrificed all his worldly prospects in order to become a missionary to the Jews, who had devoted the thirty best years of his life to the promotion of the Society's interests, whose energy and learning contributed mainly to its sudden rise from obscurity to the foremost rank among religious societies, and who was, in some sense, the founder of the Jerusalem Bishopric, should have weighed with those who might in 1858 have ascertained whether the side which he espoused was right or wrong; but they would not heed him.[8]

Almost echoing the sentiments of his brother Joseph in the publication the latter had published in the same year, Samuel displayed the same bitterness toward the society their father had helped forge and a deep resentment that those responsible for the society's policies had been indifferent to his pleas and unresponsive to any of his allegations against Gobat. This was a highly personal matter to Samuel because Rosenthal was the first Jerusalem convert of the London Society, as we have mentioned, and his reputation was important as a moral exemplar of the community of Hebrew Christians his father had strived to create. It was doubly personal since the reputation of James Finn, the husband of his sister, had also been impugned.

In the words of the father, a fair trial for Rosenthal was necessary since he "was incarcerated, exposed to violence, and denied justice." In the ideal society that McCaul had hoped to build, one should not make a distinction between a bishop and a baptized Jew for "if Jewish converts are to be thus oppressed and ruined, they will find few Jews willing to be converted."[9] In other words, the stakes were higher than the mere personal humiliation of a single convert. Such disrespect for a Christian who had been born a Jew but accepted the faith of Jesus Christ placed in jeopardy the entire life work of this missionary to the Jews.

McCaul underscored the fact that this was not an isolated incident but typified the crude and improper behavior of the Jerusalem leadership of the London Society toward baptized Jews. He mentioned how a Christian Jew had been beaten at a meeting of converts with two missionaries present; how a man named Isaak Block, considered a learned Talmud scholar, had been expelled by the bishop; and how the bishop had also condoned the marriage of an unscrupulous character named Hanna Hadoub to a young daughter of a convert. Regarding the last example, McCaul added: "I am a father and my paternal feelings may lead me to regard with undue horror the melancholy fate of Hanna Hadoub's bride."[10]

McCaul also recalled that Bishop Gobat had accused James Finn and his wife of Tractarianism, a movement emanating from Oxford associated with the Anglo-Catholic proclivities of Edward Pusey and John Henry Newman and clearly an anathema to evangelicals such as McCaul or Gobat. For McCaul, this was a totally false accusation: "Not Tractarian opposition, but Episcopal interference in the affairs of the Consulate has been the source of all the present trouble." McCaul could not help but recall that Finn was not merely a seasoned diplomat proudly representing the English government but was also a learned Hebrew scholar, who, like his father-in-law, had displayed a profound love "for the Jewish cause."[11]

Gobat and his allies, of course, denied all of these accusations and defended their innocence and moral propriety in a series of public letters.

The charges and countercharges of both parties were highly personal, but larger issues remained in the final analysis. There was the matter of the competing interests between English evangelicals and those representing the Lutheran Germans supporting the Jerusalem bishopric. Gobat, unlike Alexander, had no Jewish background and displayed little sympathy for the fate of the tiny community of Hebrew Christians aspiring to settle on Mount Zion. On the contrary, he considered a mass conversion and restoration of Jews in Jerusalem as highly fanciful, economically draining, and politically misguided with regard to the real interests of the English government. It was also obvious from his engagements with the converts themselves that he considered them to be of dubious character and ultimately unreliable as acolytes of their newly professed faith. The economic and spiritual investment McCaul had advocated in the Jewish Christian community and their proposed settlement in Jerusalem was unrealistic and unwarranted. The Protestant church would benefit more by turning its missionary gaze on the indigenous population of local Arabs living in the Middle East, one more susceptible to the blandishments of the Christian missionaries.

Whether or not Gobat's priorities would ultimately supplant those of McCaul, it was clear that in 1858 McCaul was losing the battle. He had already severed his official standing within the leadership circle of the London Society three years earlier over a budget he could no longer justify. His bitter denunciations of 1858 emerged from a position of weakness within the organization. More important, as he himself must have realized, the vision of a restored Zion and an intensified Jewish presence in Palestine so critical to his lifelong passion had lost much of its vitality and sustainability under the present leadership of the Jerusalem bishopric. McCaul could complain, and his sons continued to publicize his complaints in honoring his legacy, but from the perspective of a sickly man approaching his life's end, his aspiration of building a large community of Jewish Christians seemed as remote and unattainable as ever before. The fate of Simeon Rosenthal and his family surely signaled McCaul's own failure as a missionary to the Jews.

The Threat of Biblical Criticism

At about the same time that McCaul had experienced the personal rupture of breaking from the missionary society to which his name had been associated for decades, he encountered a new challenge in his life, one of even greater magnitude than the first. In 1860, a group of Anglican clerics published a book simply called *Essays and Reviews*, utilizing the latest findings of biblical criticism and archaeology to challenge the very foundations of a literalist reading of the Bible. Each essay was authored independently by one of six churchmen and one layperson. The most radical of the contributors was Benjamin Jowett, a fellow of Balliol College and regius professor of Greek at Oxford University. His essay "On the Interpretation of Scripture" argued that the Bible ought to be treated as scholars treated classical texts. He considered divine revelation as nonliteral and progressive; scripture was always subject to reinterpretation as each generation encountered it. Appearing almost at the same time as the publication of Darwin's famous work on evolution, the other essays in the volume also articulated from various perspectives the challenges archaeology, history, and the new sciences were posing to the veracity of the biblical account of creation and divine miracles.[12]

For an evangelical such as McCaul this book and the series of controversies that broke out in subsequent years were shocking blows to the pristine faith he had professed throughout his entire career. In a series of works written in his last years of life, he took strong issue with those who questioned the facticity of the biblical narrative, its detailed chronology, or the revelatory foundation of the miracles it described. For McCaul, this scourge of skepticism sweeping England and the Continent represented a crisis that required his full energy even in his declining years. The issue of Jewish conversion could no longer be his highest priority as he tried valiantly to prevent a disaster of major proportions.[13]

McCaul's first work defending the authenticity of the Bible addressed *Essays and Reviews* directly. Modestly entitled *Some Notes on the First Chapter of Genesis*, it had the feel of an academic discourse rather than a heated polemic against his opponents. This tone would change radically in the subsequent works, but here McCaul remained rather restrained in maintaining the historicity of the biblical account of creation and in arguing for the lack of contradictions in the two distinct accounts in Genesis 1 and 2. The biblical narrative was not made antiquated, McCaul maintained, by the progress of modern science. Moreover, the more biblical critics put forth their views on the biblical accounts, the more confusion and uncertainty reigned. He declared: "With such variety of opinion amongst the most celebrated German critics, and with nothing beyond the assertion of the essayist as to his own conviction, he will hardly blame us if we refuse to abandon the unity of the first and second chapters of Genesis, unanimously held by Jews and

Christians, by the whole Church, ancient and modern, Protestant and Romanist, until the time of [Jean] Astruc (1753); neither will he be surprised if 'men ignore a philological certainty' of the existence of which there is no visible proof."[14]

Here, as in his later works, the German critics were targeted as a source of radical heresy while the long-held testimony of Catholic and Protestant traditions was solicited to affirm what for McCaul was a consensual truth. The first words of Genesis referred generally to an unspecified duration not to a particular time frame. They did not contradict recent geological discoveries that alleged that the earth had existed "for myriads of years before the creation of man." Moses referred to an indefinite time, one exceeding the powers of human calculation. The differences between the two accounts of creation were to be explained "by the different objects which he [Moses] had in view in the two chapters. In the first, to give an outline of the history of the universe and in the second, to relate the origin and primitive history of man, so far as it was necessary as a preparation for the history of the Fall."[15]

The final conclusion of McCaul was not unexpected. Perusing some of the contemporary accounts of scientific discovery, he followed a long line of exegetes who viewed science as confirming rather than contradicting the biblical account: "Thus a comparison of the actual statements of Moses with the discoveries and conclusions of modern science is so far from shaking, that it confirms our faith in the accuracy of the sacred narrative. We are astonished to see how the Hebrew Prophet, in his brief and rapid outline sketched 3,000 years ago, has anticipated some of the most wonderful of recent discoveries, and can ascribe the accuracy of his statements and language to nothing but inspiration." One was left in a state of wonder at Moses's deep understanding of the universe, one truly superhuman. Faith had, therefore, nothing to fear from science, he proclaimed. Geology and astronomy revealed the doctrines of eternity, omnipotence, and the wisdom of the creator.[16]

McCaul's *Rationalism and Deistic Infidelity* was published at the same time as his reflections on Genesis but actually appeared even earlier in three separate letters written to the editor of the *Record* newspaper. Initially in his first and second letter McCaul took a different tack regarding German learning, claiming that the roots of the new rationalist biblical criticism emerged not from the Germans but from English and French deism. In other words, modern infidelity to scripture was to be located in the freethinking of the seventeenth and early eighteenth centuries, in the writing of John Toland, Matthew Tindal, and Thomas Morgan. The rationalism presently challenging biblical inspiration was in reality deism revived; it was an old story rather than a recent invention.[17]

However, by the third letter, McCaul distinguished between the old German learning of Philipp Spener and the Moravian brethren with that found in the writings of David Friedrich Strauss, Ludwig Feuerbach, and Bruno Bauer. Similarly, the popular writings of Gotthold Lessing, Christoph Martin Wieland, Friedrich Schiller, and Johann Wolfgang Goethe were all hostile to revelation. By the middle of the last century, McCaul contended, a disbelief in fundamental Christian doctrines arose in Germany, and its chief patrons were among the clergy. This same anti-Christianity was now advancing in England: "In the famous 'Essays and Reviews' a deliberate and well-planned assault is made upon the Church and the very existence of scriptural Christianity; and all who value either the one or the other are bound by their allegiance to their Saviour to resist the attacks of the enemy." These attacks emerged from "false friends, even holding the office of ministers of the Church." If they were honest, McCaul added, they should have left the church and if they refused, they should have been expelled. He concluded with a gloomy warning: "If the clergy or the laity falter in this matter, the doom of the Church and the country is sealed. Rationalistic Infidelity, which has been spreading silently, but surely, for the last thirty years, must prevail, the divine blessing and protection must be forfeited. Thousands will be precipitated hopelessly into unbelief, and the nation exposed to those fearful evils and that deep humiliation which followed national apostasy in France and Germany."[18]

By the end of the same year, McCaul was intensely following the repercussions of *Essays and Reviews* as they spilled over into the courtroom. One of its seven authors, Dr. Rowland Williams, was brought up on charges of heresy in the Arches Court of Canterbury in December 1861. He was defended by James Fitzjames Stephen, the brother of the famous author and critic Sir Leslie Stephen. As described in Leslie Stephen's biography of his brother, the principal charges against Williams were that he denied the inspiration of the Bible; that he specifically questioned that Jonah and Daniel had written the biblical works ascribed to them; and that he disputed the canonicity of the Epistle to the Hebrews. James Fitzjames Stephen defended his client by first arguing that the question before the court was purely legal, "that it is a question not whether Dr. Williams' doctrines were true, but whether they were such as were forbidden by law to be uttered by a clergyman." Second, the law was embedded in the Thirty-Nine Articles of the

Church of England, not, as the prosecutors maintained, in biblical passages recited in the liturgy. Third, and most important, the Articles had left open the question whether the Bible "contains" the revelation or whether it actually "constitutes" it. "Anglican clergy," he contended, "are at liberty to apply criticism freely in order to discriminate between the part of the Bible which is and that which is not part of divine revelation." As Leslie Stephen admitted, "the argument, though forcible and learned, was not in the first instance quite successful." Williams was convicted, although eventually he obtained an acquittal. Leslie also added that his brother's defense reflected his own personal convictions; he identified with the positions of his client and "believed the Church of England could be kept sufficiently open to admit the gradual infusion of rational belief."[19]

McCaul's lengthy response to Stephen focused primarily on his third point, which McCaul contended impugned the divine authority of scripture: his claim that the Bible was not the word of God but only contained it, "and to bring it down to the level of a human composition by asserting, that as the vehicle of revelation, 'it is not absolutely pure, nor from the stains and inaccuracies which appear to be necessary to everything else, which is in any way mixed up with human nature.'" For McCaul, the question whether the Bible was the word of God "is the fundamental principle upon which the whole superstructure of his [Stephen's] argument is raised." And for him, the matter for a faithful Protestant was unambiguous: "The whole scriptures" are the word of God, "not a part of them, not something contained in scripture, but scripture itself."[20] This position distinguished Protestants from Catholics who meant by the word of God both the written and the unwritten word or, in other words, the tradition. To the reader of McCaul's *The Old Paths*, the argument was familiar. He had similarly claimed that the rabbis had unjustly added their own accretions to the pure Mosaic law, which they deemed "an oral law." The Romanists and Stephen had adopted the same position, and McCaul was consistently calling out their doctrinal fallacy. To underscore his point, McCaul cited Josephus and the New Testament, claiming that "the faith of the early Christian Church was very similar, if not identical, with that of the Jews."[21] The formulation was unmistakable: early Judaism and early Christianity had been unwavering in their belief that the Bible was the word of God. Only the Catholic Church and the rabbis corrupted this belief and ultimately allowed the present biblical critics to undermine biblical authority in the author's day. Here was a direct link between McCaul's assault on the critics of biblical literalism and his previous criticisms of the rabbis. We shall return to this link below.

McCaul concluded his argument against Stephen with an intensely emotional plea to his readers. The implications of Stephen's argument were not merely theoretical or academic; they threatened the very foundations of the Christian faith and thus required a radical response:

> The present anti-biblical demonstration is not therefore a reaction, which, we may hope, according to the law of reactions, will wear itself out. It is the development of principles put into motion long before the Anglo-Catholic movement, and which have only now acquired their full momentum. It must not, therefore, be disregarded as a passing evil, but a dreadful epidemic, requiring the utmost vigilance and care to prevent its fatal ravages. The plague has begun, and can be stayed only by the combined efforts of clergy and laity. Laymen are grievously mistaken if they think that they have no duty to help in the defence of the common faith; and still more, if they think that whilst they give themselves to the promotion of missionary and philanthropic objects, or the preservation of Church rates, the faith will take care of itself. For the last fifty years the voice of the laity has been heard more and more, and the pious activity of the laity exerted in the furtherance of everything good. Most disastrous would it be if that voice were to be dumb, and that activity null only in the defence of the Bible. As the Bible, and the Bible only, is the religion of Protestants, so it is the only support of all missionary and philanthropic effort. Let scepticism increase and be taught in pulpits, and schools, and universities, and all religious societies and charitable institutions must soon come to an end. Without faith in the Bible, neither love for the heathen, nor sympathy with our own population can long continue. Without faith in the Bible the nation itself cannot exist. It is the blessing of God that gives national greatness, national happiness, and national security. But "if the foundations be destroyed, what can the righteous do?" [Psalm 11:3][22]

By 1862, only a year before his own death, McCaul faced his most formidable challenge to the notion of biblical infallibility in the person of the colorful John William Colenso, a British mathematician, theologian, biblical scholar, social activist, and advocate for native Africans in Natal and Zululand, who was appointed the first bishop of Natal for the Church of England.

In 1862, Colenso published in London the first volume of his highly provocative *The Pentateuch and the Book of Joshua Critically Examined*, immediately
evoking a storm of criticism from clergy and laity alike.[23] Two works bearing
McCaul's name quickly appeared in the following year. The first was his
thorough critique of Colenso's arguments in a book entitled *An Examination
of Bp. Colenso's Difficulties with Regard to the Pentateuch and Some Reasons for
Believing in Its Authenticity and Divine Origin*, published by Rivingtons in
London in 1863. It joined a large chorus of other critical works against Colenso including a series of ten letters submitted to the editor of the *Record*
newspaper written by Alexander's aforementioned son Joseph.[24]

The second publication was not actually written by McCaul but satiri-
cally reflected his arguments against Colenso's work. Published in Dublin in
the same year as McCaul's death in 1863, it purported to record the so-called
proceedings of a libel trial, this time involving Alexander McCaul directly.
The book, edited by J. Field Johnston, Esq., was entitled *M'Caul v. Colenso:
Libel: Report of the Trial in M'Caul v. Colenso in the Court of Proper Pleas,
Dublin, Before a Special Jury*. There is little doubt the author concocted a
fictional setting to dramatize the arguments of these two ideological adversaries by referring to his work on the title page as a "jeu d'esprit." But this is
qualified on the next page with the following line: "The reader of the following pages is requested to observe that by denominating them as 'A JEU
D'ESPRIT' is meant to be intimated the fictitious character of the machinery
employed, and not the intention to treat with levity a question regarded, in
a greater or less degree, as serious, by the community generally." In other
words, while the trial setting was no more than a literary device, the issues
raised by the dramatic debate were not to be treated with "levity." To my
mind, the arguments of the two lawyers, made with considerable flair and
wit, even nastiness at times, still reflect both of the highly publicized views
of their distinguished clients and especially conform to McCaul's opinions
represented in his other writings treated in this chapter.[25]

The plaintiff McCaul of King's College and the defendant Rev. John
William Colenso, D.D., bishop of Natal, are first introduced. The suit
accuses Colenso of "maliciously intending to injure the memory of the said
Moses who deservedly enjoyed the esteem and good opinion of the Christian people."[26] McCaul is designated as the executor de son tort of Moses,
the reputed author of the Pentateuch. As executor, McCaul "had no legal
authority to deal with the goods or the memory of the deceased, but whose
meddlings, though without authority, if characterized by honesty and

discretion, were protected by the law." The plaintiff is considered "a trustee of the Christian public, and responsible for the preservation of their ancient literature."[27]

As no less than "a trustee of the Christian public," McCaul is presented as taking the responsibility for "the historical value and dependability of the Pentateuch as a whole" in a court of law. McCaul's defense of Moses against Colenso's arguments is clearly motivated by a feeling that this work, even more than those that had preceded it, spelled doom for the English church: "The speculations of the *Essays and Reviews* were fine spun and foggy; they did not reach the million; the million did not care for them, had no taste for 'Meditations amongst the Tombs' for cloud-land ballooneries. But here they had before them a Bishop, a live Bishop, a Right Rev. Bishop, who went out to Africa for a particular purpose, and returned for a purpose particularly different. . . . The ignorant and the inexperienced were flattered by the assurance that they possessed, each one for himself, the means of demolishing that venerable structure, the Pentateuch."[28]

As McCaul's lawyer, comically named Mr. Lightside, continues in the name of the plaintiff: "It was an issue of life and death, and he would not disguise it. From time whereof the memory of man ran not to the contrary, there had been a Pentateuch. As this Pentateuch was the oldest history in the world, so there was no history of a time when there was not a Pentateuch. . . . The Divine dispensations had melted one into the other, the Mosaic into the Christian, the Patriarchal into the Mosaic."[29] Lightside admits that it is difficult to believe in the utter veracity of the Pentateuch, but it is even harder to disbelieve it: "It was hard to believe that an ass spoke. But it was harder to believe that the Jewish people were such asses as to believe he did, if he didn't. The Pentateuch itself was a miracle, a huge, uniform miracle. And looked at in this light it possessed a dignity which, in spite of all the arithmetic in the world, in spite of detected petty incongruities, would recommend it to the latest ages. This, at least, was the plaintiff's case. Therefore, he repeated, the issue was a momentous one, for, if the Pentateuch fell, the whole substratum of their common Christianity fell with it."[30]

Here is a distorting mirror cast on both the gist of McCaul's argument and an expression of the visceral feelings of the dying churchman behind it. Most interesting in his defense of the Pentateuch was the obvious connection with the Jews and their role in preserving the text. It was as if McCaul had pitted the testimony of this ancient people and his affection for them and their dignity against the heretical utterances of a misguided bishop. How fascinating was his association of the sanctity of the Torah with those who were its original bearers!

Colenso's purported attorney Serjeant Setter is then allowed to respond and to defend the integrity of the bishop's position. For him the plaintiff is wrong in insisting that this is a matter of life and death. Christianity would survive on its own strength whatever the reliability of the Pentateuch: "We quarrel not with the miraculous element in the Pentateuch. Only we insist it shall be allowed to detail its own miracles. If the Pentateuch falls, its morality and its miracles must fall along with it, but it is not with its morality or its miracles that we begin by finding fault but with the Pentateuch itself. . . . Our business is with the self-contradictions of the Pentateuch; our case is that it cannot hang together as a narrative of facts." He then provides an inventory of the numerous contradictions and inaccuracies the Pentateuch presented and its utter disdain for rational explanations and inner coherence. McCaul is not entitled to refute each and every detail by appealing to miracles: "The plaintiff is invincible. Driven from wady to wady, from Elim to Rephidim, from Kadesh to Hor, he has an unfailing resource—a reservoir of miraculous interpositions. But if miracles are to be supplied wherever necessary, I throw up my brief."[31]

Setter does not miss his adversary's referencing the Jews. In describing the alleged miracle of Moses striking the rock for water: "To the Jew indeed it might be so, with whom everything was miraculous, or nothing miraculous; to the Jew whose learning was not of the laws of nature, and who knew no history but that of one protracted national Providence. . . . The plaintiff's task is to prove the Pentateuch true, not to prove that the Jews believed it to be true." And a few pages later, Setter turns even more abusive: "The Jews were a servile, selfish, fanatical race; they were vindictive, they were bloodthirsty, they sacrificed their sons and their daughters to devils, they tumbled out of one slough of idolatry into another; they were cunning, they were credulous, they wallowed in forgetfulness of the very idea which it was their mission to keep intact and transmit to succeeding ages, the idea of pure monotheism, and will you receive the rust which they allowed to gather around it as all Divine?"[32]

Setter's rational arguments against a fundamentalist reading of the Bible suddenly take a sinister turn to something we'd see as outright anti-Semitism. Lightside had opened the door to this outburst by evoking Jewish testimony to affirm the sanctity of the Pentateuch. This allows Setter to imply that defending the integrity of the five books of Moses was synonymous with defending the Jews. McCaul's reading of scripture was Jewish at its core, Setter contends, particularly in its defense of the Torah (= Pentateuch) as the foundation of all subsequent Christian faith. It is as if Setter was arguing that by distinguishing between the morality of Protestant Christianity and the barbarity of the Hebrew culture that preceded it and that was embedded in the text, he is liberating Christianity by de-Judaizing it. There is no doubt in Setter's mind that he was exposing McCaul for what he really was: A Jew in Christian garb!

Setter closes his argument against Lightside and McCaul with one last derogatory comment addressed to the plaintiff:

> What means the insanity of this prosecution, this complaint? What means this shallow-visaged, hollow-pated rancor against the defendant? What means this foaming at the mouth of orthodoxy whenever it is hinted that the Gentiles may be in any degree enlightened, irrespectively of our church missionary militant? We are not the aggressors, if it be so. We do not compass sea and land to make one proselyte. We speak what we know, and testify what we have seen; and how much are our accusers better? Are they Hebraists? So are we. Are they churchmen? So are we. Are they in authority? So are we. In labors as abundant; in perils amongst our own countrymen; in perils amongst the Zulus; in perils of the sea; of the stock of the hierarchy; of the seed of consecrations; a Bishop amongst the Bishops; as touching the law, blameless.[33]

In the words preceding this peroration, Setter had claimed that McCaul was identifying too much with a Jewish reverence to the Pentateuch. In this passage, he alluded not so obliquely to McCaul's avocation as a missionary, one compassing sea and land to make one proselyte. In Setter's mind the roles of missionary and defender of biblical literalism were indeed the same.

Lightside does not ultimately deny the allegations of McCaul's Jewish connections; instead he seems to have powerfully embraced them. He returns to the question posed by Setter about whether what was true to the Jew should be true to the Christian as well: "I answer, in an essential, possessory sense, that it is; and that the contrary cannot be maintained until you are able to disentangle from one another the Divine and human elements which coincide in the act and fact of inspiration. . . . I tell him . . . that those old Jew stars have not gone out, but are burning brightly, and will burn brighter and brighter, until the perfect day." And finally Lightside underscores once more the Jewish origins of the notion of biblical inerrancy: "And this religious infallibility embraces a sanction openly given to the current belief of the Jews regarding some of the prominent facts in their own history. . . . Therefore, to such an extent as the Christianity of the New Testament rests for support upon the credibility of the Old; to such an extent is that credibility recognized and adopted by its Author. You cannot entirely destroy the one without disarranging the other, you cannot hold to the one and despise the other, you must abide by both or neither."[34]

In the end, the chief justice charges the jury to judge the general credibility of the Pentateuch and the mysterious and miraculous nature of Christianity. After a month, they conclude that while the defendant had exhibited "episcopal precipitancy," he had not succeeded in overturning the credibility of the Pentateuch and had not acted with malice. The damages were limited to one farthing, and the judge inserts the verdict in his notebook "to be used upon a future occasion, if necessary, and the foreman can publish it in the newspapers."[35]

In the same year he had engaged Colenso in writing and in the fictitious courtroom, McCaul published one final work on the scholarship of yet another cleric who he deemed "the head of 'the Essays and Reviews' School of Divinity." He was Dean Arthur Stanley, at the time the regius professor of ecclesiastical history at Oxford. In 1863 Stanley published the first volume of what would eventually be three of his *History of the Jewish Church*, and McCaul was apparently well enough to both notice it and review it. McCaul displayed little appreciation for the book's contribution to biblical history and theology. The lectures Stanley had delivered, he pointed out, "are manifestly the result of much thought, varied and extensive reading, study, and travel, and yet are so enlivened by the author's brilliant and ever-active imagination, that they may be regarded as the romance of sacred history." McCaul's specific criticisms of Stanley's particular interpretations of biblical passages, especially from the book of Genesis, offer little novelty to McCaul's arsenal of criticisms of the previous authors considered in this chapter. McCaul aligned Stanley with several of the authors of the *Essays and Reviews*, especially Rowland Williams and Baron von Bonsen, and even compared him to Colenso.[36]

Worthy of mention, however, were Stanley's references to Jews and McCaul's reaction to this emphasis. McCaul first pointed out that Stanley's history was an attempt to secularize the sacred, eliminate the supernatural, and depreciate the authority of scripture. But more than this mere act of secularization, McCaul maintained, Stanley had denied the fact that both the Pentateuch and the Epistle to the Hebrews were the inspired words of God; rather they were "mere vehicles of Jewish tradition, sometimes imperfect and leaving a blank." In particular, McCaul was incensed by the following line: "His doubtful qualities [referring to Jacob] exactly recall to us the meanness of character, which, even to a proverb, we call in scorn 'Jewish.'" And here was McCaul's reaction: "That nation to which we are wholly indebted for our knowledge of God, for the Law, the Prophets, the Psalms, and the New Testament, is surely deserving of a more considerate judgment and kinder treatment. It is bad to Judaize, but an anti-Judaic, heathenizing tendency is not less alien from Christianity; and this tendency is visible in all of Dr. Stanley's writings. . . . It is the same bias that causes him to suppress that supernatural element which distinguishes Moses and the Prophets from the great men of the heathen."[37]

It seems to be more than a mere coincidence that McCaul detected in at least two of the new biblical critics, Colenso and Stanley, a tendency that he understood as anti-Jewish and that their own prejudicial utterances were fully documented. In connecting his own unshakable belief in the sanctity of the Old Testament, in particular the Pentateuch, to the legacy of the Jews, both McCaul and his critics were acknowledging his strong allegiance to the Hebrew text that he considered to be the essence of true Judaism.

Here then was the vital link between McCaul's long career as a missionary to the Jews and what appeared to be a radical break in defending a literalist understanding of the Hebrew Bible in the last years of his life. Indeed, his crisis of disillusionment with the London Society and his overwhelming fear of the new rationalist theologies and their corrosive impact on evangelical Christianity ironically underscored his love for Jews and Judaism as he understood them. His unwavering defense of the Old Testament and especially the Pentateuch, or the Torah, as the Jews call it, its literal revelation and inerrancy, and its inseparable bonds with the New Testament and with apostolic Christianity was totally consistent with commitments he had made throughout his long career as a churchman. By declaring his devotion to the absolute truth of the Hebrew Bible, he was simply affirming his belief in the Jewish origins of true Christianity. This advocacy of the primacy of the Old Testament required him to undermine the claims of the rabbis that their version of "modern Judaism" was authentic. By introducing their Oral Law, they had consciously perverted the original nature of true Judaism, which was articulated in the Hebrew Bible. The rabbis were guilty of the same crime as the papists who had created their own papal traditions that often subverted and contradicted the true Christianity of the New and Old Testaments. Similarly, the new rational critics among the Anglican clergy, offering new historicist and scientific approaches in reading the Bible, were guilty of the same offense, of weakening the very foundation of Christianity, which was none other than the biblical revelation. It was thus a natural step for McCaul to move from Jewish mission to defender of the Hebrew Bible; the common thread in both endeavors was to preserve Judaism as well as Christianity in their original and purest forms. Only through this evangelical view of the Jews and the text would Christ return to redeem the world. In simultaneously attacking the rabbis and Catholics on the one hand, and the new spokesmen of biblical criticism on the other, McCaul, as he saw it, was fully carrying out God's work.

Nevertheless, McCaul's remarkable career as missionary and defender of the Hebrew Bible concluded on a sad note. He had gained some recognition for his commitment to the study of Judaism and Hebrew; he had evoked both admiration and sharp rebuke for his well-known book against the rabbis; and he had influenced a conspicuous number of acolytes, including several prominent converts from Judaism, to take up his cause in converting the Jews. In the end, however, despite his best efforts, few Jews embraced the Christian faith on the strength of his learned arguments. The project of the Jerusalem mission he had championed was plagued with turmoil and infighting; and the very sanctity of the Bible was now being challenged by forces far beyond his control. In 1863, the numerous eulogies rehearsing his impressive accomplishments could not totally obscure the fact that he died a troubled man.[38]

CHAPTER 4

The Intellectual and Spiritual Journey of Stanislaus Hoga

From Judaism to Christianity to Hebrew Christianity

In 1843, a small and obscure pamphlet was published in London with the fascinating title *Eldad and Medad* composed by a converted Jew who called himself Stanislaus Hoga.[1] The author staged a fictional dialogue between a converted Jew, Medad, and what he called a modern one, Eldad, apparently a liberal non-Orthodox Jew. Medad opened with a long discourse questioning the truth claims of any religion: "The more we reflect on the many contradictory opinions, which, as stamped coins are current in the world, the more our duty is increased to be circumspect in our belief, and neither to accept or reject an opinion without duly ascertaining its sound and weight."[2] But he was equally suspicious of any current scientific theory: "But a man in his real condition—a man who in his blindness takes unmeaning words for wisdom, and is proud to find out and give names to causes, powers, and substances, of which he has no perception: as, for instance, that something which he denominates by the words attraction, gravity, electricity, galvanism, phylogiston or . . . oxygen, hydrogen, nitrogen, etc.—the miserable, wretched, and helpless man, who is more poor than an insect, and full of wishes as an angel—a man in such condition, I saw, can do no better than read the Bible, and believe that he is a sinner, and may be pardoned." To this his interlocutor Eldad responded that maybe one would be better not reading the Bible, nor acquiring wisdom.[3]

It is hard to ascertain the real views of the author of this enigmatic dialogue from this pamphlet alone, but Stanislaus Hoga wrote considerably more, especially over the course of the next several years, addressed to both Christians and Jews and with a critical gaze at both. In addition to his extensive writings, considerable documentation exists, albeit still incomplete, that allows for a fuller reconstruction of his life and thought. I wish to argue in this chapter that this former Jew of eastern European and Hasidic origins was an original thinker on the relationship between Judaism and Christianity, a highly educated student of philosophy, science, and literature, a master of languages, including English, which he acquired late in life, and a figure quite deserving of the attention of those who study modern Jewish and Christian intellectual history in the modern era. And most relevant to the subject of this book, Hoga converted to Christianity through the agency of Alexander McCaul, as previously mentioned, and served for several years as a close associate and translator of his mentor's famous book on the Talmud among other works. The story of Hoga and the trajectory of his thinking on Christianity and Judaism were intimately linked to those of Alexander McCaul.

While several earlier scholars have noticed and written about Hoga, especially during his early years in Poland, two fuller accounts of his life and reputation among contemporaries are worthy of special attention. The first is by Beth-Zion Lask Abrahams, who offered a well-researched and comprehensive account of his life and writings with a particular focus on the English part of his life. The second, by Shnayer Z. Leiman, is an elaborate account of a story circulated in the name of the chief rabbi of Palestine, Abraham Isaac ha-Cohen Kook, about a penitent apostate who sought reconciliation with his Jewish daughter and his ancestral heritage and desperately sought a rabbinic blessing on behalf of his soul in the fading moments of his life. The story mirrors that of Stanislaus Hoga in many respects and may have been partially inspired by it, but, as Leiman conclusively demonstrated, it does not precisely fit the details of Hoga's life. What both accounts have in common, however, is their assumption that Hoga initially lived in England in a state of alienation from the Jewish community, but, in the end, he finally broke his ties with Christianity and fully returned with sincere conviction to the Jewish fold.[4]

I wish to challenge and complicate this narrative by focusing on his writings at the end of his life and on the impression he left on Jews and Christians alike in his newly adopted country. What emerged was a unique hybridity, unlike that of several other prominent contemporary converts and

Christian allies who supported his cause of Jewish-Christian coexistence, some of whom we shall consider in later chapters. Hoga revealed a rich love and intimacy with rabbinic Judaism and especially with Jewish ritual and practice; an abiding faith in the divine messiahship of Jesus; a skeptical stance toward all orthodoxies; and, finally, a considerable degree of self-doubt, restlessness, and broken commitments to even his own family leading ultimately to his self-imposed isolation from both the Jewish and Christian communities. In the final years of his life, he seemed to have surmounted his own crisis of identity through his involvement in scientific activities. To this, we shall return at the end of the chapter.

Before focusing on his later life and thought, let us recall his origins and early career. Hoga was born in 1791 as Yehezkel (= Chaskel) in Kuzmir (Kazimierz Dolny), Poland. His father, the maggid Aryeh Leib, was the rabbi of the town and a disciple of Rabbi Jacob Isaac Hurwitz, the *hozeh* of Lublin. He was clearly a wunderkind, excelling in his rabbinic studies. Through the intervention of a Danzig merchant, he was introduced to Prince Adam Czartoryski and was invited to study in his personal library, where he mastered several languages. Under the patronage of the prince, he became a mediator during the Napoleonic invasion between Jews, French officers, and Poles. He later came to Warsaw to assume the role of censor of Jewish publications, working closely with the well-known Hebraists Abraham Jacob Stern and Jacob Tugenhold, whose papers mentioned Hoga on more than one occasion. He also became the deputy of Luigi Chiarini, the anti-Talmudic writer, professor at the University of Warsaw, and head of a commission examining Jewish writings and publications in Poland. During this period, he was in close contact with Berek, the son of Samuel Zbytkower, possibly the wealthiest Jew in Poland, published several works in Polish on Jewish ceremonies, allegedly defended Hasidim against a libel in the Cracow community, and was appointed secretary of a new committee for the improvement of Jewish conditions under Alexander I for a short time.[5]

But throughout this period of time, his personal life appeared to fall apart. After marrying at a young age and having three children, he sought to abandon his family, but his father refused to allow him to divorce. He was subsequently seen in the company of a woman named Yitta with whom he had two daughters. When pressured to reveal the personal secret of his extramarital affair, he converted with Yitta and his two illegitimate children; Chaskel Meshumad (Chaskel the Apostate), as he was called in his hometown, became Stanislaus, and he and his new family soon disappeared.

At some time during his years in Warsaw, Hoga met Alexander McCaul who had been sent to the city by the London Society for Promoting Christianity Amongst the Jews. McCaul had spent almost ten years in Warsaw studying Jewish texts and engaging with local Jewish communities throughout Poland, as already mentioned. Apparently when McCaul returned to London, Hoga joined him to become an associate of the London Society, a valued author of missionary materials aimed at Jews, and a skilled translator of the New Testament and other Christian works made accessible to potential Jewish converts in Hebrew. When McCaul published *The Old Paths* in 1837, Hoga was enlisted to translate the work into Hebrew two years later. As we have seen, Hoga later acknowledged his role in the translation, even claiming to have been responsible for something more than a mere translation of McCaul's words. Be that as it may, Hoga's translation, along with translations in several other languages, including German, French, Italian, and Yiddish, made *Netivot olam*, as the Hebrew version was entitled, a source of great consternation to the Jewish community and eventually evoked multiple responses from rabbis and maskilim throughout Europe and the Middle East during the second half of the nineteenth century. Hoga's association with McCaul and his anti-rabbinic crusade represented both the pinnacle of his missionary activity and his own alienation from the rabbinic tradition in which he had been raised. Chaskel Meshumad had apparently revealed his true colors as a self-hating Jew and hostile enemy of his former coreligionists.[6]

In the immediate aftermath of Hoga's entanglement in the publication of *Netivot olam*, he seems to have disappeared again from the public arena, perhaps silently suffering the consequences of his public adversarial role against the rabbis and their vulnerable community. Yet by 1843 he appeared again with the publication of his aforementioned *Eldad and Medad* to be followed with a flurry of publications during the next four years. Culminating in a series of essays and letters to the editor of the major organ of the Jewish press, the *Jewish Chronicle*, who unhesitantly published the words of a still baptized Jew, Hoga seems to have fully regained his public voice throughout the year 1847, only to return to his private silence by the year's end. In this short period of time Hoga seemed to have radically rethought his relationship to McCaul and the London Society as well as his own notion of the organic relationship between the Jewish and Christian religions. In these same years, he gradually disclosed his most profound thoughts about his mingled identity, the place of Jews in English society, and his hopes for the political and economic security of Jews in the modern world. In the remainder of this chapter, I attempt to carefully trace the fascinating evolution of his thinking.

As I have already indicated, Hoga's first publication in this period, the *Eldad and Medad*, was yet to betray any major departure from his anti-Talmudism of the late 1830s. Medad, the converted Jew, in addition to his skeptical postures toward all religions and scientific theories, continued to voice his opposition to the Talmud and the rabbis, viewed it as the cause of Jewish suffering, and claimed that literary sensitivity and Jewish religious orthodoxy are not compatible. Eldad, the modern Jew, offered a weak defense of the rabbis, opting instead for a commitment to the Bible alone and religious observance "that can be conveniently adapted to the present circumstances."[7] Medad did acknowledge a practical wisdom and profound logic in the Talmud "which naturally ennoble the mind of a man who is entirely devoted to its study," but the Talmud was still deemed dangerous for ordinary people in perverting their natural good qualities.[8] It is difficult to identify any clear ideological position on the part of the author of this work other than to speculate that he was already voicing a kind of a dialectical conversation between his Jewish and Christian selves, his anti-Talmudism on the one hand and his appreciation of certain aspects of Judaism on the other, accompanied by the skeptical doubts voiced throughout. Whether this reading is an accurate reflection of his state of mind in 1843 or not, Hoga had clearly decided to present himself to English readers in a public way, albeit without any open break from his missionary stance and his relationship to the London Society. This, however, was soon to change.

Two years later, in 1845, Hoga published *The Controversy of Zion: A Meditation on Judaism and Christianity* in two separate editions in London.[9] Those familiar with his earlier publication would immediately sense his skeptical ideas about the poverty of human reason in attempting to understand anything beyond the natural world, or in Hoga's words: "Our thoughts are as much waking dreams as our dreams are sleeping thoughts."[10] On the other hand, he strongly acknowledged that science was the proper province of human reason, although the actual causes of gravity and light could not ultimately be fathomed.

Hoga seems here to have discovered a personal voice that was absent in *Eldad and Medad* and a boldness to declare his innermost feelings: "There are many other authors . . . who aspire for fame, for the sake of their nation, country, language, friends, and relations; but none of these can be a stimulation and spur to me, for I am so very isolated, solitary, and alone in the world, that there is not one of these subjects of which I can properly say, it is my own."[11] To overcome his lonely state, he regained his confidence in writing. He loved England and the liberty it offered individuals such as himself, and in the spirit of such openness, he sought to address the defective relationship between English Jews and Christians to create "one single community conforming to the divine will."[12]

The primary message of *The Controversy of Zion* was clear throughout: It is possible for a Jew to believe in Jesus without abrogating his observance of Jewish law. Though excluded, as he admitted, "from the pale of my nation," Hoga intended to vindicate the honor of his ancestors by offering his most daring pronouncement about the profundity of the Jewish faith: "For I am sure that the poorest Jewish school-boy in a wretched village in Poland, has a better notion of the supreme Being than all the doctors in divinity of Oxford."[13] In dismissing rabbinic ordinances as mere ceremonial law, Christians had lost sight of the deep theological message of these commandments that reminded Jews of their belief in the one God. He singled out the commandments of circumcision (*brit milah*), phylacteries (*tefillin*), and fringes (*zizit*) as particularly significant in publicizing the religious identity and the sincere faith of contemporary Jews. He even boldly pictured Jesus returning to the earth wearing fringes and phylacteries. In offering this provocative portrait, could Hoga have had in mind the biting critique of modern Jewish ritual practice published only two years earlier by Moses Margoliouth, a fellow convert and colleague associated with the London Society (and the subject of a later chapter), who had himself singled out such rituals for ridicule?[14]

The critical reason why Jews were obliged to observe the law was that it was not only their existence as a people that depended on it but Christianity itself, Hoga argued. If there was no Israel and Jewish law, there could be no true messiah either. Christ was the crown and perfection of the law. But a Jew could only believe in him through his observance of the *mitsvot*, his national covenant with God: "If you deprive Israel of its holy law, you deprive yourselves of your most holy Messiah," he proclaimed.[15] Even if the non-Jew desired to observe the law, and especially the Sabbath, he could not do so with the same conviction and the same intensity as that of the Jew who derived holiness and meaning from his ceremonial life. It was more incumbent on the Christian to insure that the Jews observe the commandments than to observe them on their own.

The ultimate conclusion, of course, was a severe indictment of the missionaries who violently attacked Jewish practice and the rabbinic foundations of contemporary Judaism. In a long speech of Satan constructed by Hoga, he reiterated his position that a gentile did not have to observe the law of Israel, but he could not be saved without believing in the eternity of Jewish practice and its direct link with the true messiah. Jews, of course, sinned in rejecting Jesus, but they would come to see the true light by being allowed to be their true selves in observing halacha. As soon as they reached this realization, they would understand the messiahship of Jesus even better than the gentiles since he was Israel's own messiah.

Hoga's last major work was the unfinished *Zir Ne'eman: The Faithful Missionary*, published in December 1847 in London. It was meant to be a serial but apparently only this first issue was printed. With the apparent absence of any subsequent issues, Hoga the author seems to have suspended his publishing career.

The subtitle of the journal already reveals the author's intent: *A Monthly Periodical, Illustrating the Value of Judaism, with a View to Opening the Eyes of Some Deluded Christians in England to the Doings of the (So-Called) "London Society."* In publishing this text, Hoga was coming clean, so to speak. He fully declared his sins to the Jewish people, his contribution to the foundation of falsehood, as he called it, and his final wish not only to repudiate the London Society but to replace it with a "new temple of truth." In declaring his final break from the London Society, he had two goals in mind: to encourage Jews to resist the enticements of the missionaries and to uphold their practice of Jewish law, in the first place, and, and in the second, to plead for the civic emancipation of the Jews, a goal the missionaries had resisted in their zeal to convert Jews to the "true faith."[16]

Hoga spelled out his grievances against the society with which he had been associated for so long in considerable detail. The society was a pious fraud, raising huge sums of money and then placing them in the hands of a few phony missionary converts who were totally ineffectual in their conversion of other Jews. They preyed only upon poor and vulnerable Jews who had no other recourse but to accept their blandishments. This time he explicitly mentioned the author of *The Old Paths*, although without recalling McCaul's name. He mocked him for his ridiculous claim that Reform Judaism was a path to conversion that he had orchestrated. The unnamed missionary pretended to convert Jews by pointing out the deficiencies of rabbinic Judaism but, in the final analysis, they did not convert. He also noted in passing that the Hebrew version of McCaul's anti-Talmudic tract, supposedly prepared by Hoga himself, was unjustly called a mere translation. One might understand this as a veiled assertion that McCaul was not the sole author of the book, at least in its well-read Hebrew version.[17]

Hoga's ultimate message to McCaul and his associates was almost spelled out before the book abruptly ended, obviously unfinished. The London Society, so he contended, failed to convert Jews not because their hearts were hardened but because the unsophisticated missionaries never bothered to understand the true convictions of their Jewish victims, their pristine faith, their glorious liturgy, and their high moral values. It was questionable, Hoga contended, that Christianity actually brought a higher morality to the world; instead it wrought cruelty and erroneous principles. Only in the author's own era and in the new surroundings of English society had it overcome its fanaticism and revealed its high moral mission. In the end, carefully crafted books spelling out the cardinal principles of Christianity and how they fit together could communicate the Christian faith more effectively than missionaries ever could. What was required was a plain and forthright composition written in Hebrew to address the Jewish objections to the missionaries rather than an obscure recitation of metaphysical doctrines. Hoga seemed to be suggesting that he would undertake such a project properly explaining the evidence of Jesus Christ to the Jewish community. He would address the enduring truths of Christianity and show how human salvation depends on it. But alas, the proposal remained only that as Hoga's discussion abruptly came to an end.[18]

The Faithful Missionary was Hoga's final publication and the last articulation of his thoughts on Judaism and Christianity. However, during the same year 1847, specifically between March and November, Hoga submitted several short articles and letters to the editor of the *Jewish Chronicle* that were surprisingly published in this major periodical of Anglo-Jewry. The fact that his work was easily accepted by Jews was proof enough for Beth-Zion Lask Abrahams that Hoga had by now become a sincere and full-fledged Jew. As she wrote: "His return to Judaism must have been complete by now, for that periodical would certainly not have given space to a known apostate."[19] Shnayer Leiman reached a similar conclusion as he wrote: "Most important he was a genuine *baal teshuvah* who lived his last years as a recluse, disowned by Jews and Christians alike."[20] To my mind, both of these conclusions were unwarranted. Hoga may have imposed upon himself a reclusive life in his final years, although, as we shall soon see, even that conclusion is not self-evident; but he was hardly disowned by Jews who read him and even praised him in the Jewish press, at least through 1847. Moreover, there is no evidence whatsoever that he relinquished his faith in the Christian messiah while advocating Jewish practice and excoriating the missionaries. Despite his mingled identity, I would argue, the Jewish press saw him as a scholar and as a worthy ally. Their full acceptance of his published views testifies to a degree of editorial tolerance perhaps less prevalent in our own day but obviously present in mid-nineteenth-century England.

Hoga first appeared in the pages of the *Jewish Chronicle* on March 19, 1847, intervening in a heated discussion on the derivation of *Elohim*, the plural name of God in the Torah, that had previously gone on for some time between John Oxlee, a deeply learned Christian cleric sympathetic to Jews and rabbinic culture, and two Jews, Samuel Lee and Tobias Theodores, a regular contributor to the first Anglo-Jewish periodical, the *Voice of Jacob*, and its successor, the *Jewish Chronicle*. The fact that Oxlee had often written for both Jewish newspapers belies the assumption that only Jews were invited to write in the Jewish press, even on matters of great theological controversy between Jews and Christians, such as the name of God. In fact, only two years later, in May 1845, the same Theodores wrote a long and most favorable review of Oxlee's impressive publication *Three More Letters* in the pages of the *Jewish Chronicle*, defending the right of Jews to practice Jewish law without Christian harassment. At the beginning of the review, Theodores made the following extraordinary statement worth citing in full:

Within these few years, and in this country, the Rector of Molesworth [John Oxlee], Charlotte Elizabeth [Tonna], and Stanislas Hoga have labored for Jewish conversion, speaking in the same tone of kindness towards the Jewish people, of respect for the Law of Moses, and of reproof against the measures heretofore resorted to for weaning the Israelites from the religion of their fathers [an explicit reference to the activities of the London Society]. Whereas formerly, the vilification of the Mosaic Law and of Jewish observances were considered the most approved means wherewith to instill an attachment to Christian principles. The gentle and amiable zeal of Charlotte Elizabeth, the cutting irony of Hoga, resulting from an unfortunately correct knowledge of the world as it is; and the elaborate erudition, as well as the bold speculative energy of the tolerant Rector—all tend to establish the gross error of those who,

on Christian grounds, consider it warrantable to absolve a son of
Abraham, under any moral circumstances, from obeying the Mosaic
commandments.[21]

Theodores's statement should erase any doubts about the Jewish establishment press's self-interest in welcoming Hoga into its credible list of contributors. Theodores not only connected Hoga with Oxlee and Tonna, two
Christians who, as we shall soon see, strongly defended the integrity of Jews
practicing their laws but nevertheless sought their ultimate conversion to the
religion of Jesus, but he openly identified him as a man who had labored for
Jewish conversion, hardly a characterization of a Jew who had wholeheartedly
embraced Judaism. Theodores and his editors obviously considered all three
friends and allies of the Jewish community in the battle with the anti-
Talmudic activities of the London Society despite their own Christian
agendas.

Hoga's discussion of *Elohim*, whether calculated or not, was written in a
way not to offend Jewish sensibilities. Both in his initial piece and in two
follow-up entries composed in May and June of 1847, Hoga argued that while
it is natural for human beings to perceive of God as a plurality, in essence,
God's true being is that of a perfect unity and is the foundation of the Mosaic
religion. In distinguishing between fallible human perception of God and his
actual singular reality, he impressively brought the testimonies of ancient and
recent philosophers from Orpheus and Pythagoras to Kant and Newton.
While eschewing any discussion of the Christian Trinity, Hoga pointed out
that Jews were not commanded to believe in something that contradicted
their reason, but they were obliged to observe the commandments transmitted by their forefathers.[22]

By August 1847, Hoga printed a prospectus of *The Faithful Missionary*
already articulating his multi-prong attack on the ideology and tactics of the
London Society. He included as well an unflattering reference to *The Old
Paths*, a text he himself helped to create, at least in its Hebrew translation, by
pointing out how the missionaries have reduced it to the "rank of an advertisement of universal salvation pills."[23] In September, he focused his attention
on the vicious campaign of the London Society to block Jewish emancipation. He denied the notion that Jews could not properly serve the nation as
members of Parliament, pointing to the great success of the recently
appointed Baron Rothschild. While underscoring the deleterious political
consequences of the actions of the London Society, he continued to heap

insults on his former mentor Alexander McCaul, whom he called "the chariot and horseman of the London Society" and whose assault on the Talmud did not hold water. More than in any of his writings, he appeared to fully embrace his connections with the Jewish community in this essay, perhaps because its focus was on the ethnic and political identities of Jews in English society.[24]

Finally, in November of that same year, he penned his final piece in the *Jewish Chronicle* on the potential impact of Moses on Plato, disagreeing with his friend Oxlee and siding with a Jew named Hertz Ben Pinchas who believed that Plato was indeed indebted to Mosaic law. Hoga offered the following in introducing his intervention: "Now, as I am so exceedingly delighted to see brotherly love between Jews and Christians, I am very sorry to perceive some misunderstanding between a most estimable friend of the Jews (though too learned and wise to be a doctor, and too pious and sincere to be a bishop), on the one hand, and an enlightened Israelite whose writings testify alike to his talents and his excellent feelings, on the other."[25] Oxlee wrote two rejoinders to Hoga, but Hoga, despite his personal expression of good will, was not to be heard from again. Oxlee, however, did acknowledge Hoga's disagreement with his position in the following intriguing way: "The regret so kindly felt and expressed by Mr. Hoga, respecting one of your valued contributors and myself, equally befits the scholar, the Jew, and the Christian." Was Oxlee alluding respectively to the three participants in this discussion of Plato and Moses—Hoga, Hertz Ben Pinchas, and Oxlee himself? If so, he designated Hoga neither Christian nor Jew but simply scholar, perhaps suggesting both the erudite image he cut among Jews and Christians as well as his ambiguous status between both communities.[26]

We might round out our discussion of Hoga's image among contemporary Jews and Christians by offering some final observations on two reviews of Hoga's *Controversy of Zion*, the first penned by a convert from Judaism and a missionary writer and the second by a Jew. In the first case the author was Ridley Haim Herschell, the editor of the missionary newspaper the *Voice of Israel* and, like Hoga, a former Jew with roots in eastern Europe. Herschell found the book painful to read especially coming from the pen of the famous translator officially employed by the London Society. While he did not wish to hurt the feelings of "our respectable and highly talented brother," as he called him, and acknowledged errors of Christians in dealing with converts, he still believed that sincere Christians and converts had overcome prejudice as "brothers and sisters of faith in the Christian church." He, of course, took exception to Hoga's fanciful notions of Judaism, what he called "the sunny hours of childhood," and Hoga's absurd pronouncement about the superior knowledge of Jewish schoolchildren over Oxford divines. On the contrary, he claimed, "a well-instructed Sunday-school child knows more about God than a whole assembly of rabbis."[27]

In contrast, the author of the second review was Jacob Franklin, the editor of the *Voice of Jacob*, published between 1841 and 1846 and, like its eventual successor the *Jewish Chronicle*, a periodical composed by Jews and promoting Jewish interests. After some reluctance, he welcomed Christian authors and readers who supported his Jewish newspaper, especially Charlotte Elizabeth Tonna who became his close friend.

Franklin had written a brief notice of *Eldad and Medad* a year earlier, but he devoted a longer review to *The Controversy of Zion* as soon as the first edition appeared. Franklin was quite aware of Hoga's background but was fascinated by the argument of the book despite the fact that Hoga had left the Jewish fold. Here is how he justified the attention he was giving the book, distinguishing between the character of the author and the quality of his argument:

> Under the title, an exceedingly curious pamphlet challenges our review. It is issued at the cost of a penny only. And because we think that it ought to have an extensive circulation among Christians, we willingly give it such notoriety as our columns afford. Mr. Hoga's learning and ingenuity did not, as is said, find their appreciation among his brethren [the Jews], and in carrying them to another market, he forfeited the "portion and inheritance in Israel." It is not, therefore, with the writer that we have to deal, but with what he has written; prominently, in contrast as it stands, to that vilification of the Jews and Judaism, which another deserter from our ranks has recently given to the English public.[28]

Franklin was referring to Hoga's contemporary the aforementioned Moses Margoliouth who had recently published *The Fundamental Principles of Modern Judaism Investigated* (1843), a devastating critique of Jewish ritual practice, derogating especially the commandments of fringes, phylacteries, and *mezuzah*, the container housing biblical verses on the doorposts of every Jewish home. I have mentioned a possibility that Hoga had responded to this book directly in *The Controversy of Zion*. Be that as it may, Franklin certainly noticed the contrast between the divergent approaches of the two converts: Hoga was vigorously defending the perpetuity of the Mosaic ordinances, affirming especially the same rituals Margoliouth had dismissed, and as Franklin put it, Hoga wrote "so pertinently, and so quaintly, as to be even entertaining as well as argumentative." Franklin was especially taken by Hoga's claim that Jews understood Jesus better than Christians because he was Israel's messiah and exclaimed: "And this is the language of one who is himself a baptized Jew!" Franklin also pointed out the high price of the pretentious, "regal, Episcopal" Margoliouth book in contrast to the low cost of the sincerely modest Hoga pamphlet. To the editor of a Jewish periodical navigating the troubled waters of Jewish-Christian relations in the mid-nineteenth century, bad apostates deserved rebuke while good ones needed to be recognized and even appreciated for their defense of the Jewish cause.[29]

After 1847, as I have noted, Stanislaus Hoga seems to have stopped publishing and he was not heard from again. This is especially surprising given the polite and pleasant demeanor he displayed in his exchanges recorded in the *Jewish Chronicle*, as well as the degree of acceptance of his views by Jews and Christians alike. But unless more of his writing is discovered in the future, we are left to ponder his utter silence at the end of his life. Thanks, however, to the diligent research of Beth-Zion Lask Abrahams, we know the date of his death, January 21, 1860, and the place of his death, 98 Charlotte Street, London.[30] What was he doing in the last thirteen years of his life?

According to Abrahams's research in the London Patent Office, and also based on evidence still accessible online, Stanislaus was an inventor, registering three separate patents in 1858 and five others between 1852 and 1857. His applications describe the nature of these inventions: separating gold from ore; creating an instrument for ascertaining the existence of gold in the earth; coating the surfaces of the cell of galvanic batteries and also the surfaces of crucibles; applying power in locomotion by which a given force may in its effect of overcoming resistance be increased and multiplied; inventing electric telegraphs; and more. One might dismiss this evidence as referring to another Stanislaus Hoga if not for the fact that several of his contemporaries, such as Mrs. Finn, the daughter of Alexander McCaul, had mentioned his scientific interests in passing, as we have seen, and Hoga himself often referred to science and the natural world in his own writings.[31]

Our account of the journey of Chaskel Meshumad from Kuzmir to London, from Hasidism to evangelical Protestantism, from associate of the London Society to passionate critic, and from Christian anti-Talmudist to a defender of the halacha accompanied by a faith in the messiahship of Jesus still remains incomplete. But one thing is clear: Hoga did not necessarily die a broken, lonely, and despised man, rejected universally by Jews and by Christians. His unique brand of Jewish Christianity was recognized and even appreciated by some, and he apparently found a way to bring together in his own mind and heart his Jewish and Christian selves. His final refuge, however, was science, and given his remarkable intellect, he proved capable of making the unexpected transition from theologian/translator to scientific inventor. We might recall, in closing, his prescient remark in *The Controversy of Zion* of 1845: "Science is the only object in which a Jew may excel to the satisfaction of the whole world."[32] By the time of his death in 1860, Stanislaus Hoga had apparently discovered his peace of mind in the neutral nontheological space of scientific inquiry. And Hoga would eventually be followed by many other talented Jewish individuals who sought the same path, the same recognition for their intellectual accomplishments, and the same entrance into European society.

CHAPTER 5

The Christian Opponents of McCaul
and the London Society

John Oxlee and Charlotte Elizabeth Tonna

Tobias Theodores's remarkable statement cited in Chapter 4, linking Stanislaus Hoga with John Oxlee and Charlotte Elizabeth Tonna, is the starting point of this chapter.[1] A Jewish testimonial praising a convert to Christianity along with two contemporary Christian writers in the pages of a journal for Jewish readers is unusual in its own right. That it was offered in the midst of a positive review of Oxlee's petitionary letters addressed to the archbishop of Canterbury was even more noteworthy and calls for further comment about this exceptional Christian cleric and his equally incomparable colleague Charlotte Elizabeth Tonna. One recent scholar has already noted the link between Hoga, Oxlee, and Tonna and includes them in a community he labels as the "Hebrew-Christian Movement."[2] There are obvious similarities among all three and several others he writes about in his pioneering study. But for the purposes of this book, I want to examine the two, especially the relatively unstudied Oxlee, as original thinkers and actors, articulating their sense of Christianity in its historical and contemporary connections with Judaism, without any formal affiliation with each other. Moreover, I see both as consciously articulating a new Christian relationship with Judaism in stark opposition to that of the London Society in general and to Alexander McCaul in particular. In a study examining McCaul against the background of his followers and opponents, theirs are significant voices.

The Rector of Molesworth

John Oxlee (1779–1854) was the son of an affluent farmer in Yorkshire. After excelling in his Latin and theological studies, and after his ordination as a minister of the Church of England, he devoted himself to the study of classical Hebrew literature, especially the Talmud and kabbalah. He was clearly a kind of philological genius, having allegedly mastered in one way or another some 120 languages. After serving several small parishes, he was ultimately assigned the relatively insignificant rectory of Molesworth in Huntingdonshire, which offered him modest income but also the welcome opportunity to pursue his intellectual interests, especially those related to his impressive mastery of Jewish sources. He not only authored several books, some of which originated as public letters, but he was also a regular contributor to various academic and Christian periodicals, along with several Jewish ones as well. Despite his obvious isolation from the major universities and the clerical seats of power and influence, Oxlee used his pen to enter the public arena of theological discourse and debate, and in this, he was relatively successful.[3]

Oxlee's most ambitious work was *The Christian Doctrines of the Trinity and Incarnation Considered and Maintained on the Principles of Judaism*, consisting of three volumes published over a span of thirty-five years.[4] In the introduction to the first volume, Oxlee lamented the fact that the Greek and Latin fathers were ignorant of Hebrew and that this condition continued until the Reformation when Christian scholars were finally capable of revealing to the world "the dark recesses of that gigantic fabric of Jewish superstition, the Talmud; which, for anything that modern Hebraists can effect toward leveling it with our understandings, must henceforth be contemplated with as much admiration and stupor as a colossus or a pyramid."[5] Oxlee's apparent ambivalence, perceiving the rabbinic tradition as both a gigantic fabric of superstition and a colossal pyramid, was perhaps meant to anticipate a hostile or at least indifferent reaction to his endeavor by his Christian readership. But, as he explained, he was not addressing Christians alone. While he was not writing "with the vain expectation of converting the Jews," he still hoped to diminish their religious prejudices against Christianity and to excite "an inquiry amongst them into the merits of the question." Moreover, proving that Christian principles derive from Jewish ones was another way of confirming "the truth of our faith."[6]

Since Jews and Christians concurred on most articles of faith, he argued, it was only incumbent on him to focus on their basic differences of doctrine:

FIGURE 3. John Oxlee. Reproduced from William Smith, ed., *Old Yorkshire* (London: Longmans, Green, 1882). By permission of the British Library.

the notions of Trinity and Incarnation. Regarding these, it was possible to find intriguing parallels to Christian doctrine in midrashic and kabbalistic literature. So in the case of the Trinity, "the unsearchable and ineffable mystery of the Trinity is, in metaphysics, the same with that of the three higher numerations of the cabbalist."[7] And similarly, "in the belief and description of the divine agency and regenerating influx of the Holy Spirit of God, the Jew coincides with the Christian; and on many occasions, the language of the cabbala is highly capable of illustrating and expounding the sense of the Gospel. The sole difference betwixt us is, that we profess to obtain the gifts of the Spirit through the medium of the Word incarnate; whereas they reject the doctrine of the incarnation and profess to obtain them by faith in the Word merely, like the saints of old before the coming of our Saviour."[8]

Notwithstanding the impressive erudition and scope of his intellectual project, Oxlee's doubts about the success of his endeavor were highly palpable by the close of the third volume, where he apologized in a postscript for the thirty-four-year delay between this and the previous volumes. He admitted he was not writing a popular book, having sold only eight copies in the last three years, as he pitifully acknowledged.[9] Nevertheless, he mentioned by name a small group of clergymen who reviewed the work favorably.[10] Perhaps more in line with the general response to the book were the pointed criticisms of none other than Samuel Taylor Coleridge, who dismissed entirely the work's basic premise that Christianity was enhanced by rabbinic endorsement: "To what purpose then are the crude metaphysics of these later Rabbis brought forward, differing as they do in no other respect from the theological dicta of the Schoolmen, but that they are written in a sort of Hebrew." Oxlee could only respond to this by accusing his critic of taking too much opium; but the famous writer with his well-publicized addiction had obviously touched a raw nerve.[11]

Oxlee continued to explore the connections between Judaism and Christianity in several of his other works. One of his most unusual articulations is found in a pamphlet published five years after his death by his son, the Reverend John Oxlee, perpetual curate of Oversilton, diocese of York, entitled *The Mysterious Stranger; or, Dialogues on Doctrine*. Its first part is labeled *Dialogue the First, Between the Jew Rabbi and the Stranger*. Oxlee opened this work with a scene somewhere on "the high road between London and Edinburgh," depicting a mysterious Christian philosopher with a large golden crucifix. The stranger dresses in special clothing on Friday and meditates on Saturday without ever entering the local cathedral.[12] This unusual

behavior elicits the curiosity of the local rabbi Mordechai who thinks the
stranger might actually be a Jew. They soon engage in dialogue, and in the
course of their conversation, the stranger declares: "The Law of Moses is
the Word of Wisdom, the Body of the Schechinah, and whoever violates a
single letter of it, or refuses to pay homage to it, blasphemes the Great Name
of God, and insults the Almighty." The rabbi questions his allegiance to the
law and particularly the Sabbath while wearing a cross. The stranger's
response recalls Oxlee's earlier tome. His Christian doctrines in no way
diminish his commitment to the divine unity: "Know you not, that in the
Divine language of the Cabbala any effect or emanation of the supreme
essence may be called a Son, while the cause of that effect or emanation is
called a Father. . . . The cabbalists maintain not only a trinity, but a quinity
of divine persons, and yet they are never accused of denying the unity."[13]

The rabbi seems swept up by the words of the stranger and imagines
for a moment that he is conversing with "R. Judah Elai, or R. Simeon Ben
Yochai, or one of their scholars." When he comes to his senses, he becomes
irritated and plans to depart. The stranger's final words encapsulate his
primary message to the rabbi: "If you cannot embrace the Gospel, then
adhere to the Law. If you cannot become a sincere Christian, then continue
to be a devout and candid Jew; and do nothing to dishonour the name of
that God who called Abraham out of his country and gave Jacob his stat-
utes." Mordecai was about to condemn the man as an apostate, "but, calling to mind how admirably he had described the beauties of the Sabbath,
his conscience smote him, and stifling his prejudice for a moment, he
replied, 'The stranger is a learned and wonderful man.' Being asked if he
was a Jew, he answered, 'I cannot tell.' Being asked if he was a Christian,
he replied, 'I cannot tell.' "[14]

The ambiguous identity of the mysterious stranger, neither strictly a Jew
nor a Christian, but somehow inhabiting a space betwixt and between both
religious communities precisely captured Oxlee's rich understanding of both
Judaism and Christianity, their interdependence, and his strong polemical
stance vis-à-vis the London Society. These themes had preoccupied Oxlee in
his most well-known publications, a series of three and then three more
letters addressed to the archbishop of Canterbury regarding the futility of
converting the Jews in the manner McCaul and his colleagues had so aggres-
sively pursued. In these writings, Oxlee shifted noticeably from his previous
scholarly fixation with the doctrinal parallelism of the two religions to a
public posture defending the integrity of contemporary Judaism and Jewish

legal practice and the fallacy of Christians who sought to proselytize Jews by denying their very essence as practioners of the Mosaic law.

The first series of letters to the archbishop appeared in 1842. From the beginning, Oxlee introduced himself as a patron of the London Society for Promoting Christianity Amongst the Jews, not yet its critic. Citing impressively from a wide array of Hebrew sources, Oxlee reviewed the long and tortuous history of the Jewish-Christian debate, especially the fifteenth-century disputation of Tortosa as related by Solomon ibn Verga in his classic work, the *Shevet Yehudah* (Rod of Judah).[15] Why, he asked, did Christians fail to convert Jews, despite all of their efforts in this regard? His answer was unambiguous:

> There must be some earthly cause, and that cause, I hesitate not to say, is the bigotry and unauthorized presumption of the Christian Church, in demanding that the sons of Jacob, before they can become Christians, should cease to be Jews; that they should abandon the Law of Moses in order to embrace the Gospel of Christ. . . . I boldly assert, on the contrary, that the Law of Moses never has been authoritatively abrogated, nor ever will be so abrogated. . . . To us, who are the seed of the Gentiles, sprung not from Abraham, but from Adam, the authority of the New Testament is everything; the oldest and the only covenant which we have to plead with God, being the gracious overtures of the Gospel, through the mediation and satisfaction of our Lord Jesus Christ. But with the posterity of Jacob the case is not so. They received their Mosaic covenant, or the Law, directly from heaven, by the ministry of the angelic host, with the audible voice of the living Jehovah himself, and in a way and manner so miraculous and glorious, as to find no parallel in the history of the world.[16]

Such a law, Oxlee added, might be allowed to die a natural death but can never be formally abrogated. Indeed, in the author's time, the law has not only failed to disappear; it has flourished, "actually professed at this day by no less than seven million of the children of Israel, being more than double the number of those who received it at the first from Mount Sinai." The proper Christian behavior toward contemporary Jews was thus obvious: "How then, I would ask, can we conscientiously exhort the Jew, on embracing the faith of the Gospel, to forsake and abandon that Law, which was not only commanded by God at the first, and enforced by the very last of the Jewish prophets, but also strictly enjoined and practiced afterwards both by Christ and his twelve disciples?"[17]

Oxlee offered several historical explanations for how the estrangement of Judaism from Christianity developed, including the initial persecution of the first Christians by the rabbis, as well as the later savage maltreatment of the Jewish community by the Christians. He pondered why Christians, both past and present, held such an utter distaste and aversion for anything Jewish. In Oxlee's words, "the less Jewish, the more Christian; and the less we have to do with the Law of Moses, the more intimate we become with the Gospel of Christ."[18] In raising such a question, he entered deeply into the psychology of the Jewish-Christian relationship of mutual recrimination and repudiation based on intimate albeit painful encounters with the other. When the mysterious Christian stranger of Oxlee's dialogue embraced the Sabbath, he reversed the equation of the less Jewish, the more Christian, and he left his rabbinic interlocutor in an utter state of confusion and ultimately receptive to embracing Christianity from an entirely different perspective.

Oxlee actively promoted the practice of Jewish ritual by Jews, including the observance of the Sabbath, circumcision, dietary laws, and Jewish festivals, and approved of their interpretations of the Bible in a literal and plain sense. He was aware that the Christian mission would never reach the majority of Jewish believers, but he still imagined a future scenario where the law and gospel were united—neither a modern Judaism nor a modern Christianity —but "the pure law and the pure Gospel," two religious systems blended into one, with the Nazarene church at the center performing every divine precept contained in the Old and New Testaments and providing a model of perfection by which all other Christian churches would gradually approximate its biblical standard.[19]

In his enthusiastic embrace of Jewish law, Oxlee could not ultimately avoid parting company with the London Society with which he had initially identified himself. And so he proclaimed "if the London Society . . . should continue to be activated by the same ignorance, bigotry, and prejudice, which has hitherto marked all similar movements; whatever missionaries they may appoint, whatever collection of money they may make, whatever public speeches they may utter; their efforts, I am confident, will ultimately miscarry, and terminate in disappointment." Anticipating that his sharp criticism might be misunderstood, he backtracked a little in acknowledging the good intentions of the London missionaries: "There is no such thing in the world as absolute evil; and even from the most diabolical conspiracy, there will often accrue something beneficial, beyond all human expectation. How much more naturally, then, may something good be anticipated from the exertions of a Society, whose motives of action cannot be impeached; and whose sole end and design is the enlargement of the kingdom of Christ?" Oxlee hoped that the number of "circumcised prelates and priests" would multiply so that they should form an independent Nazarene community, instructing and converting their own brethren, and ultimately erecting their third temple in the Holy Land.[20]

It was the same Jacob Franklin, the editor of the *Voice of Jacob* and close friend of Charlotte Elizabeth Tonna, whom we discussed in Chapter 4 for his praise of Stanislaus Hoga in the pages of his Jewish journal, who quickly responded to Oxlee's first set of letters. On March 31, 1843, he reviewed Oxlee's work, opening with the following incredible lines, which I cite in full:

> The author was unable to even publish an ad on this booklet in *The Jewish Intelligence* (the official periodical of the London Society). This evasion does not surprise us, especially after reading these powerful arguments, with which the Conversionists could not even hope to grapple with any chance of success. Under these circumstances, we consented to lend such aid as we could afford, in order to bring this Christian appeal under the notice of our Christian readers, assuring them, emphatically, that they will not be accounted guiltless, who shall continue their support of "the way and manner hitherto practiced" for enticing Israel from his fealty, if they neglect to seek after, and to search diligently the reasoning of the venerable and learned Rector of Molesworth.[21]

As discussed in Chapter 4, Franklin was not averse to publishing Christian authors in his Jewish periodical if he felt they served the larger interests of the Jewish community. But in this case, the circumstances were even more unexpected. Oxlee, a member in good standing of the London Society, had simply asked the editors of the society's journal to publicize his new pamphlet in the pages of their publication and they had refused. He had obviously challenged the very core of their missionary aspirations and tactics and they could obviously not tolerate such dissent. Instead, Oxlee turned to his Jewish friend Franklin to disseminate his opinion in a journal written for a Jewish readership, in Franklin's words, "in order to bring this Christian appeal under the notice of our Christian readers." That Oxlee had enlisted the support of a Jewish editor to broadcast his Christian message is remarkable in itself; that he assumed that he would reach Christian readers by publishing in a Jewish journal seems even more surprising. It provides further evidence of the potential avenues of communication available to at least some Jews and Christians in nineteenth-century England.

What followed was Franklin's appraisal of the Christian cleric:

> Mr. Oxlee appears to be an honest minded teacher of the religion he professes; a scholar of varied attainments and profound research, superior to the expedients which he exposes in others, who have the same end in view: that is, to induce the Non-Christian world to recognize Jesus as the Messiah. He at once confesses the impiety of undermining the Israelite's fidelity to the ordinances of God; he declares his conviction as to the enduring character of the Divine covenant with our fathers; and he repudiates the fiction,—that any later revelation has superseded the requirements of that covenant. He is, however, still a Christian, and he would have us so far the same, as to superadd to the original, and as yet unchanged, tenets of our religious faith—the belief in a triune Godhead.[22]

Franklin did not challenge this dogma as long as Christians did not violate the Jewish community by cajoling the Jewish poor and defenseless, by kidnapping Jewish children, or by performing other dastardly acts. On the contrary, "the Jew will listen to his Christian brother, who, addresses him in that spirit of amity and of legitimate design, advocated by the author of these letters, pray God to lead such discussions to the discovery and manifestation of truth."[23] In promoting Oxlee's strong disagreement with the aspirations and tactics of the London Society, his appreciation of Jewish scholarship, and his preference for the plain meaning of scripture associated with Jewish exegesis, Franklin consciously chose to downplay the fact that this evangelical cleric still sought to gain Jewish souls and still shared the same ideal of proselytization professed by his colleagues in the London Society. In the same way it was possible for a Jew to distinguish between a good or at least benign convert and a bad one, one could also differentiate a good missionary from a bad one. Allies and enemies, for Franklin at least, were never absolute, only relative, and in this muddled public forum of diverse Christian voices, Jews had to listen attentively and discern carefully who spoke in their best interest and who did not.

Two years later Oxlee published a sequel to his three letters to the archbishop, simply called *Three More Letters Humbly Submitted to the Consideration of His Grace the Most Reverend the Lord Archbishop of Canterbury* [. . .]. He opened by confirming the account of Jacob Franklin regarding the reception of his prior publication by "the committee of that society of which your Grace is the acknowledged and highly distinguished patron." He had attempted to advertise the publication of his 1842 pamphlet but was refused by them: "that they could not think of giving any publicity to a pamphlet, containing statements so derogatory to the honour of our blessed Saviour."[24]

Oxlee related how offended he was but went on to say:

> By chance, I got to know of the Anglo-Jewish press in London, and of a recently instituted journal called *The Voice of Jacob*; an interesting Jewish periodical, conducted with great ability by Jewish editors, in support of Judaism; and which the Christian reader, if he really wishes to learn what is progressing amongst the Jews, ought constantly to read, in preference to *The Jewish Intelligence.* The proprietor, then, of *The Voice of Jacob*, being applied to, and thinking, perhaps, that my Letters had been refused publicity in *The Jewish Intelligence*, because they contained more truth than might be quite welcome to the views of the Committee, readily consented to have them advertised in his own periodical; and not only so, but in three successive numbers recommended them to the perusal of every Jewish professor, with so much effect, that I presently had the satisfaction to receive letters, not only from London, but from Liverpool, Oxford, and Birmingham; thanking me for my efforts, extolling the truthfulness and importance of the argumentation, and even expressing a hope, that the sons of Jacob would thereby be reminded of their religious duties, and roused to the performance of them with more strictness and sincerity.[25]

Oxlee, a Christian author working in relative obscurity, had ironically found a receptive readership among Jews! Having being spurned by the London missionaries, he was embraced by a Jewish editor who not only publicized his critique of his Christian colleagues but made him a kind of celebrity, at least among Jewish readers. As Franklin had reached out to support his public stance regarding the Christian mission toward the Jews, Oxlee reciprocated in kind by acknowledging the support while celebrating the new publicity he had gained from an unexpected source. Perhaps more unusual than his actual argument in support of Jewish ritual practice was the way it was now disseminated through the organ of the Jewish press. Both Franklin's initiative to publish the message of a Christian cleric whose ultimate concern was the Jewish acceptance of Christian faith and Oxlee's satisfaction in gaining a receptive audience through that initiative offer a remarkable glimpse at the ways in which Jews and Christians could align themselves while promoting their own self-interests in midcentury London.

In the main, Oxlee's new publication did not stray from his earlier themes, although he added longer discourses on "vulgar conceptions of the Godhead and the belief in the Diabolarchy."[26] Oxlee, however, added a new twist in suggesting that the Jews had a purer vision of the Godhead and attributed little to the devil in contrast to the corrupted views of contemporary Christians. As before, he relied heavily on Jewish sources and returned repeatedly to the parallelism of the kabbalistic and Christian notions of a Trinity, a "more simple, intelligible, and necessary development of the Godhead." To the Jew, accordingly, "the Christian tenet of the Trinity ought to recommend itself as worthy of admiration and belief, not only for its truth but its simplicity." So too, the doctrine of the Incarnation "so far from being incompatible with, is capable of being fully demonstrated on the principles of Judaism." And the doctrine of vicarious atonement was likewise embedded in rabbinic Judaism. The gospel thus became in Oxlee's formulation "a glorious appendix to the Law, rendering it efficacious and complete," and "thus forming one universal Israelitish family of true worshippers."[27]

In his third and final letter, Oxlee emphasized the need for contemporary Jews to regain the Holy Land, "that the divine promise awarded to you of retaining the land of Canaan, as a perpetual inheritance, may be firmly ratified and established, and that your restoration to the divine favour may be visibly demonstrated and confirmed, by your once again possessing the patrimony of your forefathers."[28] He returned to the theme that Jews need not cease to be Jews by affirming the Christian faith. He called for a renewed study of scripture based on a competent knowledge of Hebrew and Greek sources. And, most important, he insisted that Jews and Christians cease "from mutually despising and reviling each other because of their religious differences." Gentile "tyranny" exercised over the Jewish convert "is nothing else than Gentile ignorance, Gentile bigotry, and Gentile folly."[29]

Ultimately, he returned to his explicit criticisms of the actions of the London Society, first involving its bishop in Jerusalem and McCaul's faithful disciple Michael Alexander: "To imagine for a moment, that the Anglo-Prussian Protestant Church, now attempted to be established at Jerusalem under the episcopal rule of Dr. Alexander, can ever form a nucleus around which the dispersed Israelites may ultimately be collected in the land of Palestine, as converts to the Christian faith; is highly preposterous and absurd." Then he addressed the predicament of the London Society in general, its constant shifting, dissimulation, and hypocrisy, and its ultimate betrayal of its original ideals of Christian benevolence. In lurid detail, he described the present internal politics plaguing the organization and the discrepancy between its published reports of "wonderful conversions and baptisms of adult Jews" and the actual reality on the ground. Moreover, the leaders of the London Society "seem ever prepared to practice any delusion, and to keep secret any counsel, so long as it has a tendency to augment their funds and the number of the conversions; but how these Jewish converts are to dispose of themselves in the future, whether they are to intermarry with the sons and daughters of Israel, and so keep themselves and their posterity separate and distinct from the Gentile Christians; or whether they are to intermix . . . they are cunningly silent, and never venture to promulgate a word for fear of damaging their interests or causing the dissolution of the Society itself." Instead, Oxlee advocated the actual return of Jews, the retention of the separate identity of the Nazarene community in Palestine without the interference of church officials, as well as the opportunity of Jews with the support of Christian rulers, perhaps the Russian emperor, to practice their own law. We have already discussed the specific context of the bishopric of Jerusalem and McCaul's enormous disappointment that his own dream of a tolerated and respected community of converts in Jerusalem had not been fulfilled. Writing thirteen years earlier, Oxlee voiced his strong opposition to this "preposterous and absurd" idea.[30]

Very soon after Oxlee had published *Three More Letters* it was reviewed in the pages of the *Jewish Chronicle* by Tobias Theodores, a review partially discussed in Chapter 4 and alluded to at the beginning of this chapter. Here, as we have seen, the Jewish reviewer linked Hoga, Oxlee, and Tonna together. But he also gave special attention to Oxlee's second set of letters. It is worth quoting how he summarized Oxlee's theological stance:

The revered author proposes to fit Christianity for an approximation of Judaism by the removal, after a system by him proposed, of all that the "Christianity of the day" contains of a heathenish origin; and to prepare Judaism for a reconciliation with Christianity by grafting upon the former such Christian dogmas as are considered true by the author, and moreover, already extant, as he is persuaded, in the more recondite systems of Jewish theosophy. For the author does not consider Judaism alone to stand in need of conversion; he ascribes corruption quite as boldly to the Christian Church of the present day.[31]

The summary is interesting in presenting an ambivalent reaction to Oxlee's interreligious project. On the one hand, Theodores appreciated Oxlee's accusations against the present church in calling it corrupt. On the other hand, he was totally unpersuaded by Oxlee's prodigious effort to find support for Christian dogma in the utterances of kabbalists and *darshanim* (Jewish homilists). Even if such tenuous links were correct, why would Oxlee assume that the "recondite systems of Jewish theosophy," as he called them, carry any authoritative weight for most Jews? For "Judaism is no more bound to acknowledge the reveries of its Cabbalists than Christianity can be expected to recognize the phantasmas of its Rosicrucians, of some of its Swedenborgians, of its Jacob Boehme, of any of its numerous illuminati." He cited the anti-kabbalistic treatise of the seventeenth-century Venetian rabbi Leon Modena, recently published "by the learned Dr. Furst at Leipzig to prove that the oldest among the Cabbalistic works are of a modern origin."[32] He proceeded to demolish Oxlee's other parallels between kabbalah and Christianity, an enterprise, he pointed out, pursued by earlier Christian thinkers since the days of Petrus Galatinus.[33] The plurality of God's name could not be considered Trinitarian in the ordinary use of language. The doctrine of the Incarnation was also "a stranger to Israel." So too was the doctrine of vicarious atonement alien to Judaism; the repentant himself atoned for his sins. Judaism likewise had no place for a sacrificed, divine messiah as depicted in Christianity. In summing up Oxlee's study of the theological principles of Judaism, it is quite clear that they were thoroughly Christian, "that the tradition whence they are said to be derived, might be expected to have come from the fathers of the Council of Trent, rather than from the Rabbies of Sura, Nahardea, or Pumbetitha."[34] Labeling Oxlee's principles as Catholic rather than rabbinic must have surely elicited the ire of the book's author, but Theodores still reserved kind words for Oxlee at the end of his review:

Having thus negated all the doctrinal postulates made by the Rev.
Mr. Oxlee, we deem it a duty and a pleasure to assure the Rev.
gentleman, that our feeling towards him is not that of systematic
opposition. We cheerfully pay him the tribute of our gratitude, if it
be worthy of his acceptance, for the brotherly affection with which,
so unlike the majority of his predecessors in Jewish-Christian controversy, he addresses the members of the house of Israel; of our
respect for the sternness with which he pleads the sacred cause of
conscience against arrogance and usurpation; of admiration for the
varied learning with which his well-stored mind supports him in the
struggle for that which he holds and confesses to be the truth . . .
we hail in him a believing priest of the Church Tolerant, the gradual
establishment of which, within the memory of this generation,
opens a new phasis of the world's ecclesiastical history; a church that
has as yet but few followers, but under whose banner are sure to
collect tribes and nations to whom the Roman Eagle and the British
Lion, the Cross and the Crescent never penetrated; within whose
capacious halls all honest minds shall surely be admitted, on terms
of mutual respect and mutual forbearance, to join in the great universal hymn to the one Father of all . . . when He, who alone pos-
sesses the truth absolute, shall, in His wisdom, see fit to hush even
the last sound of dissonance among men, and to reinstate harmony
upon her long-forsaken throne—never again to be disturbed![35]

Theodores had dismissed Oxlee as a bad theologian but had praised him
as an important political ally in the struggle for Jewish political rights in
England. His balancing act of appropriate criticism and commendation illu-
minates why astute journalists such as Franklin and Theodores viewed
Oxlee's convoluted and unconvincing reflections on Judaism and Christianity as still worthy of notice and appreciation in the fight for Jewish survival.

Oxlee seems to have won the hearts of other Jewish readers as far away
as the American continent. As early as June 1843, the Jewish publisher Isaac
Leeser of Philadelphia had received a copy of the *Three Letters* from his
English associate Joseph Rodriques Peynado and noticed the "bold stance it
takes against the system which has been so much patronized in England, of
bringing the Jews to Christianity by an appeal to them to forsake the Mosaic
law."[36] Several years after the death of John Oxlee, the *American Hebrew
and Jewish Messenger* offered an enthusiastic endorsement for an anticipated

biography of the man to be written by his son, suggesting that it would be especially popular "amongst Israelites of the United States." It continued:

> The Rev. Mr. Oxlee opposed, single-handed, but with the most powerful effect, the whole conversion society. He did not enter the battle-field unarmed, but with the best weapons to conquer,—God's law and our time-honored commentaries,—he fought—he conquered. The Israelites throughout the world owe a debt of gratitude to the Divine of another faith who spent the best part of his life to become conversant with the Hebrew law; who studied the Talmud and kindred learned works, for the sole purpose of familiarizing himself with their laws, their probity, their past chequered condition, and their future glorious prospects. In short, no Israelite, that wishes to be informed what the refined mind—the sound scholar— thinks of his religion should be without the biography of the late Rev. John Oxlee.[37]

Absent from this profile of Oxlee was any reference to his obscure and unconvincing ruminations on the Jewish parallels of Christian dogma. Oxlee was remembered fondly for both his public stand against the missionaries and for his sound scholarship and his refined mind. Only a month later, the *Jewish Chronicle* offered its own encomiastic homage to the Christian pastor, raising the bar of scholarly accomplishment even higher:

> The late John Oxlee was an extraordinary scholar. Had preferment in the Church been given by merit and not favour, John Oxlee would have adorned an episcopal chair, instead of being suffered to go through life unacknowledged by the Church which he so zealously served. We believe that since Buxtorf no Gentile excelled him in rabbinical lore. But what particularly endears his memory to the Jewish scholar was the candour of the deceased. Having studied the Scriptures in the original language, he had discovered the groundlessness of many assertions of Christian divines, and candidly and publicly admitted the correctness of the Jewish interpretations of the questions at issue. He was as opposed to the conversion delusion as the Jews themselves. We therefore willingly reproduce the subjoined sketch of the life of the deceased.

What followed was a biographical sketch written by a John Dowson for the *Whitby Gazette* a month earlier.[38]

By the time of his death, the heroic image of Oxlee as a brilliant Hebraist who defended the integrity of Jews against the conversionists seems to have displaced entirely the earlier academic criticisms of his recondite scholarly work. The irony of John Oxlee's legacy as a public figure and scholar was that it was shaped in large part by his Jewish not Christian readers. They were the ones who deemed him a champion of their interests and elevated his intellectual profile as a scholar of Judaism far beyond his actual attainments. The author who had lamented the fact only a few years earlier that no one had bothered to purchase his three-volume magnum opus was now lionized by the Jewish press as the most extraordinary scholar, unrivaled in his knowledge since the time of Buxtorf, and the public defender of the Jewish community. Oxlee had ultimately gained some of the recognition he had sought all his life, albeit not from his own coreligionists but from a beleaguered community who viewed him as a friend and ally.

Charlotte Elizabeth Tonna

In addition to Oxlee and Hoga, Charlotte Elizabeth Tonna (1790–1846) was the final person included in Theodores's collective portrait of the three friends of the Jews and opponents of the conversionists. Unlike Oxlee, Tonna is not an unstudied figure in the history of nineteenth-century politics, religion, and literature. In recent years, historians of gender have noticed her public role in the fight for human rights and social reform, often articulated in the journals she edited, especially the *Christian Lady's Magazine*. While she hardly professed feminist views, her public profile as a woman, and one impaired by deafness, was well recognized and appreciated. She has also been studied as a Protestant evangelical writer, who strongly advocated the restoration of the Jews to the Holy Land as a precondition for Christ's second coming. Some twenty years ago Hilary L. Rubenstein wrote a thorough and thoughtful account of her deep involvement with Judaism as well as with individual Jews during her relatively short lifetime. Most relevant was her description of the close and even intimate relationship she had with Jacob Franklin, the editor of the *Voice of Jacob* and a figure, as we have already seen, at the forefront of Jewish-Christian dialogue. In what follows, I offer only some important expansions on Rubenstein's account.[39]

FIGURE 4. Charlotte Elizabeth Tonna. Engraving by T. Bonar, frontispiece from *The Works of Charlotte Elizabeth*, 6th ed., vol. 1 (New York: M. W. Dodd, 1848). By permission of the British Library.

At first glance, it might appear odd to place Tonna in the company of John Oxlee. On the few occasions where she addressed him in print, her remarks were highly uncomplimentary. Her first mention of Oxlee's work appeared in a brief note in her *Christian Lady's Magazine* only a year after his first three letters to the archbishop had been published. She wrote the following: "Another Clergyman [she had previously mentioned the work of Rev. W. Pym in the text], the Rev. J. Oxlee, has published a pamphlet on which he calls the Jewish question [a clear reference to *Three Letters*]. The practical working of which would be to dissolve Christianity in Judaism, and then to evaporate the latter into nothing. From his doctrine and deductions we heartily dissent. He certainly has shewn up the falsehood and absurdity of certain ancient 'fathers.' But he ends by out-doing them all."[40]

Two years later she offered a more detailed explanation of her distaste for Oxlee's writings. She related that some of her friends had recommended Oxlee's *Three More Letters*, "which is said to be obtaining a wide circulation among the Jews under the supposition that it exposes the sentiments of a section of the Christian Church on points in controversy between them and us." But after reading the work, she reacted with anger and horror. In startling language she proclaimed: "We believe and hope that the views held by the author of that pamphlet are peculiar to himself; that no other clergyman of the established church, nor lay-member of it, nor any individual of any denomination professing to hold any creed in accordance with the Holy Scriptures, is tainted with heresies so fanciful as those which, alas for the state of ecclesiastical discipline among us!—a beneficed minister of the established church has not feared to proclaim in a document addressed to the Primate of that church [the archbishop of Canterbury]."[41]

What set her off was Oxlee's disquisition on the devil and his attempt to disprove the personal existence of Satan. By labeling such a belief "a horrid, damnable and blasphemous superstition," Oxlee, in Tonna's eyes, had flatly contradicted the literal meaning of scripture and was justifiably deemed a heretic. While she acknowledged that Oxlee was a very learned man, she proclaimed, nevertheless, that one who departs from the word of the living God necessarily becomes a fool.[42]

Tonna had clearly noticed that "a portion of doctrinal truth" was intermingled with such an error, but by undermining the foundation, the remainder of the small book could not nullify "the pernicious character of the work, as contradicting, in many points, the direct word of God." Tonna was also unaccepting of Oxlee's position of offering one gospel to the Jew and another to the gentile, as she put it, since neither gospel was the one Paul preached. She also felt a sense of unacceptable compulsion in Oxlee's design to offer the Jew a way to find Christian faith:

> We strenuously as ever, protest against forcing the conscience of the Jew on points where God has seen fit nationally to distinguish him from every other branch of the human family . . . we protest against compelling, or even asking him to change his Sabbath, to lay aside the seal of the national covenant, to cease from observing the commemorative or the anticipative ordinances; or in any way to Gentilize him whom God hath been pleased to send into the world a Jew; but the system of theology on which Mr. Oxlee grounds his advocacy of a sustained distinction is very far indeed removed from anything that we can recognize as scriptural.[43]

She closed with the following denunciation of his treatise: "We hope that some faithful brother will, however, be found . . . to tell this erring minister his fault, and to shew him that his wild system has no shadow of a foundation, either in 'the twelve tribes of Israel' or in 'the twelve apostles of the Lamb.' "[44]

It is perhaps not surprising that Charlotte Elizabeth Tonna failed to appreciate the virtues of Oxlee's work and the genuine ways in which their attitudes toward Christianity and Judaism were actually quite close. A literalist when it came to reading scripture, who could not accept any deviation from fundamental Christian doctrine, she was not a scholar of rabbinic Judaism. She had not studied the midrashim and Talmud as Oxlee had done, and she was certainly not adept at kabbalah and medieval Jewish thought. She probably did not recognize the esoteric Jewish doctrines and sources he readily discussed and would not have found in them the Jewish religion with which she identified, that based on the Old Testament alone. She could hardly fathom Oxlee's intricate excurses on the parallels between Christian and Jewish doctrines. While like her, he defended the integrity of Jewish law, encouraged Jews to practice the ritual commandments, and favored a restoration of unconverted Jews in the Holy Land to precede the Second Coming, she obviously missed the resemblance of their ways of thinking and their shared disdain for the conversionists and the London Society. They were in fact fighting on the same side, as Theodores had quickly ascertained.

I would like to underscore Tonna's allegiance to the same values that Oxlee held by focusing on a public controversy in 1843–44 in which she engaged with yet another figure we encountered in Chapter 4 and one whom we will meet at greater length in Chapter 6: Moses Margoliouth. The reader might recall the comparison Jacob Franklin, Tonna's friend, had made between the good convert, Hoga, and the bad one, Margoliouth. Franklin clearly despised the latter, this former eastern European Jew who had repudiated his heritage, ridiculed contemporary Jewish practice, and supported McCaul and the London Society throughout most of his long career in the Church of England. It is clear that Tonna too was fully at odds with his position and the feeling was mutual.

To fully appreciate the context of the heated exchanges between Tonna and Margoliouth, it is necessary to trace and reconstruct a series of essays and letters published in the *Christian Lady's Magazine* beginning as early as January 1843. In that month Tonna had published an essay entitled "Fringes and Phylacteries," commenting on an incident in the town of Hertford regarding certain Christians who had ridiculed the Jewish commandments of fringes and phylacteries. She vigorously defended the rituals as sacred obligations "laid on the children of Israel by the God of Abraham, Isaac, and Jacob." Regarding the fringes, she added, what "a touching sight to behold the men of Israel in their synagogues, not one, down to the youngest boy, being without the scarf to which these fringes are attached: and they, together with the rolls of the law, are all that is left of the past!" She even expressed the wish to own such a scarf but repressed the feeling "because we felt they were holy unto Israel, and no Gentile has a right to put them on." And she thus concluded: "God would keep His own peculiar nation distinct to the end of time, and this could not be if Gentiles took upon them the badges, and entered into the covenant prescribed for Israel alone."[45]

Several months later, in May of 1843, Jacob Franklin, the Jewish editor of the *Voice of Jacob* and Tonna's friend, addressed a letter to her as editor of her journal. She published this immediately and warmly welcomed it. Franklin was particularly incensed by an address given by Hugh McNeile, the well-known Irish Anglican clergyman and the dominant spirit of Liverpool evangelicism. Franklin had been told by "a venerable inhabitant of Liverpool" that McNeile had made the following public statement regarding the Jews: "although they bowed down not to idols, they worshipped not the true God, and . . . they were, as the Unitarians were, idolaters."[46]

Franklin understood quite well the special bonds between Tonna and McNeile. While Tonna had been born into an English evangelical family, she experienced her "conversion" while living as an adult in Dublin among Irish Anglican evangelicals before moving back to England. She was therefore closely associated with the "Celtic fringe" of British evangelicalism, as Donald Lewis called it, and Hugh McNeile was her ongoing mentor. McNeile's essays often appeared in her journal, and only a month earlier, Tonna had even devoted a touching panegyric to him.[47]

Tonna responded by fully identifying the author of the letter who had signed simply as "Jacob" as Jacob Franklin, the founder of a free Jewish press in England. She called on McNeale to either retract the statement or show he had never made it. She was confident in McNeile's love of the Jewish people:

> He was among the very first boldly to proclaim, and has been among the very firmest steadily to uphold, the direct literal application to the literal Israel of those glorious promises . . . he has unflinchingly maintained the doctrine of Israel's coming restoration, and the unclouded glory to be shed over them, and reflected from them, under the literal, personal reign of their Messiah; and in the quiet family circle of his own happy home, we have again and again rejoiced in the glow of a spirit as warmly affectionate towards God's ancient people, as, we humbly hope, is our own.

She expressed her discomfort of often being accused of "too Judaizing, as some call it." But she protested the charge, since her interest was not in "Judaizing" the gentiles but rather in not "Gentilizing" the Jews. She again repeated her wish that Jews should not abrogate the ritual of circumcision nor the wearing of fringed garments.[48]

In the next issue Tonna published McNeile's public response to Franklin along with a private letter he had addressed to her as well. In the first, he expressed his love of the Jewish people and his intention not to offend Jewish sensibilities. Indeed he did not consider his comparison of Jews with Unitarians and idolaters as insulting. Christians like him were ready to forgive Jews for neglecting the Holy Scriptures and for wasting their time on Talmudic fables; Jews might also forgive the Christian church as well for its "heaping reproach upon Israel instead of seeking the peace of Jerusalem."

In his longer epistle to Tonna, McNeile offered justification for the conversionists, arguing that no one can rightfully claim that a Jew without baptism can be saved. In so doing, he drew from his book of popular lectures on the prophecies distinguishing ancient from modern Judaism.[49] For McNeile, "Modern Judaism comprehends the opinions, traditions, rites and ceremonies, which began to be received and practiced before the destruction of the second temple; were afterwards enlarged and embodied in the Cabalistic and Talmudic writings; and have been professed and followed by the great body of the Jewish People, without any material alteration, down to the present day." This version of Judaism, according to McNeile, opposed biblical truth and was preoccupied by human traditions alleged to be divine and "reengaged by most palatable superstitions." He cited examples of modern Judaism's false notions located in the Ashkenazic prayer books of the Jews, referring especially to an eyewitness account of the London Society missionary Mr. Ewald: "When Mr. Ewald visited the Jewish synagogue at Hebron a few months ago, he found a copy of the prayer which they offer up for Sir Moses Montefiore and his Lady." When Ewald read the prayer, he turned to the Jews in his presence and claimed this was, in fact, idolatry. McNeile's claim thus did not fall far from the mark: Jews did not actually bow down to idols, but they do not worship the true God. Nevertheless, he held a deep sympathy and prayerful affection toward them, as he proclaimed. As we shall soon see, Moses Margoliouth had clearly read these lines, which he cited, and was perhaps influenced by McNeile in his main work on modern Judaism.[50]

Tonna was pleased by this dignified response, defended her own position regarding the national restoration of the Jews to the Holy Land, and expected the great body of Jews to repudiate the Montefiore prayer. She also referenced a letter she had written to the bishop of Jerusalem, Michael Alexander, who had just been installed in his new position.[51]

At about the same time as these exchanges with Franklin and McNeile in 1843, Tonna had published this letter to Michael Alexander, also the target of Oxlee's criticism. Alexander had converted from Judaism and was ordained at Lambeth Palace in 1841 in the presence of both his mentor Alexander McCaul and Charlotte Elizabeth Tonna. McCaul had previously been offered the Jerusalem bishopric but had nominated Alexander instead since he believed that the position should only be held by a person born a Jew. As we have noted earlier, Alexander was subsequently appointed the bishop of the United Church of England and Ireland in Jerusalem and arrived in the city in 1842. He proceeded to consolidate the Protestant presence in Jerusalem, opening several institutions under his authority, but subsequently became a controversial figure by stirring up the other major churches in the city to compete with him and by antagonizing the small local Jewish community who felt threatened by this apostate missionary in their presence.[52]

In the opening of her letter, Tonna challenged Alexander and his personal relationship to the Jewish people:

> In your person, the Christian Church of the circumcision is once
> more planted on the height of Zion; in your person, the reproach of
> seventeen centuries is there rolled away from the Israel. Call you
> what we will, my Lord, you are a Jew, a circumcised Jew, and your
> dear partner, the wife of your bosom, is a Jewess, a descendant of
> Levi; your daughters who, under the Lord's blessing, are growing up
> as the polished corners of the temple, are Jewesses also. Here I pause:
> for I feel that something is wanting to complete the picture. My
> dear Lord, hear with me while I respectfully and affectionately put
> once more the query—Why are not your sons also Jews?[53]

In labeling Alexander's church as a church of circumcision, by explicitly mentioning the bishop's circumcision, and by questioning why Alexander had not circumcised his sons, Tonna was making a critical point: that while Christians and Jews were obligated to observe the moral law, Jews in particular had an additional obligation of keeping the ritual commandments stipulated by biblical decree and exemplified by both Jesus and Paul. The gospel never abrogated the law for Jews, and as she put it, "it seems unjust to rob a Hebrew boy of his birth-right, because his parents have obtained a better inheritance."[54] Surely this was meant as a biting criticism of the way the bishop was raising his sons, indeed, his entire congregation.

Tonna's view was identical with that of Oxlee, whether she had noticed it or not. Both were committed to preserving the Abrahamic covenant for Jews that the gospel never abrogated. This meant preserving the national character of the Jewish people, allowing them to repossess their land as divine inheritance, of encouraging them to observe the Sabbath and festivals, and expecting them to perform the circumcision as the most visible sign of their eternal covenant. At one point Tonna acknowledged that she could not properly observe the Jewish festival of Passover: "Yet I am a Gentile; I could not properly partake, because my fathers were not brought out of Egypt by the visible arm of the Lord; but I believe that every individual of the seed of

Abraham ought to observe it."[55] In short, she claimed, just as she could not be a Jew, it was unwarranted to demand that the Jew become a gentile. She implored the bishop to practice Jewish ritual, including circumcision and the wearing of a fringed garment, and to impart these commandments to his children, since these were the practices of Jesus and the apostles. The ultimate restoration of the Holy Land could only be engendered by Jews reclaiming their birthright.

Despite these obvious similarities between Oxlee and Tonna, they had contrasting styles of expressing themselves and very disparate educational backgrounds in Judaism: Tonna relied exclusively on biblical texts, which she knew intimately and related to passionately; the more academic Oxlee made his case with an armory of rabbinic and kabbalistic sources. Nevertheless, each in his or her way offered a common challenge to those churchmen such as Alexander McCaul who argued that Jews should convert, shed their Jewish identity, and cease observing Jewish ritual. Both challenged the viability of a Protestant church in Jerusalem made up of converts blended together with other Christians and ceasing to preserve their ethnic and religious character.

Alexander never responded to Tonna but Moses Margoliouth did. Sometime between June and November 1843, he published his most important work challenging the very foundations of modern Judaism, perhaps, as I have suggested, an echo of McNeile's well-known publication and certainly mindful of the latter's designation of the Jews as idolaters. Margoliouth then published another pamphlet only a year later directed against Tonna, replete with advertisements promoting his larger work accompanied by approbations from several churchmen praising the book and its author.[56]

By November 1843, Tonna had noticed Margoliouth's book and his personal attack against her positions on Judaism and the Jews. His challenge came prior to the publication of her letter to the Jerusalem bishop but addressed the very same issues she had voiced there. She immediately responded to him in kind. She first identified him as "a Jewish gentleman who, having been born and educated in Poland, was led to investigate and to embrace the Christian religion," arrived in England where he was converted by the London Society, and was looking forward to his ordination from the Church of England. She summarized the main themes of his book directed against the contemporary Jewish practices of fringes, phylacteries, and *mezuzah*, and then added:

> After reiterating, and that we are sorry to say in a most irritating
> tone, and in a sense in which he never dreamed of using it, the term

"Idolaters" as applied by the Rev. Hugh M'Neile to the Jewish people; after roundly charging them with worshipping their fringes, and passing a severe sentence upon the nation of Israel, the author thus turns upon a very humble, but very honest and devoted ally of theirs. [He writes of her:] "Strange to find, however, there are good and pious Christians, who profess to love the Jews, and would yet conceal from their view their precarious state *for fear of hurting their feelings*; and would even insist that the converted Jew, who is taught by the Spirit which giveth life, and not by the letter which killeth, should still wear the fringed garment . . . which the Rabbis have so adulterated, that it must have become an abomination in the sight of God.[57]

Clearly offended by Margoliouth's questioning of her motivation in supporting Jews and Jewish observance, she offered a vigorous defense of her advocacy of Jewish rituals, adding "we should have been delighted to have seen Mr. Margoliouth, with a Talith on his shoulders, bearing a palm-branch in the London Synagogue during the feast of Tabernacles, just past, and uniting in the Hosannas of his brethren; and in those beautiful scripture lessons and prayers to which he would indeed have attached a deeper spiritual meaning than many of those around him, but to which no conscientious Christian could refuse as hearty an Amen as we uttered."[58] She underscored the inconsistency of his lamenting the ignorance of Judaism on the part of English Jews while writing an English book for them and for Christians excoriating the Jews for errors unknown to them.

She revealed as well her discomfort at her friend McNeile's unfortunate choice of epithets to describe the Jews. She recalled her long and intimate friendship with him and expressed her pain in taking a position on the Jews that might contradict his. Margoliouth, in describing the "Talith" as an idol for some Jews, had surely twisted McNeile's words to the detriment of both him and the Jews: "Mr. Margoliouth is young and zealous, and learned, and clever, and has spent a great deal of time in deeply exploring a vast deal of rubbish, which nineteen-twentieths of all his brethren would readily repudiate; but surely this is not the way to do them good, by bearing false witness against them as a body, even to the capital crime of idolatry, because some fancy that putting the fringe of the Talith to their eyes will help to preserve their sight." Such a conclusion was equivalent of accusing an old woman of witchcraft for nailing a horseshoe to the door for good luck, she added.[59]

In the end, Tonna objected most to the bitter tone of Margoliouth's book, his speaking ill of his Jewish brethren in England, and his personal attack on the courageous editor of the Anglo-Jewish press, Jacob Franklin.[60] For Tonna, Jews deserved support and deliverance, not vituperation, while being allowed to preserve their own nationality, something Margoliouth and his stinging barbs would not allow.

In the following year, as we have said, Margoliouth took the opportunity to answer Tonna, this time not addressing her comments on his book but rather her public letter to Bishop Michael Alexander. He opened by declaring that since he did not expect the bishop to answer Tonna personally, he had taken up the gauntlet. He felt especially qualified since he was a Christian Israelite, one born a Jew who was confirmed in the faith of Jesus after reading the articles of the Church of England in their Hebrew translation. Jews who had embraced Christianity did not seek an earthly Canaan, as she had described, but a heavenly Jerusalem, far more sublime than the earthly reward she imagined. Her dogmatic view that Israel's ordinances were perpetual was based on the faulty notion that Hebrew Christians are still heirs to the land of Israel according to some national covenant, but this too was misconstrued for one becoming "a partaker in the kingdom of Christ."[61]

Margoliouth repeatedly mentioned Tonna's close Jewish associate Jacob Franklin ("your elder brother Jacob") and the latter's slanderous references to him in the *Voice of Jacob* as well as Tonna's own negative references to him in her *Christian Lady's Magazine*.[62] He took exception to these attacks and declared: "Pardon the liberty I take in addressing to you in the language of brotherly Christian advice and remonstrance, and in venturing to suggest that you may perhaps have overstepped the limits of your sphere in challenging the whole Church in your letter to the Bishop of Jerusalem."[63] Had he meant by this comment her limits as a Christian woman? How did a personal appeal to a bishop constitute an attack on the entire church? He proceeded to challenge her notion that Jesus and Paul believed that Christians should uphold the old law. For converted Jews, he argued, the new covenant they embraced surely abrogated the old. A close examination of scripture demonstrates how Tonna's position was untenable. He responded to her previous attack against his book on modern Judaism and located her same arguments in the parallel criticisms of Franklin against him, a kind of echo of each other. Modern Jews, particularly those who observed the rabbinic commandments of fringes, phylacteries, and *mezuzah* did not worship the true God but were idolaters. By emphasizing her wish for Jews to practice Judaism, she had lost sight of the need to promote Christianity among the Jews in order to save their souls. Her belief in the eternality of the "commemorative ordinances" of Israel was unscriptural and arbitrary. He particularly singled out for ridicule the "hoshannas" recited on the Jewish holiday of Sukkot, while repeating the account of his colleague Ewald about the prayer to "Sir Moses Montefiore and his lady" and his designation of such practice as idolatry. Tonna had also known of this story but thought it had been repudiated by most Jews. But Margoliouth then located the reference in the official sacred service of the London Jews. The prayer for Montefiore, he thus argued, was typical of the flawed worship of most modern Jews, a kind of modern idolatry fabricated by the rabbis meant to distance Jews from their biblical roots and the true Christian faith.[64]

Margoliouth's response illustrated the huge gap between the conversionists of the McCaul camp with which he identified and their critics who, while aspiring to ultimately convert the Jews as well, had insisted that the Jewish commitment to the law was still valid. Margoliouth, of course, had personally practiced rabbinic ritual for much of his life and well knew the difference between the idealized portrait of biblical legislation Tonna and Oxlee had evoked and the real one shaped through hundreds of years of rabbinic exegesis. Neither Tonna nor Oxlee was very transparent about what specific laws contemporary Jews should practice and by whose authority they should determine what the law required. Indeed, even Oxlee, with his impressive knowledge of rabbinic sources, was never precise about the actual law Jews were supposed to uphold as opposed to some abstraction of divine law that would be fused in his mind with the divine gospel. Would it be based on the *Shulhan Arukh*, on Ashkenazic or Sephardic custom, on the authority of the rabbis of Jerusalem or the chief rabbi of London, or perhaps the Reform rabbi of the same city? Margoliouth alone understood that the contemporary practice of Jews living in the nineteenth century was radically different from that practiced by biblical Hebrews or by Jesus himself. This, of course, had been the ultimate message of McCaul's assault on rabbinic Judaism. Margoliouth, his faithful disciple, had personally affirmed this message by abandoning Judaism for Christianity. He had crossed the boundaries of the law; but had he cast off his Jewish identity altogether? We shall explore this question in Chapter 6.

Before closing this chapter, however, there is one final document worth considering regarding Charlotte Elizabeth Tonna's relationship to Jews and Judaism. This is the remarkable obituary penned by her devoted colleague and friend Jacob Franklin in the pages of his Jewish journal the *Voice of Jacob* on the occasion of her untimely death from cancer in 1846. This is a text unlike any other regarding the history of the Jewish-Christian dialogue in this era, and perhaps in any era. We have already seen in the entangled histories of Jews and Christians in mid-nineteenth-century England the possibilities of close alliances and intimate contacts crossing conventional social and cultural boundaries especially in the pages of the Jewish press. But Franklin's homage to a pious Christian lady was indeed a unique outpouring of personal affection as well as a sincere affirmation of the hopes and prospects of Jewish-Christian coexistence in the wake of centuries of mutual hatred and recrimination.[65]

Franklin's tone throughout was incredibly frank and open. He understood from the start that Jews and Christians alike would view with suspicion the friendly relations between the two editors: "Many pious Jews shook their heads, and blamed the confiding disposition which had been, in other cases, so often and so Jesuitically abused. It boots not here to note the illiberality with which some, not pious, have assailed a friendship which they could neither understand nor appreciate . . . she too has been by her Christian brethren suspected and taunted of 'Judaizing' and of compromising her Christianity for the sake of Jewish favor!"[66]

Franklin the Jew could admire the deep and abiding faith of Tonna the evangelical Christian. He appreciated that she had begun, like her other colleagues, as a conversionist but was ultimately transformed by her real encounters with living Jews:

> When, however, she came to know Judaism and the Jews from direct investigation—to understand their obligations, their polity, their hopes, and their expectations—she ceased to desire the estrangement of a single soul from the Synagogue, as at this day disciplined. True, she held fast by her own faith, and hoped and prayed that the Synagogue might be brought to adopt it; but she did not and could not expect the realization of what she prayed for, until our national restoration to Zion under the Messiah. For the hastening of that great day she joined the Jew in prayer; and she fulfilled her mission when she exhorted Israel to be faithful in all things to the unrepealed and unrepealable covenants of his God, in their traditional integrity, and when she helped to rouse the slumberers in our ranks to a consciousness of their high vocation, and to a yearning after the

fulfilment of their appointed destiny, according to the promise of the All-faithful One.[67]

In offering her distinctive voice on behalf of the Jews, she suffered great indignities, private slights and public rebukes, even hostility, according to Franklin. But she persevered in withdrawing her support from the London Society, challenging the bishop of Jerusalem, standing up for the rights of beleaguered Jews around the world, advocating an Anglo-Jewish version of the Bible, and more. As a supporter of the Jewish press, she even helped to soften much Jewish prejudice toward honest Christians like herself.

Franklin's final words encapsulated the hopes her life represented in his mind for the future of Jewish-Christian relations: "And though the humble seed, scattered in the hour of shade by those of different faiths, may not have sprung up into favour in their own day, still is it permitted to fellow-labourers in such a vineyard, to realize, even now, the consciousness that the plant they have sown and watered shall bear fruit and flourish, when their voices, become mute meanwhile, shall be privileged to swell the harmony of universal creation, worshipping Israel's God 'with pure lip and with one accord.' "[68] Whether or not Franklin's eulogistic and impassioned rhetoric conveyed the actual reality of Charlotte Elizabeth Tonna's contribution to as well as the limits of Jewish-Christian dialogue in her lifetime, he had authentically and sincerely conveyed the depth and intensity of a singular friendship between a Jew and a Christian, not an insignificant accomplishment in the socially divided environment in which he lived.

CHAPTER 6

Moses Margoliouth

The Precarious Life of a Scholarly Convert

Of all the converts Alexander McCaul would have considered among his small coterie of disciples, Moses Margoliouth (1818–81) was surely the most accomplished. Author of numerous learned tomes on biblical literature, Jewish history, Jewish-Christian polemics, and theology, of works of travel literature, and even a novel, Margoliouth's name was familiar to Jews and Christians alike. As we have already seen, his fiery rhetoric had antagonized both the Jewish editor of the *Voice of Jacob*, Jacob Franklin, and his close Christian associate Charlotte Elizabeth Tonna, the evangelical writer and editor.[1] But they were clearly not his only adversaries. Despite his obvious talents as an engaging and prolific writer, in his public career and private life as a Christian clergyman he met with professional failures, economic instability, and even open and veiled aspersions on his moral character. Margoliouth, as we shall see, also displayed a restless spirit, a high opinion of himself that some might call arrogance, along with a contentious and polemical style in dealing with those who disagreed with him. Those painful moments of his life when he struggled with economic insecurity and a negative image projected by his detractors, when he failed to advance in the hierarchical world of the English Protestant clergy, were surely related to his eastern European Jewish origins, his obvious accent and physical appearance, as well as his conspicuous support for the cultural achievements and political rights of Jews. But these were exacerbated as well by his own personal style, charming and upright to some, but devious and untrustworthy to others.

FIGURE 5. Moses Margoliouth. *Portrait of the Author with the Marble Head of the Empress Lucilla* by Lewis Ferriere, British vice-consul at Tunis, 1847, in Moses Margoliouth, *A Pilgrimage to the Land of My Fathers*, vol. 1 (London, 1850), opposite title page. By permission of the British Library.

Despite the numerous references to Margoliouth in modern Anglo-Jewish historiography, a significant scholarly study of his life and thought still does not exist.[2] I can hardly do justice to the many dimensions of his career and intellectual accomplishments, especially his classic histories of Anglo-Jewry, in the confines of a single chapter. But I hope to make a strong case, nevertheless, for his importance as a Jewish and Christian thinker. In describing his life as a convert with conflicting loyalties I am aided by the abundance of printed and manuscript materials that survive to tell his story in rich and colorful detail. In particular, his amazing account of his travels to the Holy Land as well as his partially autobiographical novel depicting the clerical life of a young English seminarian offer the historian a deeper insight into the mind and self-image of a highly ambitious convert struggling to define himself simultaneously as a Jew and a Christian throughout his life. McCaul eventually lost contact with Margoliouth toward the end of his life, but Margoliouth never forgot his teacher, as his writings fully testify. In emulating his teacher's ideological and academic paths, he remained a devoted acolyte of his distinguished Christian mentor and a worthy advocate of McCaul's missionary theology.

Early Career

Moses Margoliouth was born in Suwałki, Poland, in 1818,[3] and grew up in the home of a local merchant of some means who seems to have supported him financially even after he left his native Poland and the Jewish fold. At the young age of sixteen, he married Chaja Goldberg, and their first child, Miriam, was born the following year. Margoliouth initially left Poland alone in 1837 with the apparent reluctant blessing of his parents. He ended up in Liverpool where he met a missionary who encouraged him to convert. With the support of an unknown benefactor, he matriculated at Trinity College, Dublin, and also later studied in London at McCaul's seminary at Palestine Place. In 1843, even before he was ordained as a minister in the Church of England, he published his first book. It was entitled *The Fundamental Principles of Modern Judaism Investigated*, and it was clearly intended by its clerical and financial backers to introduce the young and talented convert scholar to the Christian world as an articulate spokesman of the Christian mission toward the Jews. To this end, it was appropriately dedicated to McCaul himself and was introduced by Henry Raikes (1782–1854), chancellor of the diocese of Chester, an active evangelical preacher and philanthropist who would remain a supporter of Margoliouth through much of his career.[4] The long list of subscribers, which followed Raikes's preface to the volume, including "His royal highness the prince Albert" and "His majesty the King of Prussia," bore the markings of the London Society for the Promotion of Christianity Amongst the Jews who evidently engineered this "coming-out" publication for their highly promising candidate for ordination. The fact that the work was published in well-crafted English only six years after Margoliouth had arrived from Poland and was also well illustrated and carefully divided into separate sections—an autobiographical sketch, the core arguments followed by a summary of the 613 commandments in rabbinic Judaism, as well as appeals to both Jews and Christians—argue strongly for the editorial intervention of this well-funded organization.

Margoliouth's backers would not have been disappointed by the final result. In his opening memoir, Margoliouth offered the testimony of his life's experience to convince his Jewish brethren of the truths of Christianity. In addition to his early education in Suwałki, he related how he had continued his rabbinic studies first in the neighboring towns of Pszeroszla (Przerośl) and Grodno, and then in Kalvarija, Lithuania. While living in the latter town he met two like-minded students who loved to read Hebrew books with him and who subsequently introduced him to the Hebrew Bible with the New Testament distributed by missionaries. He added the specific information that his two friends were from Königsberg and that their fathers had acquired the Bibles from J. G. Bergfeldt, the representative of the London Society in their city and well known for his efforts in widely distributing the society's publications among the local Jewish population.[5] No doubt this early encounter with the New Testament, which Margoliouth continued to study, was a triggering event in his initial decision to leave Poland and ultimately to convert.

Following in the footsteps of Saul of Tarsus, he proclaimed, he had not renounced the errors of modern Judaism lightly "without mature and prayerful investigation." He revealed specifically what sparked his lifelong urge to embrace the faith of Jesus when he first stumbled on the words of Psalm 24:8: *Adonai Ezuz* (God is strong). Only later was he to realize the revelatory nature of the phrase since *Ezuz* in Polish is Jesus. In a matter of a few years, he not only journeyed from his hometown to Liverpool and London but from traditional Judaism to evangelical Christianity. Despite his repudiation of his family and their Jewish roots, they did not sever their relationship with him altogether.[6] On the contrary, he continued to correspond with his father, mother, and siblings, and to visit them in future years, long after his formal break from Judaism. His ability to retain these intimate relations despite his apostasy might offer some insight, as we shall later see, into how he constructed his own self-image as a converted Jew during his many years as a Christian cleric.

The underlying theme of his devastating critique of contemporary Jewish practice was the distinction he made between ancient and modern Judaism. Following McCaul's lead, he claimed that the modern version of Judaism practiced by contemporary Jews was distorted and false, invented by the rabbis and having little or no basis in scripture. Following McCaul's attack on the Talmud, published only six years earlier, Margoliouth set out to prove his contention by focusing on three basic rituals of the Jews, fundamental in defining their religious identity in the present time: the commandments of *tefillin* (phylacteries), *ẓiẓit* (fringes), and *mezuzah*. Offering a detailed exposition of each ritual, he attempted to prove that "there is not the least shadow of evidence" that current practice and belief bear any relationship with those of ancient Judaism. The phylacteries were viewed as magical charms and amulets; the fringes were enveloped in fables regarding the dyeing of their blue thread; and the *mezuzah* was falsely considered "a sentinel to keep away evil spirits and fairies." Such practices were not only idolatrous, contended Margoliouth, but especially in the case of the prayer shawl, "the rabbinical talith bears a close affinity to the Popish scapular; in its supposed virtues, it may be called a rabbinical scapular." This was only one instance of many to demonstrate that rabbinic law should rightfully be labeled "Jewish Popery," again a striking echo of McCaul's arguments.[7]

What appeared to be idolatry in both Catholicism and modern Judaism was indeed so: "Perhaps the reader will be able to fancy the ludicrous sight of a synagogue full of Jews, sometimes of thousands, all at once engaged in kissing their fringes. . . . Here again we see a great affinity between Popish Christianity and rabbinical Judaism. Popery enjoins its votaries, 'kiss the crucifix, and exalt it everywhere; yet pretend that you do not adore it, but Him who died on it.'"[8] Margoliouth referred to the Reverend H. McNeile's aforementioned designation of the Jews as idolaters and the naive and false appreciation of this practice by Charlotte Elizabeth Tonna in this context. He concluded: "It is God-like love to tell them plainly the dreadful situation in which they are placed; and it is God-less liberalism to act a contrary part."[9]

But following Margoliouth's bitter denunciation of modern Jewish practice, he appeared to shift direction to clearly acknowledge, in contrast to his mentor McCaul, that not all of rabbinic Judaism was unworthy of Christian attention. This digression arose when describing the members of a Talmud study society adorned with fringes and phylacteries. In a long note, he offered a positive sketch of such Jewish literary associations that focus on the study of the Talmud and then further explained the various branches of rabbinic literature: Mishnah, Gemara, and *aggadot*. Only the latter was deserving of abuse since "it consists of all the allegories, absurdities, fables, indecencies, and wonders found in Talmudic lore." However, the Babylonian Talmud in its entirety got a better review "for it is an extraordinary Babel, or most inconceivable mixture of political economy, ethics, a little astronomy, logic, metaphysics, jurisprudence, allegories, and fables of the most ridiculous and contemptible nature . . . whilst at the same time it contains many valuable truths, and many other subjects worthy of attention." And finally Margoliouth offered the following portrait without any reservation at all: "It is indeed a wonderful scene to behold a Jewish Beth Hamedrash [house of study] in Poland on a Saturday afternoon; to see ten or twelve large tables surrounded by pious Jews who have a zeal for God. Were even their greatest enemy to witness such a scene, he would be struck with their piety. It would inspire him with a spirit of love and affection, and his prejudice would be turned into sincere respect for the Jewish nation; but, the fact is, their real state is far from being known and considered by the majority of British Christians."[10]

How might we understand his praise of the Talmud and students of the Talmud in a treatise designed to denigrate the rabbis and their twisted interpretations of Jewish rituals? Was this merely an inconsistency on Margoliouth's part, a nostalgic throwback to his youth as a student in a Polish yeshiva? Was he merely distinguishing between the cerebral and rational activity of the rabbis in contrast to their fabulous and irrational lore, which he abhorred? McCaul, too, as we have seen, shared this blatant inconsistency to some extent: ridiculing the Talmud and its immoral statements, on the one hand, while waxing eloquent about the acute intelligence and moral fervor of Polish Jews, on the other. Such remarks were indeed confined to a footnote that might be passed over by the reader who focused on Margoliouth's central argument. Yet the remaining sections of this, his first book, also abounded with inconsistencies. Had he come to criticize his former coreligionists or to praise them? Apparently he intended to do both.

Upon concluding his examination of the three rituals, he surprisingly offered his readers a full summary of all of the 613 commandments of rabbinic Judaism, hoping "a more complete translation of them into English will be acceptable both to English Jews and Christians. It will also serve as a synopsis of all Jewish customs and ceremonies."[11] The listing of the commandments spanning some eighty pages was passed over without comment, derogatory or otherwise. Did he expect English Jews to consult his synopsis after tolerating his insulting description of their ritual life? And what use would this unaided summary be to Christians who had been led to believe that rabbinism was indeed nothing more than popery?

In the next section addressed to the "House of Israel," Margoliouth attempted to save face with the Jews whom "I esteem, respect, and love, with unequalled affection," while distinguishing them from modern Judaism, which "I found to be wanting, and unworthy of professing followers of Moses and the Prophets . . . contrary to the will and word of the living God." He was realistic enough to expect only hatred and calumny from Jews since "this is the frequent experience of the converted Jew, either from your public journals, or private conversation."[12] He lamented the fate of previous converts such as "Rabbi Moses," the son of the Hasidic rabbi Shneyer Zalman of Lyady, who was deemed insane by community officials for converting to Christianity, or a Mr. Cohen, a missionary to the Jews of Smyrna, who endured considerable suffering at the hands of the grand rabbi of Constantinople.[13] Nevertheless, Margoliouth would persevere in his invitation to his Jewish brethren to accept the word of Christ: "Let us never forget that Christianity, as well as Judaism, is of Jewish origin, and that both were once confined exclusively to our nation. The Author of Christianity was a Jew; the glorious company of the Apostles were Jews; the noble army of primitive martyrs were Jews; the infancy of the Christian Church was Jewish." And thus in the words of McCaul, he acknowledged "that we are disciples of the Jews, converts to Jewish doctrines, partakers of the Jewish hope, and advocates of that truth which Jews have taught us."[14] The argument that conversion to Christianity was an affirmation of Jewishness no doubt resonated personally for Margoliouth in his simultaneous embrace of his Jewish and Christian selves. But could it prove effective in encouraging other Jews to approach the baptismal font? Most Jews who read *The Old Paths* were unpersuaded that McCaul was a "partaker of the Jewish hope"; such was clearly the fate of this book as well.

The final section of the book was addressed to Margoliouth's Christian readers. He opened with an apology for perhaps sounding too Jewish for a seminarian soon to be ordained a Christian cleric: "My dear Christian readers, I humbly trust that in addressing a few words to you in behalf of my nation, I shall not be chargeable with having imbibed early national prejudices, which I cannot get over, and that I am therefore still anxious to elevate the Jewish nation above their level, being puffed up with national pride." Here he transparently revealed his own self-awareness of the contradictory nature of his narrative, both denying and then affirming the integrity and viability of the Jewish tradition. But this self-awareness did not inhibit in the least his lavish praise for the Jewish community that followed. He admired Jews "for their genius, for their love of learning, and for their literature; and when I am to speak of Jews abstractedly from Judaism, words fail me to express my admiration for them. . . . You will not be surprised therefore . . . when I tell you that it grieves me to find that many Christians connect with the idea of the Jew all that is absurd and ridiculous, and even boldly speak of their literature (which evidently they never fully examined) as a mass of absurdities."[15]

Fully aware of the inconsistency of appreciating Jewish literature while debunking Jewish practice, Margoliouth drew the analogy that Greece and Rome excelled in the arts and sciences although their religions were filled with superstition. Jews, too, he proclaimed, excelled in the sciences although they were hardly recognized among the "Sapientissimi" of the cultures of the world. And, he asked, why do those Christian scholars who pass over the Jews in silence falsely blend the name Jew with the idea of Judaism?[16] For Margoliouth, the distinction was clear: Judaism is about religious belief and practice, but Jewishness entails literary and scientific accomplishment. Here he unambiguously offered a secular definition of Jewish identity, one based on ethnicity and culture. By separating religion from culture, Margoliouth has seemingly found the strategy to declare his own allegiance to Jews in his new role as a minister of the English church. But as we shall see, the distinction in Margoliouth's own life was never so clear-cut; the name Jew and the idea of Judaism, as he put it, were so intimately linked that even he was unable to surgically separate the two.

Citing generously McCaul's appreciative words on Jewish learning and those of his son-in-law, James Finn, as well, Margoliouth offered a vast inventory of Jewish literature from antiquity to the present. This included the

Bible itself, the Hellenistic Jewish writings, the Mishnah and Gemara. He singled out the brilliance of Josephus and Philo and the exceptional community of Jews in Alexandria. Most prominent of all in his depiction were the Sephardim of Cordova, Seville, and Granada, the illustrious students and translators of ancient philosophy: "They were the means, therefore, of the old classics being actively disseminated amongst the Western Colleges of Christendom." They excelled in the study of astronomy, and especially in biblical commentary that left its enormous impact of Christian exegesis until this day.[17]

This led Margoliouth to lament the deficiencies of seminary education for English divinity students with respect to Hebrew literature. He offered a short inventory of Hebrew books worthy of being introduced into university courses, almost all of them written by medieval Spanish Jews, including the Hebrew poetical writings of Samuel ha-Nagid, Solomon Ibn Gabirol, Judah ha-Levi, Abraham Ibn Ḥasdai, Judah al-Ḥarizi, and more. But the list continued into the modern era with such names as Joseph Penso de la Vega and Moses Ḥayyim Luzzatto of Amsterdam, and in his own lifetime, the maskilic essayist and poet Naphtali Hertz Wessely. He compared the latter's *Shirei Tifferet* with the work of Milton: "I have read them both and have no hesitation in saying that they are equal to each other, with the only difference, that Wessely is not so profuse in mythological terms as Milton. Wessely, like Milton, did not think rhyme a necessary adjunct, or true ornament of a poem, or good verse; and therefore rejected it, which makes the poetry of the Shiray Tiphereth exceedingly sublime, in as much as the author felt himself at liberty to express his noble ideas more fully than he would have done under the bondage of the modern trammels of rhyming."[18]

Margoliouth closed his reading list with prose works of such luminaries as Saadia Gaon, Rashi, Abraham Ibn Ezra, David Kimḥi, Maimonides, Gersonides, and Isaac Abravanel. Even the Jewish contribution to music was mentioned, a subject to which he would return in his later writing. But almost as if to stop himself, he reversed course to close with the warning to his Christian readers that they should never forget that men of wisdom know not God, and that the real state of the Jewish nation is not so laudatory: "The very lamp of life, which was entrusted to them, they exchanged for false and delusive fire." It was the London Society that was required to rescue them, to show sympathy for their "desolate posterity," to display them affection by acquainting them with their melancholy state "that they might flee the wrath to come."[19]

Margoliouth suitably closed on the right note in his role of devoted Christian missionary to the Jews, but there is something strikingly discordant about the radical shift in his narrative from an enthusiastic recounting of medieval and modern Hebrew poetry recommended to Christian readers to the conventional debasement of Jewish spiritual blindness. One might understand this contradiction better by seeing him through the lens of Christian Hebraism, the long-held fascination with Jewish learning by Christian scholars. Margoliouth was undoubtedly a scholar drawn to Jewish sources both because of his love for the Jewish intellect and for their significance in better understanding Christianity. Yet loving the Jewish mind might only explain a part of Margoliouth's Jewish preoccupations. He also loved Jews, including members of his own family, and, as we shall see, even "the idea of Judaism" as well.

Pilgrimage to the Holy Land

In 1844 Margoliouth was ordained as a minister of the Church of England and, after a brief stay in Liverpool, was offered the rectorate of Glasnevin, near Dublin, which he gladly accepted. By this time his wife and daughter had joined him, and he witnessed the birth of his son. What appeared to be an ideal location to pursue his scholarly work apparently became unbearable after three short years, however. By the summer of 1847 he had decided to set sail for North Africa and the Middle East with his ultimate destination the Holy Land and the consecration ceremony of the new Protestant chapel in Jerusalem under the direction of Bishop Samuel Gobat. He may have been bored by the small provincial parish or more likely was desirous of regaining his own independence in what was becoming for him an intolerable marriage with his wife Chaja. Whatever his ultimate motivation, he traveled for almost a year, recording in a large batch of letters his variegated experiences with people and places. He soon edited a large sampling of this correspondence and published a book entitled *A Pilgrimage to the Land of My Fathers* in London in 1850. This substantial work, while summarized by Peter Jones,[20] has not been studied in depth by any scholar and needs to be contextualized within the history of Christian travel literature to the Middle East of the nineteenth century. While this task is beyond the scope of my present inquiry, I would like to utilize this rich source to explore some of the themes already touched upon in the first section of this chapter, particularly Margoliouth's vision of himself as a Christian and a Jew, as a convert and missionary. What is especially fascinating about his travel account are the conversations with Jews, Christians, and Jewish converts that allowed him to express himself in a relatively informal and spontaneous way, somewhat different from that of his more scholarly or polemical writing. Of course these letters were edited and formatted for publication, and some were undoubtedly translated into English, thus distancing them even more from the originals on which they were based. Nevertheless, they appear to be presented in a relatively haphazard manner and offer glimpses of rather unexpected personal encounters and reflections. As a source of self-reflection and self-imaging, A Pilgrimage offers the historian a wealth of insight into Margoliouth's thoughts.

I begin by noting the large percentage of letters addressed to Margoliouth's own family, particularly his mother and father, his brothers Herschel, Joshua, and Israel, and especially his daughter Miriam. He wrote to each with great affection and love almost as if his dramatic departure from Judaism had never taken place or, at least, with the expectation that his family had come to tolerate and even respect his new station in life as a minister of the Christian faith. He indicated that these family letters, other than the ones to Miriam, were written in Hebrew and then translated. Notably missing is even one letter to Chaja, indicating a total break from his Jewish wife, a fact ultimately substantiated in a series of unpublished letters documenting the history of their unhappy marriage written some ten years later.[21]

He wrote, for example, to his brother Joshua on the state of the Jews of Paris, his first major stop on the Continent. He included "an epistle to our dear mother which will acquaint you with my mind respecting the fair daughters of Jacob in this city." In the same letter, he imagined he was communing with her face-to-face and sent his most affectionate salutation to his dear father, promising to write him when he arrived in Metz. The letter to his father followed, composed with great excitement since this was the city of his paternal ancestors. He had chosen to visit this city, he wrote, for "I know of nothing more delightful than for a child to be able to comply with his affectionate parent's wishes."[22] One might be tempted to react cynically to such a declaration to a father who had painfully witnessed his son's departure from his ancestral home and faith, but the letter has an air of sincerity about it, with the additional information that Margoliouth's ancestor from Metz was none other than Tobias Cohen, the well-known eighteenth-century Jewish physician, distinguished graduate of Padua's medical school, and author of the Hebrew medical textbook *Ma'aseh Tuviyah*. Margoliouth searched for a copy of this precious volume in Metz to send to his father but could not find one; he eventually succeeded in locating one in Constantinople, Tobias's later home.[23]

The same letter included the following precious closing:

> I intend writing to my dear mother and sister from Lyons, when I shall give them a little more information about the Israel of France. But remember, I shall expect a long letter from you whilst in the island of Melita, now known as Malta. You will find reference made to that island in the New Testament, in the last two chapters of the Acts of the Apostles. I expect you, Joshua, Herschel, and Israel, will give me all the information of interest, with respect to the present state and future prospects of our nation scattered through Russia and Poland.
>
> I am, my dear father,
> Your very affectionate son,
> Upon whose heart thou art a seal [based on Psalm 3:3][24]

This casual information passed between son, parents, sister, and brothers might appear somewhat bizarre to the modern reader. There is no indication of tension or awkwardness in the relationships between family and apostate son. Moses promised more reports about the Jewish situation in France for his mother and sister; he in turn requested to know more about "our nation scattered through Russia and Poland." More surprising was the casual way he told them of his planned journey to a city important for Christian history and documented in the New Testament. Would Jewish parents from Poland find such communication of interest or might it have been received with a certain degree of unease? Nevertheless, his words revealed quite surprisingly the open lines of communication between the family members and Moses, a high degree of toleration on the part of the parents and siblings in referencing Christianity and its sacred sites and texts, and a special interest on Moses's part in learning about the life of "his scattered nation" despite his formal divorcement from the Jewish community.

Moses had previously copied brief letters from his brother and father during his early months in Liverpool that already indicated their openness to him even after he had told them of his conversion. In the first, his brother Herschel wrote: "I must acknowledge that I do not find any unrighteousness in your letters, but, at the same time, they are beyond my comprehension; therefore, I know not what to do. I have resolved by the help of God, to come to England, and to hear from your mouth more of your tenets, for I am very anxious about them."[25] Whether Herschel ever came to England is unknown, though his son Gershon (George) eventually joined Moses in England and followed his example by converting.[26]

The father's letter was even more poignant: "I received your last letter, which revived my spirits; seeing, though I forbade you several times (in severe terms) to write me anymore, still you have persevered in writing; therefore I beg of you to pardon my past letters. And I assure you for the future, that as you were when at my house the dearest of all your brothers, and the beloved of my soul, and my heart and soul's chief desire was to make you a chosen vessel in the sight of God and men; with the same love and affection I love you still, and I will continue to do so until my life's end."[27] There is some reason to wonder whether Margoliouth had included (or embellished) these short excerpts in his first written justification of his conversion in order to underscore the sincerity of his actions. They apparently were originally written in Hebrew (or Yiddish) and then translated by Margoliouth himself. If they are indeed authentic, they reveal a remarkable adjustment on the part of both Margoliouth and his family to his new life as a Christian, the powerful bonds of family loyalty, and the security Margoliouth must have gained in knowing that his exit from Judaism did not mean that he would be cut off from his immediate family.

Two additional facts confirm this family situation. In the first place, it appears that Margoliouth did receive financial support from his father, who funded his initial journey to England and perhaps his trip to the Holy Land as well. He subsequently found Christian donors to support his needs but suffered considerable economic hardship in later years after the death of his parents. Second, in 1856–57 on his way to Russia, Margoliouth returned to Suwałki, his native town in Poland, visiting his mother and his brother Herschel who were still alive. Such a visit more than suggests that his ties to his family continued long beyond the letters published in his travel volume.[28]

Beyond the intimate relations to his own immediate family that *A Pilgrimage* purported to display lay a complex web of connections Margoliouth forged between three distinct communities, sometimes in tension with each other, sometimes intermingled and overlapping. I refer first, of course, to Margoliouth's kinship with Jewish converts like himself, betwixt and between the two religions, who especially viewed their mingled identities as a source of pride and moral virtue but sometimes of alienation and pain. I refer as well to Margoliouth's empathy with Jews of all backgrounds and persuasions, a feeling that especially rises to the surface when he encountered historical places of collective Jewish memory, Hebrew books and manuscripts, and especially worship services, Hebrew liturgical poetry and music. Finally, there remained a profound sense of his Christian commitment, his sincere conviction in the tenets of his adopted faith, his devotion to missionizing, and his excitement in seeing Christian holy sites while simultaneously repudiating and distancing himself from Christian practices, particularly Catholic or Orthodox, that offended his religious sensibility as an evangelical Protestant. The portrait of Margoliouth that emerges from these diverging and converging alliances is one of complexity and ambiguity, one dynamically evolving over time as he met and encountered variegated people, places, and objects that stimulated particular aspects of his religious, cultural, and professional identity. I offer some specific illustrations of each of these competing and intersecting loyalties that defined his personhood as reflected in his travelogue.

One of the longest accounts of his encounter with Jewish converts was offered almost at the beginning of the volume describing his aforementioned visit to Paris. After speaking about the city's Jewish population, he turned to consider "Christian Jews" and especially one particular family. Here is his description of their first meeting:

> Christian Jews are here comparatively a considerable number; but it is to be regretted that they strive to conceal that they ever were Jews. I became accidently acquainted with a highly respectable Judeo-Christian family, while examining a Hebrew manuscript in the Bibliothèque Royale. I was copying a few lines into my notebook from an unfolded volume. A patriarchal-looking gentleman, leader of a large party of both sexes—whom I took as a visitor—passed by me several times; the old man, I observed, cast a bewitching eye, at each of his rounds, on the books before me. He at last mustered courage, and came up to me, saying:—"You must be desperately fond of Hebrew lore, since you take so much trouble in wading through so voluminous a book, so that peradventure you might find something to copy which is worth having." My reply was: "It is natural for a Hebrew to indulge in a predilection for his national tongue, and to be zealous in sifting out even a solitary pearl from a

mountain of sand." I followed it up by quoting Jarchi's [Rashi, the medieval Jewish commentator] simile in commenting on Gen. xxx-vii. i. By the time, I finished my reply, my friend's large family encircled me. The aged gentleman observed: "Pardon me, Sir, I was not aware that you are a Hebrew; I took you, from your dress, for an English clergyman." "You are not mistaken in your surmise," was my rejoinder, "I am not the only Hebrew that am privileged to be a clergyman of the Church of England."[29]

The family was pleasantly surprised by his answer and the eldest son put his arm on him and said: "I trust you have neither any engagement nor any objection to prevent you accompanying us home; my venerable father, my aged mother, my dear sisters and young brothers, are all suppliants for the pleasure of your company." Margoliouth accepted their invitation. They waited for him as he copied five more lines of the manuscript he was reading. He took the arm of the eldest sister and they departed together.[30]

All of the elements of the first encounter are already familiar to the reader of Margoliouth's works: his passion to read Hebrew books and manuscripts whenever he could find them; his declaration that Hebrew was his national tongue; the ease in which he cited classical Jewish literature, in this case a line of Rashi's Torah commentary; and the pride in acknowledging his position as a "Hebrew" clergyman of the Church of England. Attracting people like him with similar backgrounds and entering into an intimate conversation with them was a quality Margoliouth displayed not only in this instance but throughout his travels.

Margoliouth subsequently learned about the history of the family. They had left Spain in 1492 as baptized Christians but declared themselves Jews in Leghorn years later. When their great-grandfather was near death, he enjoined his family never to neglect the study of Hebrew and to detest all idolatry, especially that practiced by Catholics. He revealed to them a manuscript of the New Testament that he had kept secretly in his possession with his own markings on it. His children were caught by the Inquisition for possessing the manuscript but eventually fled Lisbon for Amsterdam. Years later, the family almost miraculously came into possession of the same manuscript of the New Testament owned by their great-grandfather. Their discovery triggered their return to the Christian faith and they were baptized by a Protestant minister.

In the course of intense conversations with the family about their secret background, Margoliouth was urged to reveal his as well, as they spent hours together in their splendid Parisian home. He was eventually led to their private library where he viewed an old Hebrew manuscript of the Old Testament and the precious manuscript of the New of their ancestor. They prayed and studied together as "Christians of the House of Israel." Margoliouth left a deep impression on the entire household, and he too was transformed by this encounter.[31]

On a carriage traveling to Bourges, Margoliouth met three young German men who had recently graduated from a university. They reluctantly admitted that they had learned a little Hebrew. He quickly sensed that they were Jews; when he asked them, they denied it, "but not without a betrayal of embarrassment." Upon arriving in Bourges, they visited the cathedral together, and Margoliouth described the subsequent conversation that followed: "When we arrived at that really splendid edifice, I asked my friends, who professed to be Christians, to explain to me the meaning of several New Testament historical representations, in paintings as well as in sculpture; for I told them that I was a Jew, and expected Christians to instruct me in such matters. However, my friends were not well versed in the New Testament; and it was not till I expressed my unqualified surprise that well-educated Christians should be so unacquainted with their scriptures, that they confessed to me that they were *Yehudim* [Jews]." In a later conversation with his crestfallen Jewish friends, Margoliouth added: "They were chagrined that they were found out. The reason they did not like to be recognized as Jews was, that in France, with all the boasted strides of civilization and liberality, the Jew was still held in execration."[32]

On his way to Marseilles, Margoliouth engaged a priest in conversation and in the course of their conversation, he took out a copy of a Jewish prayer book, "expecting by this means to originate a friendly conversation with reference to the analogy between Romanism and modern Judaism." To his surprise, he learned that the priest could read the Hebrew prayers. Margoliouth responded: "Pardon me, I took you for a priest of the Church of Rome; but now it is plainly manifest to me that you are a Rabbi of some Jewish congregation." "You are right either way," he replied, "I was a Rabbi of a Jewish congregation till my thirty-sixth year and for the last twenty-five years, I have been a minister of the Lord Jesus." Given the priest's impressive credentials, Margoliouth was shocked that he had rejected the Protestant faith over the Catholic "whose doctrines and practices are in direct opposition to Jehovah's divine behests." The priest acknowledged the negative practices of the church but nevertheless felt the obligation not to abandon his flock. Margoliouth concluded: "In short, he is a Protestant, an Obadiah in the household of Jezebel."³³

Margoliouth also offered an account of a different kind of encounter regarding the burden of his Jewish-Christian identity, this time with a Jew. He related that he had received a request from the English Jew Abraham Benisch, at the time the coeditor of the *Voice of Jacob*. Benisch's coeditor was none other than Jacob Franklin who, as we have seen, had severely criticized Margoliouth's book on modern Judaism. Benisch had learned that Margoliouth had in his possession an actual portrait of Maimonides and sought its whereabouts for a biography of the medieval sage he was preparing, totally oblivious to the potential slight Margoliouth might have felt in dealing with him. Without hesitation, however, Margoliouth copied a letter written by the Italian scholar Isaac Samuel Reggio (1784–1855) documenting the background of the portrait with a copy of the portrait itself. In the aftermath of this kind gesture Margoliouth felt abused particularly because of his convert status. And thus he wrote:

> But did Dr. A. Benisch acknowledge that he was indebted to me for Maimonides' likeness, as well as for Reggio's letter? No, no. I am a Christian Jew; it would be an acknowledgment that converted Jews have been misrepresented, as to their characters and principles. Besides, what would the Jews, at large, say? "Dr. Benisch was actually applying for information on Jewish literature to a M'shumad (an apostate), and we have all along maintained that converted Jews know nothing about our learned men, and that it is only the ignorant who are entrapped in the conversion nets." I can understand all this; but common justice asks, "Is it right?"
>
> Dr. Benisch assumes an air of impartial honesty, liberal in his views, uncompromising in his independent principles, and yet publishes the "Life of Maimonides," embellishes it with the information I readily furnished him with, and never mentions that such a person as the author had anything to do with it. . . .
>
> I would have taken no notice of the whole affair . . . were I not anxious to point out the unjust treatment which the converted Jew experiences from the hands of his unconverted brethren. Had I, or any other Jewish convert, been guilty of an apparent fault, how

publicly would the Jewish convert's name sound in the Jewish magazines![34]

Notwithstanding such treatment by some Jews, the overriding impression Margoliouth left his readers regarding Jews and Judaism was decidedly positive, including the manner in which he was received by other Jews. In Tunis, for example, he was invited to a Jewish wedding where he was introduced to the chief rabbi of the Portuguese synagogue. The Jews standing around them kissed the sleeve of the rabbi and then kissed his as well, "and they therefore honoured unwittingly my apostate coat with ardent kisses." He subsequently met the parents of the groom and bride and was even introduced to the bride. He added: "I was not only invited but forced to partake of everything I saw before me." In the course of his conversation with his hosts, he openly discussed Christianity, the essential difference between Protestantism and Catholicism, and even freemasonry, an affiliation Margoliouth enjoyed during much of his life.[35]

When the wedding ceremony finally took place, Margoliouth felt great comfort and joy since he well understood the ritual and the accompanying recitation of prayers. Its discordant melodies "would prove irksome, if not disgusting to the uninitiated Gentile," but to Margoliouth they were familiar and pleasing. Gazing at the beautiful bride, he conjured up the image of a Hebrew woman with timbrel in hand conducting "an orchestra of Zion's daughters." He extolled the art of minstrelsy among "the children of the Hebrew race" never suppressed by oppression. Jewish musical talent continued until his day through the brilliance of Rossini, Meyerbeer, and Mendelssohn, he added, relying on the testimony of Benjamin Disraeli whom he cited.[36]

Jewish music was clearly a vital conduit linking him to even the most ordinary of Jews. On board an overcrowded steamer heading for Beirut, he encountered a large group of Polish Jews on their way to Israel and watched them "davening" with prayer shawls and phylacteries. He was especially taken by an older Jewish woman engrossed in reading her prayer book: "She hopes for Israel's restoration and laments over their present degradation . . . all in such rapid succession, that she carried me along with her." When she concluded her prayer, she continued to hum to herself "the beautiful alphabetical Passover hymn (beginning with the Hebrew lines 'El b'nai beitkha be'karov')." He added: "Several times this day, I caught myself accompanying her in it."[37] Elsewhere in his narrative, he transcribed Hebrew melodies and sent them to various Christian friends, including his own daughter, so they might learn and perform them. At the Jewish fast day of Tisha Be'Av, he reproduced for his readers its most famous elegy "Eli Zion" in the original Hebrew with musical annotation and English translation.[38]

It was not only Jewish liturgy that captured his heart but also a deep awareness of Jewish space and again the Hebrew book. Two more examples must suffice. Traveling on horseback to Mount Lebanon with his Christian companions, Margoliouth was overtaken by emotion when peering at the mountain before him: "I was overcome; and looked very thoughtful. I felt several times as if I could leap down from my horse and throw myself on the ground, and press my lips to its burning clods. But I controlled myself, and therefore held my peace, but it was pain and grief to me. I had no brother Jew with whom to exchange feelings. Though my friend Mr. Woodcock is a good and pious man, he cannot possibly feel the same emotion in his breast as one of those to whose ancestors this land was given for possession."[39]

Margoliouth's most significant encounter with a rare Jewish book was undoubtedly his viewing of the famous "Damascus Keter" during his visit to Damascus. He had initially learned of the existence of the manuscript from the rabbi of Smyrna, Turkey, Ḥayyim Palachi (1788–1868), who had welcomed him into his house and had given him one of his Hebrew books that mentioned the priceless treasure. This manuscript of the entire Hebrew Bible was copied in Burgos, Spain, in 1260. At an unknown date this ornate codex reached Damascus where it was securely protected in the synagogue. It was inspected by the Jewish scholar Alexander Harkavy in 1886 and by Avinoam Yellin in 1919. That Margoliouth had already seen the manuscript (on not one but on two separate visits, the second with his Christian colleagues) in 1848 is quite remarkable. He related that due to a chance meeting with a young rabbi in the streets of Damascus, he gained entrance into the sealed chamber where the manuscript was stored. He wrote: "I have seen almost all of the manuscripts in various national libraries in Europe, but this one deserves the palm for beauty and execution. I kissed it several times after I finished examining it." He was then treated as a dignitary, meeting the richest Jew of the city, Rabbi Farḥi, in his home as well as other Jewish notables.[40]

Of course, these intimate meetings with rabbis and other Jews could not mask Margoliouth's identity as a minister of the Church of England. As we have seen, he dressed appropriately as a Christian cleric and was immediately recognized as such even when he flaunted his Hebrew knowledge and Jewish literacy. And, indeed, he well understood his role as a Christian missionary seeking converts to his own brand of Christianity wherever he went, leading services in Jerusalem and for other Christian congregations, and offering consolation and spiritual support when called upon by fellow Christians. When visiting the synagogue of the port of Bizerte, Tunisia, for example, he met two old rabbis "basking in Talmudic heat" who allowed him to teach the Old Testament and relate its passages to the messiahship of Jesus. According to Margoliouth, they claimed they were not equal to stand in his presence. He also related that after his sermon in the synagogue, other Jews were afraid to refute him and were beginning to be won over by his persuasive argumentation.[41]

On the steamer heading to Beirut where he had sung with the old Jewish woman, he also confronted a group of Jewish pilgrims, including a rabbi Elvira, and engaged with them about the meaning of Old Testament verses and their Christological message. He offered the Jews a Hebrew translation of the Book of Common Prayer, and led a Protestant service. Mixed among the pilgrims was a Pole whom he later learned was named Yozeph Danowski, who had been born in his native town of Suwałki and was a neighbor of his father. After warmly embracing this man, they engaged in conversation about the dubious value for Yozeph of "spending so much time with wretched Jews." Provoked to respond, Margoliouth excoriated Christians who persecuted Jews: "Since Jesus was a Jew, is not Christianity, therefore, a Jewish religion? And should not Christians rather pity, than hate and curse them." His Polish compatriot was not only convinced by his words but begged his forgiveness for his thoughtless remark.[42]

I offer one final example of Margoliouth's narrative that might bring together in a rather untidy manner the various stands of Moses Margoliouth's religious, ethnic, and professional identity found in *A Pilgrimage to the Land of My Fathers* as he actually presented them. Toward the end of his narrative, Margoliouth finally describes his arrival in Jerusalem, entering through the Hebron gate. He goes first to pay his respects to the Protestant bishop, the Reverend Samuel Gobat, and then visits his dear friend the Reverend F. C. Ewald, the well-known missionary of the London Society. When first seeing Jerusalem, he recites Isaiah 60:19–22. He then descends the Mount of Olives and chants Rabbi Judah ha-Levi's "beautiful elegy, my favorite, 'Zion Halo Tishali'" ("Won't you ask after, O Zion, the weal of your captives?"), the medieval Jewish poet's most famous Hebrew poem. Soon after on Good Friday he pays a visit to the Church of the Holy Sepulchre, but instead of being uplifted, he is horrified by the crude reenactment of the ceremony of

the crucifixion, which he labels "a blasphemous farce." He is particularly
disgusted by what he calls the Christian pranks of dancing, shaking, quaking
dervishes, and Christian fire worshippers. In the end, he enters the Protestant
service of Bishop Gobat to listen with reverence to his sermon on the Resur-
rection. And finally he relates how, on Easter Monday, he runs into a group
of Jewish converts in the Armenian church and listens to their agonizing
stories. He then reacts: "Alas! Little do gentile Christians know of the bitter
trials which fall to the lot of the Jewish converts. . . . Does anyone, possessing
a modern share of common sense, think that a Jew would embrace Christianity simply because he had a desire to be hated, and traduced and maligned
by the members of the Synagogue, and suspected and despised by the members of the Church?" These few pages describing his encounter with his
beloved Jerusalem, remarkably encapsulate the entire gamut of his emotions:
passionately reciting Isaiah and his favorite Hebrew poet; feeling alienated by
a Christian service not his own but warmed by the presence of his Protestant
bishop's homily; and finally underscoring the misery of Jewish converts to
Christianity, hated and persecuted by Jews and Christians alike, surely an
expression of his own life experience as well.[43]

Recollections of an English Cleric

Upon his return to England in 1848, Margoliouth worked in a variety of
parishes, in each case, ending in failure and reassignment as he struggled with
various clergymen and others who sought to undermine his authority and
good name. In the early 1850s he was charged with mishandling funds in the
parish of Wybunbury and was forced to resign as curate.[44] In 1860, he was
accused by Charles Burney, the vicar of Halstead, of other improprieties that
appear to be both economic and perhaps sexual as well. The vicar's accusations were probably triggered by Margoliouth's allegations that Burney had
plagiarized a sermon of another cleric.[45] In each case, Margoliouth was
required to defend himself by turning to those who had supported him in
the past to testify to his moral character. These public skirmishes surely took
their toll on his reputation and emotional state. They were exacerbated even
further by economic instability and the need to procure funding for himself
and his literary projects while at least partially subsidizing the wife and family
he had essentially deserted and who had moved years earlier to Paris.[46] There
is no doubt that Margoliouth's public image as a foreigner and a converted

Jew contributed significantly to his professional failures. In his own defenses of himself, he was fond of the phrase "the so-called friends of Israel" in referring to those who sought to harm him. As we shall see, he used the same phrase to refer to those who hypocritically despised all converted Jews while professing to love them, including members of the London Society for the Promotion of Christianity Amongst the Jews, the organization that had essentially launched his career.

Amid all the turmoil that plagued his life by the early 1860s, his quiet separation from Chaja Margoliouth and his family now became a matter of public record. Chaja, with the support of several Jews including a London rabbi, wrote to the bishop of London complaining of Margoliouth's delinquency in supporting her and her family. Her letter prompted a vigorous defense from Moses himself offering in great detail the history of their failed marriage and its ultimate disintegration, her crude attempts to accuse him of marital infidelity, and her futile effort to regain entrance into his life. While Margoliouth vigorously claimed that his conversion and decision to become a Christian minister had nothing to do with their mutual alienation from each other, it was no doubt a factor in their initial breakup and his departure for the Middle East.[47] Over a decade later, having taken up residence in London to return to his literary projects, his enemies within both the Christian and Jewish communities apparently would not allow him peace and security.

It is precisely in the midst of this relatively low period of his life that Margoliouth wrote *The Curates of Riversdale: Recollections in the Life of a Clergyman; Written by Himself.* Clearly meant to be a novel with fictional characters and plots, it could hardly mask the personal experiences the author incorporated into his narrative. It is quite fascinating to consider the possibility that Margoliouth, now a middle-aged man facing private, professional, and economic challenges, sought the outlet of a satiric novel perhaps to poke fun at his adversaries and to overcome, or simply escape from, his personal miseries. One possible clue that strengthens this suggestion is a quotation attributed to the Duke of Wellington placed at the beginning of the work: "I should like to tell the truth, but if I did, I should be torn to pieces, here or abroad."[48] Whatever his motivation in composing this work at this juncture, the so-called novel well reflected prominent aspects of his life, his career, and his ultimate concerns. Like his travelogue, his first and only experiment with a fictional genre offers another rich opportunity to the historian to probe Margoliouth's understanding of himself.

The main character of the novel is a young man called George Holdsworth who attended Jesus College, Oxford, was a serious student of the Hebrew language, and was awarded the so-called Kennicott Hebrew scholarship for his achievements.[49] In the opening chapter, a conversation takes place between an editor and the reluctant writer in which the latter is encouraged to publish his book in novel form in order to protect his real identity. What is interesting is that while all the main characters bear fictional names, the author agreed to depict several well-known individuals as they really were. They included the colorful Richard Whatley (1787–1863), the bishop of Dublin; Samuel Gobat (1799–1879, the aforementioned Protestant bishop of Jerusalem; Johann August Wilhelm Neander (1789–1850), the German theologian who corresponded with Margoliouth during his travels; Giuseppe Caspar Mezzofanti, the Italian cardinal and prominent linguist; and Edward Pusey (1800–1882), Protestant churchman and regius professor of Hebrew at Christ Church, Oxford. It is safe to assume that the individuals on this list were easily recognizable in clerical and academic circles and, in some cases, were personally known to Margoliouth.

The character George relates that since leaving Oxford, he has traveled to Germany, Russia, Turkey, and Greece, has witnessed the coronation of Alexander II in Russia, and has also visited Egypt and Jericho. Upon graduation, he was named a curate at the parish of Christ Church, Riversdale, but before taking up his post, he went off to visit a distant relative, the bishop of Kilcurragh, who lived on an estate near Dublin. It is obvious from the start that each of these details closely approximates those of Margoliouth's actual life: his university education, if not from Oxford then from Trinity, Dublin; his outstanding Hebraic credentials; his sojourn in a country parish near Dublin; his relationship with the bishop of Kildare, perhaps a stand-in for Kilcurragh, his journey to the Middle East and especially Russia; and his witnessing the Russian czar's coronation. In many respects, despite his Christian origins, George Holdsworth bears a strong likeness to Moses Margoliouth.

But the identification is not so simple. The most fascinating and mysterious character of the novel is introduced to George during his visit to the bishop's house in Ireland. His name is Benedict Monteleone, and he is about to be ordained and assigned a curacy at St. Peter's also in Riversdale. The bishop introduced him to George: "By the bye, you will have an opportunity of displaying your Hebrew laurels before a clever connoisseur in such matters. Monteleone is supposed to be one of the best Oriental scholars in Europe.

He is of Spanish-Hebrew extraction, a graduate of several foreign universities, as well as of Trinity College, Dublin."[50] Monteleone and Holdsworth become friends. Monteleone, of course, also resembles Margoliouth: a graduate of Trinity College, Dublin, a true master of Hebrew literature, and an especially enlightened convert. In contrast to the Ashkenazic author of the novel, however, Monteleone stems from Sephardic culture, so revered by Margoliouth in his *Fundamental Principles*.

The two new friends engage in conversations on biblical criticism, Islam, polemical literature, and other theological subjects. With the bishop, they visit an invalid Christian woman named Miss Neville who is consumed with visions of rebuilding the Temple of Jerusalem, of restoring the Jews to their homeland, and of identifying with Deborah, "the 'Mother of Israel.'"[51] Could this be a not-so-veiled allusion to the deaf Charlotte Elizabeth Tonna, who shared similar visions and directly confronted Margoliouth in public debate as we have seen?

Interspersed within the narration of the principal characters is a colorful portrait of the clerical life of Ireland, with its superficial, self-serving, arrogant, and inebriated clergymen. George records the following remark from one of them in his intoxicated state: "We Irish are gifted above all people. . . . We were, and are, an isle of saints. It is the Papists alone that were and are the scum and dirt of the land."[52]

Back at the Riversdale parish, George finds a kind and intelligent mentor in his rector Dr. Radcliffe. In striking contrast is the neighboring rector Mr. Alslop who mentors George's friend and fellow student Verity. Alslop is the insensitive teacher who ignored his curate and treats him with disrespect. He is also the bigot who cannot countenance Jewish converts. Upon meeting Monteleone, he announces: "I do not like Monteleone. I do not think that he is a sincere Christian; he is Curate to a man for whom I have no respect at all. Archdeacon Godfrey, his rector, is a man—whatever scholarship he may possess—who has not one particle of the learning of the Spirit; he takes no interest in our great Protestant associations and meetings. Monteleone is just like the Archdeacon in this respect. He does not care even for the spiritual welfare of his brethren after the flesh."[53]

It soon becomes clear why Alslop resents Monteleone. He had asked him to speak at the annual meeting on behalf of "the Friends of Israel Association," but he rudely refused. "No respectable Christian Jew can possibly identify himself with that association," Monteleone added. "Its existence is an insult to the Church. I do not think much of their converts, whom their agents parade in their speeches on platforms." Alslop also volunteers the information that Monteleone had challenged his precipitous baptism of a Jew named Hashbaz Eisenschwartz, an ignorant blacksmith from Posen with a shady career of business practices. But Alslop rejected the criticism: "It was enough for me that Eisenschwartz was again in business; he does well as a Tobacconist. A Jew is a Jew all the world over, whether he goes by the name Monteleone or Eisenschwartz." In the end Alslop humiliates himself by preaching on the theme of the pope as Antichrist, mistranslating a key Hebrew phrase that he had learned from "an eminent Hebrew scholar" named Eisenschwartz.[54]

Beyond focusing on the primary circle of close friends of George Holdsworth, Margoliouth presents a flashback to another circle, that of the previous generation of his sympathetic mentor Dr. Radcliffe and his friends. Besides Radcliffe, they include Verity's late father, a professor at Cambridge and a Lord Montacute, a wealthy English heir. All three were particularly inspired by Benedict Monteleone, the late father of the young curate with the same name. Radcliffe tells the young Verity the story of how the old Monteleone, also a brilliant scholar, taught them all the Hebrew they knew, how ethical and giving he was, and how "he was a Christian Jew of the Apostolic stamp." The friendship of the three became "a threefold cord" through their relationship with the Jewish Christian. Radcliffe advised the young Verity never to speak ill of men of Jewish origin nor to speak with the young Monteleone about his late father at all. If he dares disparage his national origins in his presence, the rector continued,

"he will bring before you, in bold relief, the officials of Missionary and Church Building Societies with an accuracy frightfully true. . . . You will feel so humiliated as not to have a spark of patriotism left in you. He will make you acknowledge that the Church was holy, just, and good as long as her Deacons, Priests, and Bishops were Jews; that she become depraved, unrighteous, and bad as soon as she became Gentilized. Be very careful also how you talk of the 'Friends of Israel' who are interested in the conversion of their countrymen; he positively loathes the phrase 'Friends of Israel' and abhors the 'Friends of Israel Association.' He takes pains to make himself disliked by 'those platform friends' " as he calls them, 'to be spared the service of an illustration by those pious mountebank mouthpieces.' "[55]

There is nothing subtle or hidden about Margoliouth's unflattering portrait of the hypocritical Alslop who professes Christian charity through his "friends of Israel" association while speaking ill of all converts who allegedly retain their Jewish markings even after their baptism and ordination. Nor does the noble Dr. Radcliffe hold back in his condemnation of the same "friends" who turned out to be the worst enemies of the convert Monteleone. Anyone reading this work in 1860 would realize instantaneously that the author was speaking about his so-called "friends" associated especially with the London Society and their futile and cynical attempts to convert vulnerable Jews, to present them as learned and able missionaries, and then to question and undermine their status as Christians in the first place. No doubt Margoliouth in these depictions was speaking from experience and referring explicitly to the kind of ugly relations with certain Christians that had plagued his entire career in the church. Consider one example, by way of comparison: the aforementioned case of Charles Burney, the vicar of Halstead, one of Margoliouth's chief tormentors, whom Margoliouth had labeled "my deadliest enemy and [who] has persecuted me for the last two years with a perseverance of which a Herod or a Nero would be proud." When Burney made his unsubstantiated accusations against him, "a few of the so-called 'friends of Israel' not only gladly believed the accusation but cheerfully repeated the same."[56]

The novel concludes, however, on a more positive and hopeful note as most of the principals congregate at the home of Dr. Radcliffe and his wife for a dinner party. Margoliouth had already introduced the mysterious but beautiful mother of the young Monteleone who, along with her son, was an honored guest of the evening. Dutton, a young Christian student mentored by Monteleone, was asked to present what he had learned from his gifted teacher and proceeds to offer a competent oration on Hebrew sacred music to the sympathetic guests in attendance. Monteleone eventually takes over the lecture, tracing the history of ancient Hebrew music from the biblical Yuval to the end of the Babylonian captivity with vast erudition and eloquence. In the course of his remarks, Monteleone explicitly referred to a list of authorities on Jewish music, including the Jews Abraham Ha-Cohen of Zante (1670–1729), Moses Mendelssohn (1729–86), and Leopold Zunz (1794–1886), along with the Christians Martin Luther (1483–1546), Immanuel Tremellius (1510–80), Myles Coverdale (1488–1569), and Ernst Wilhelm Hengstenberg (1802–69). The evening concludes with the recital of a Hebrew hymn by both mother and son followed by a solo performance of an Aramaic hymn by the mother. We have already noted Margoliouth's infatuation with Jewish liturgy, Hebrew poetry, and music, evidenced in his travelogue as well as in his scholarly publications. If there could be any doubt about the striking resemblance between Monteleone and Margoliouth beforehand, the former's allocution on the music of the Hebrews leaves no doubt at all that the character of Monteleone was created to articulate the author's ultimate concerns. With this moving scene, the first volume of a supposedly longer but unfinished work abruptly comes to an end.

The Ultimate Futility of the Christian Mission

In a previous chapter, the reader will recall, Jacob Franklin, the Jewish editor of the *Voice of Jacob*, had explicitly distinguished between two types of converts: those who left the Jewish faith out of conviction but continued to defend Jewish interests even after their apostasy and those who despicably supported the missionary assault on the integrity of Judaism and subsequently became bitter enemies of the Jewish community. The good convert Franklin had in mind was the aforementioned Stanislaus Hoga; the bad convert was none other than Moses Margoliouth. Focusing exclusively on Margoliouth's first book, *The Fundamental Principles of Modern Judaism*, and recalling his heated exchanges and those of his close friend Charlotte Elizabeth Tonna with Margoliouth, Franklin could hardly conclude otherwise.[57] But as this chapter has tried to demonstrate, Margoliouth's relation to Jews and Judaism was much more complex than Franklin could ever have imagined, and especially over time, he too came to deplore the same missionaries with whom he had been identified at the start of his career. In order to demonstrate conclusively this pronounced shift in his attitude, I would like to explore briefly several of Margoliouth's other works written in the period between 1843, the date of publication of *The Fundamental Principles*, and 1860, the year *The Curates of Riversdale* appeared. This may offer a corrective to the incomplete and negative portrait drawn by Franklin and confirm the suggestion that Margoliouth, through the course of his long career, came to embrace his Jewish roots and defend Jewish interests, albeit in a manner different from that of Stanislaus Hoga.

We have already noted that there is no hint whatsoever of any wavering loyalty to the missionaries of the London Society in Margoliouth's first publication. This was also the case with respect to his well-known multivolume history of the Jews, published in London in 1851. This impressive accomplishment, along with his other works on Anglo-Jewish history completed over a lifetime still await a serious scholarly assessment with respect to both their level of historical research and, more important, their impact on Jews and Christians alike. In the context of this chapter, my focus is solely on Margoliouth's testimony regarding the London Society. He wrote:

> Whatever over-zealous, alias mistaken friends, or open foes, may say and write against the Society, a calm and deliberate view of its operations must lead to the inevitable conclusion, that the Society effected the most important changes in the civil, political, literary, and religious conditions of the Jews in this country. Its supporters were the means of removing a great portion of the load of prejudice which oppressed the Hebrew race in this realm, and thus originated a general kind feeling in the breasts of the English towards the Jews; and thus paved the way for the removal of civil and political disabilities, which disabilities will doubtless ere long be remembered no more. The Society, by their publications, doctrinal and controversial, led many of the House of Israel to examine the traditions of the Talmudic fathers, which led many of their provincial Rabbies in this country, as well as in other parts of the world, to profess the religion of Christianity. And to no other instrumentality can the reform movement, amongst the Jews, be ascribed, but to the London Society for Promoting Christianity amongst the Jews; so that the improvement, or change, in the literary and religious character of the English Hebrews must be ascribed to that Society as the cause.[58]

This strong positive endorsement of the London Society, echoing the society's own claims in encouraging conversions and even establishing Reform Judaism in England, would have warmed the heart of Margoliouth's mentor Alexander McCaul who had professed similar sentiments. He was, of course, aware that not everyone would agree with his assessment referring to "over-zealous, mistaken friends" or "open foes," but he quickly dismissed such opposition in offering his unrestrained praise of the organization.

However, several years earlier, his approval seems to be have been accompanied by some reservations and doubt. In 1847, immediately prior to his departure for the Holy Land, Margoliouth inaugurated a missionary publication that he called the *Star of Jacob*, perhaps meant to counter Franklin's

Voice of Jacob. Margoliouth's ambitious publication was doomed from the start. It lasted for a half a year and was aborted entirely when he departed England. In one issue, in the course of his reporting of a recent anniversary meeting of the London Society, Margoliouth politely offered a series of proposals for making the society "more profitable." He suggested that advocates of the London Society should be well acquainted "with the present literary, political, civil, and religious condition" of Jews everywhere beyond the borders of Great Britain. They should possess a fair knowledge of Jewish literature as well as "the trouble Jewish parents take, and the expenses they go to, in order to educate their children"; they should be willing "to run to the end of the world in search of some who know not the Gospel" and should not neglect those "who live with us in the same cities and streets"; but they "must love and show regard" for Jews in their hearts not only in public.[59] These prescriptions addressed to the London Society seemed innocuous enough although they appeared to suggest that all was not perfect with respect to its mission to the Jews. Professing love for Jews not only in public but in one's heart might be another way of saying what was increasingly on the mind of Margoliouth as the years passed: Be wary of those who publicly call themselves "the friends of Israel." They might not be such good friends at all.

Such mild advice appears to have been abandoned by Margoliouth some ten years later and replaced with unrestrained and bitter denunciation of those missionaries who had acted unjustly toward him and other converted Jews. In 1856, a small book of two epistles was published in London with the title *The Anglo-Hebrews: Their Past Wrongs and Present Grievances*. It included a postscript and was simply signed by "a Clergyman of the Church of England." Historians who have noticed this work have attributed it to Moses Margoliouth, and there seems to be little doubt that it came from his pen. There are obvious similarities between the historical narrative of this work and Margoliouth's other works of history. Indeed, the author fully acknowledged this fact by citing Margoliouth on two occasions as his major source.[60]

What was unique about this work was its powerful appeal to the English public in demanding political rights for Jews in England and its sharp denunciation of the failures of the London Society. Given its explosive message, it is understandable why the author published the work anonymously. Its message, in many respects, was similar to *The Curates of Riversdale*, published only four years later. In both cases—whether hiding the name of the author or publishing an indictment of the so-called "friends of Israel" in the form of a novel seemingly allowed Margoliouth protection from those who would seek retribution for his unpopular stands. Clearly by 1856, he had grown disillusioned with the present condition of Jews in Great Britain and felt personally responsible for speaking up. He also had learned from his own bitter experience how intolerant Christians could be in failing to welcome the small community of Jewish converts in their midst.

After presenting a sweeping history of the persecution and discrimination against Jews in England from the Middle Ages until the nineteenth century, Margoliouth provided a more focused account of the last fifty years, the remarkable integration into English society of several prominent Jewish families such as the Goldsmids, Rothschilds, Salomons, Montefiores, and others, along with the frustrating and futile efforts to gain full political equality for the Jews of Great Britain. After recounting the persistent discrimination displayed toward Anglo-Jews, he turned to address the mistreatment of Hebrew Christians like himself, and particularly that stemming from the London Society.

He estimated that there were some three thousand Jews in England who had converted: "many have quietly joined the Church, and take care to shun 'the friends of Israel,' who are the mouthpieces and pen-and-bottle-holders of that Society. And I know many respectable Hebrews, who are almost Christians, and would have been such altogether, were it not for the unjust grievances which many of their Hebrew-Christian brethren endure."[61]

He proceeded to describe in greater detail how the London Society functioned:

> The principal means which the Society used . . . for the conversion of Jews in this country are schools for children of poor parents, and operative institutions. The first institution was that of a shoe-making school, the next a bookbinding establishment, to which was eventually added a printing-press. . . .
>
> Some [of the converts] . . . aspired to the office of missionary. But the principal actors of that Society dreaded lest the missionary should become proud, and they took every opportunity to warn their friends not to show such and such an one [sic] too much attention.[62]

He offered several specific examples of converts who were abused and then continued:

But the Hebrew Christians who suffer most from the mouth-pieces of the Society are those who have embraced Christianity independently of their machinery, especially if they happen to be men of talent. A regular system of persecution is brought to bear upon them. Their reputation is damaged without mercy; for the agents of the Society run to and fro through the country, at the expense of the charitable, to attend public meetings, and they have therefore many opportunities of ruining any man who is obnoxious. . . .

I once asked a Hebrew Christian, a minister of the Church of Scotland, an ex-missionary of that Society, "Tell me what is your candid opinion of the London Society for Promoting Christianity amongst the Jews." His reply: "My candid opinion is, that it is the most gigantic humbug I have ever read of or heard of; it out-Barnums Barnum. Their agents, like the scribes, Pharisees, and hypocrites of old, compass sea and land to make one proselyte; and when he is made, they make him out to be twofold more the child of hell than themselves."[63]

Margoliouth concluded by addressing the Jewish community: "I say then again to you, my Anglo-Hebrew fellow-subjects, be not bitter against your Hebrew brethren of the Christian faith. Their grievances are far keener than yours."[64] In the postscript, he cited his fellow convert and ex-missionary of the London Society Nathan Davis: "It is to be deplored that persons professing to be friends of the Jews, and who get their living by that profession, should act the part of Haman and try in every respect to trample upon poor Mordecai."[65] It well encapsulated the outrage Margoliouth had finally expressed in most glaring and explicit terms.

Margoliouth had begun his long career in England as the "poster child" and faithful emissary of the London Society, displaying his impressive knowledge of Judaism to argue forcefully for the futility of modern Jewish lore and practice. He believed then in the integrity of the organization that had supported him and the righteousness of its cause. His experience as a parish minister and associate of the London Society ultimately revealed a reality of discrimination and hypocrisy he had never imagined. Margoliouth attributed the constant trials and tribulations he faced in Christian society not to his own deficiencies, which, of course, were noticeable, but to the unbearable intolerance he felt from his fellow Christians, especially the clergy, despite the sincerity of his own conversion and the impressive scholarly credentials he brought to his work on behalf of the church. Ironically, it appears that the more alienated he felt among Christians, especially his so-called "friends of Israel," the more he felt comfortable with his roots in Judaism, with its intellectual culture, its literary legacy, and its lyrical sensitivity. His writings as a whole testify to his hyphenated status as a believing Christian at peace with the faith of Jesus but unable and unwilling to disengage from the Jewish collective past or the present plight of his former coreligionists still struggling for civil rights in midcentury England.

CHAPTER 7

The Jewish Response to McCaul

Isaac Baer Levinsohn

Until this point, the focus of my inquiry has been the missionary Alexander McCaul himself, his assault on rabbinic Judaism, and the complex web of some of his closest Christian and Jewish-Christian associates. I now turn directly to some of the contemporary Jewish readers of his provocative book. What makes the McCaul missionary offensive especially interesting for the intellectual and cultural history of nineteenth-century Jewry is the remarkable Jewish response it elicited. Three of the most important writers of the Haskalah, the Jewish Enlightenment, in eastern Europe felt the need to pen significant and lengthy Hebrew responses to McCaul: Isaac Baer Levinsohn, Samuel Joseph Fuenn, and Eliezer Zweifel. I have identified at least seven additional responses to McCaul written by other Jewish intellectuals across the continent and one, by Raphael ben Elijah Kassin, the rabbi of Aleppo and Baghdad. There are undoubtedly more, as well as numerous notices and shorter responses in Jewish periodicals. As mentioned earlier, McCaul's formidable polemic would ultimately do less damage to the welfare of the Jewish community than the insidious Damascus blood libel of the same epoch, on which McCaul had published a sympathetic defense of the Jews. Yet like the Damascus affair, the McCaul affair was highly publicized all over Europe and elicited an intense transnational response from Jewish leaders and intellectuals across the continent.[1]

Most fascinating was the role of the maskilim in their counterarguments against McCaul. These were the same Jewish critics of traditional Judaism who had challenged petrified and ineffectual rabbinic authority; had objected

Figure 6. Isaac Baer Levinsohn. From the Abraham Schwadron Collection at the National Library of Israel, Jerusalem. By permission of the National Library of Israel.

to the excessive preoccupation of yeshiva students with Talmud study at the expense of the acquisition of general culture; and had excoriated the parochialism and narrow-mindedness of their coreligionists as due to Talmudic obscurantism and cultural isolation. These same critics of the Talmud now felt obliged to defend it, to argue for the very humanity and moral sensitivity that McCaul had claimed was lacking in the Talmud in the first place. Defending traditional Jewish mores as embodied in the Talmud while criticizing its stranglehold on Jewish culture forced these intellectuals to perform a delicate balancing act in which they strove to define their own Jewish identities, their relationship to the ancient sources of their tradition, and a new and bold strategy to transform Judaism at its core. The Jewish counterattacks against the English missionary thus represent thoughtful and nuanced articulations of what Judaism meant in the context of their own societies and how it could still retain its authentic values while reforming itself in the light of the new exigencies and challenges of the modern era. These texts are thus important as contributions to modern Jewish self-reflection, especially because they originate among Jewish thinkers beyond Germany, thus offering a different perspective from those of the more thoroughly studied German Jewish thinkers.

Isaac Baer Levinsohn (Ribal, 1788–1860) wrote two responses to McCaul's work against the Talmud. The first he called *Ahiyah Shiloni hahozeh* (Ahiyah the Shilonite, the Seer), composed a few years after the Hebrew publication of McCaul's book (*Netivot olam*, 1839) but only published in Leipzig in 1864 after the author's death. He spent twelve more years working on his massive *Zerubavel*, which he completed in 1853, a highly detailed response to each chapter of McCaul's composition. It too was published posthumously in Leipzig, a year earlier in 1863.

Levinsohn, the so-called father of the eastern European Haskalah and also dubbed the Russian Moses Mendelssohn, is not an unstudied figure in modern Jewish history. Born in Kremenets, Ukraine, where he spent most of his life in poor health and poverty, he was well known for his political efforts to convince the Russian government to improve the educational and economic plight of its Jewish minority. He was also hailed for his attempt to disseminate enlightenment ideals within the Jewish community, especially his clarion call for Jewish internal reform entitled *Te'udah be-Yisrael* (A Testimony in Israel) published in 1827. This work was followed by many more, including especially his large-scale *Beit Yehudah* (House of Judah), a defense against the blood libel, satiric attacks against the Hasidim, polemical writings against Christian missionaries, and a significant correspondence with scholars all over Europe.[2]

Yet despite his well-deserved place in the history of nineteenth-century European Jewry, a full and comprehensive treatment of Levinsohn as a Jewish thinker still does not exist. The most authoritative studies of him in recent years have focused on his programmatic and political role in the Haskalah movement. I refer specifically to the scholarship of Immanuel Etkes, Michael Stanislawski, and Eli Lederhendler, and most recently Eliyahu Stern, who have emphasized his collaboration and interaction with the Russian government and primarily treated his publications, especially the *Te'udah*, as publicist writing designed to secure political goals.[3] There is no doubt that Levinsohn wrote in a political context and that his ultimate aim was to enhance the economic and social situation of his community while raising its educational level. But one might question Levinsohn's ultimate effectiveness in this political role given his relative distance from the vital centers of Haskalah activity in eastern Europe and the limitations imposed on him by his declining health and economic status. Much of the extensive writing that has shaped his lasting legacy, informed by an extraordinary mastery of rabbinic literature in all periods and a strong grounding in contemporary scholarship in German, Russian, and Polish, was published after his death. But except for some useful summaries of these works written many years ago, no one appears to have deeply studied Levinsohn's original reflections on Judaism as a whole.[4]

My effort here is only a modest beginning of such a larger project and primarily focuses on Levinsohn's responses to McCaul. In my attempt to treat him primarily as a modern Jewish thinker and not merely an advocate for political rights and reforms, I follow the brief but important comments of Eliezer Schweid who saw Levinsohn in conversation with Albo, Mendelssohn, and even Geiger, as well as Shmuel Feiner who discussed his work as a historian.[5]

According to his nephew and biographer David Ber Nathanson, Levinsohn's *Aḥiyah* was meant to serve as an introduction to the larger work *Zerubavel*. Both works addressed McCaul directly, although they were also designed as general defenses of Judaism, the rabbis, and the validity of Jewish law for modern Jews. According to Nathanson, Levinsohn was responding to the plea of English and French Jews, especially Moses Montefiore, to respond forcefully to the infamous English missionary. Despite his lack of an adequate library and ill health, he took on the responsibility with remarkable devotion over a long period of time. Given the importance assigned to it by the author, it ultimately became the third part of his even larger work, the *Beit Yehudah*.[6]

Ahiyah and *Zerubavel* are also different in size, form, and content. *Ahiyah* was written in the form of a fictional dialogue between a learned Sephardic Jew and a Lutheran nobleman and military officer, the latter open-minded and tolerant of all religions. Their exchange focused primarily on matters explicating modern Judaism in terms understandable to a Christian, while concluding with a concise summary of how a Jew expects Christians to behave in relating to contemporary Jews and Judaism. Levinsohn had hoped it would be translated into English through the intervention of Montefiore in the same manner as his earlier work on the blood libel, but apparently no translation ever appeared.[7] *Zerubavel*, on the other hand, was a long and detailed response to McCaul written primarily for enlightened Jews with rabbinic knowledge. Its exposition in four parts numbering hundreds of pages each was meant as the final and conclusive answer to the dangerous missionary, and it appears to cover its subject exhaustively.

By way of introducing the two books, I would like to focus on five themes that well illustrate Levinsohn's unique approach to the Jewish-Christian debate as it emerged in his own lifetime. I consider as well a sampling of the books Levinsohn was reading in constructing these works in a brief appendix at the end of the book, many of which he cites as well in his other compositions. They testify to his wide erudition, his expertise in ancient and modern history, as well as his familiarity with contemporary Christian and classical scholarship. They provide at least a partial picture of his bookshelf and the kind of sophisticated arguments he was able to construct based on his wide-ranging reading.

The Qualifications of a Rabbinic Scholar

Early on in *Zerubavel* we find a discussion of what constitutes rabbinic literature, and specifically by what categories the rabbis divide the divine commandments (*mitsvot*). The astute reader realizes immediately, however, that Levinsohn was really speaking about something else: the qualifications necessary to study rabbinic literature in the first place and what in fact such study entails: "a knowledge of the science of Talmudic logic and knowledge of the source of the language of the Mishnah and Talmud and their grammars; an expertise in [Near] Eastern languages and their grammars; and also some knowledge of Greek and Latin and related fields; an expansive and complete knowledge of the histories of each nation and language, of their laws, customs, and ways of life; their fields of knowledge and the foundations of their religious beliefs, their idolatrous practices and similar things."[8] He adds that a student of the Talmud needs to know something about how the work is put together, its organization and forms of expression, and its myths and expressive styles found in Near Eastern civilizations in general. A student should also master rabbinic history and the political context of its culture, the different types of legal expressions, and how they are organically linked in the whole system the rabbis create.[9]

According to these criteria, few yeshiva students in Poland and Russia would have met Levinsohn's minimal standards for Talmud study. He had in mind a new image of a rabbinic scholar, one grounded in linguistics and grammar, in classical and ancient Near Eastern languages, and in comparative history and religion. It was a standard of scholarship that required an intimate knowledge of rabbinic texts alongside the training of the university, and one that few could meet, including many of his fellow maskilim. It, of course, was meant to highlight his unique education, which would be thoroughly demonstrated on every page of his long work. But most important, it was meant to discount McCaul's qualifications. The cleric who had surpassed most of his Christian contemporaries in mastering rabbinic texts had not and could not achieve Levinsohn's level of Jewish scholarship.

Levinsohn listed ten shortcomings that made McCaul's rabbinic scholarship highly suspect. According to Levinsohn, McCaul didn't understand that the Mishnah alone was the Oral Law. He did not distinguish between actual and theoretical law, between halacha (law) and *aggadah* (myths, fables), or between simple and exaggerated statements especially common in ancient Near Eastern cultures. He had no real understanding of rabbinic chronology or the specific context of particular rabbinic utterances. He did not appreciate that the Oral Law and liturgy were not identical, and that law and custom were not the same. He did not take into account regional variations and the heterogeneity of different Jewish cultures over time. He was deficient in his knowledge of the ancient history of Judaism and Christianity. And even more conclusively, he was a poor reader of rabbinic texts, citing them out of context, misquoting passages, omitting critical references, and claiming individual exegetical opinions to have legal status when they did not.[10] Levinsohn had redefined rabbinic scholarship to meet what he saw as the standards of his time. He had not only dismissed his opponent's qualifications as a rabbinic scholar; he was also arguing that rabbinic culture could no longer be studied by anyone in isolation from other fields of knowledge. It needed to be integrated into the study of the languages and literatures of the ancient world. Rabbinics, moreover, could not be divorced from the study of ancient Christianity and vice versa. In his polemic with his opponent, Levinsohn had articulated a new definition of the *talmid hakham*, the rabbinical scholar of his day, one equally applicable to Christians and Jews alike.

The Futility of Religious Polemic

Levinsohn sought not only to question the qualifications of his polemical opponent but to dismiss the very polemic in which he was engaged. It is immediately clear to the Jew Mizraḥi, one of the two interlocutors in the fictional dialogue in *Aḥiyah Shiloni ha-ḥozeh*, why the Christian Alphonso had requested a meeting: it is to present him with McCaul's *Netivot olam* for his comments and perhaps thus to persuade him of the truths of the Christian faith and the falsities of his own. It is at this point that Levinsohn sought, through the voice of Mizraḥi, to undermine completely the proposed terms of such a conversation between Jew and Christian. Mizraḥi not only refuses to read McCaul's book; he objects strenuously to the idea of discussing the merits of one another's faith, of entering into any debate over matters of conscience, no matter how cordial or respectful. In the first place, any Jewish-Christian "conversation" is not a dialogue of equals but an exercise of power relations where the dominant majority has the upper hand over its minority. Mizraḥi compares such a debate to one between a master and his slave. The latter is doomed to lose.[11]

Mizraḥi further argues that Judaism did not remand salvation to Jews alone; if a person is moral, he can be saved. Debates are superfluous since there is no reason to vanquish one's opponent. Each religion should follow its own path in fulfilling God's will: "I will go according to my religion and faith which I inherited from my father and in which I will die and be buried." This is the reason Mizraḥi refuses to read polemical works but prefers to read history or simple accounts of the other's religion. Both religions have produced scholars who have penned polemical works. On the Jewish side,

Mizraḥi mentions a long list of luminaries from Saadia to Mendelssohn, but in the end each has proven to be ineffectual.[12]

Mizraḥi subsequently concludes that

> neither side [in an argument between the two religions] is capable of convincing the other to accept the religion in which one was raised from birth. This is because both rely solely on tradition without any rational argument. The first might say that I received such and such [a tradition] from my ancestors and my wise and righteous teachers who saw the divine presence face-to-face, while the other might claim he received such and such [a tradition] from his fathers and wise and righteous teachers to whom God revealed himself and walked in their camps. One fortifies his tradition on the basis of stories of supernatural signs and wonders of which he was told happened to his ancestors and teachers. The other side opposing him will make fun of him and be suspicious of him, claiming, "How could your eyes be blinded from the light of truth? Who would be impressed by such signs?" His opponent will likewise fortify his tradition on the basis of such stories of signs and miracles. . . . Who then will not acknowledge that with such arguments these debates have no meaning and one will never vanquish the other? The more one side promotes its stories to strengthen its tradition the more its religion will be weakened in the eyes of the other.[13]

Mizraḥi further claims that useless debates between theologians weaken faith and encourage atheistic views such as those found in the writings of Voltaire and his contemporaries Julien Offray de La Mettrie and Victor de Riqueti, Marquis de Mirabeau. The weak opponent who ended up debating, as the case of Mendelssohn illustrated, did so against his will. Instead of disputation, Jews and Christians need to acknowledge their common roots and their shared human condition: "Let us come together and extend a hand to each other; we have one father and one God created us." Jews and Christians share a common religious foundation despite their doctrinal differences, and together they are in the best position to combat the atheism that exists in the world.[14]

In acknowledging the futility of hundreds of years of debate between Jews and Christians and the damage such encounters had wrought, especially to the Jewish side, Levinsohn adopted an irenicist tone and a plea for mutual toleration seemingly unique in the annals of Jewish-Christian polemical literature.[15] He had, of course, given voice to the obvious reluctance of early generations of Jewish disputants to participate in such forums where defeat was the only possible outcome. He had dismissed their courageous actions as futile and self-defeating, arguing that beliefs could not be articulated or defended through rational discourse, and that ultimately faith rested on received traditions and internal conviction. There is a certain irony in this strong formulation of Levinsohn. This same author had often claimed that Judaism was based on rational foundations, transparent and self-evident to even the outside observer in contrast to the dogmatic, esoteric, and inflexible doctrines of the church. But here, Judaism too appears to be based on miraculous stories sanctified by a collective tradition impervious to critical scrutiny. And equally ironic is the plea to abandon all debates between the two faiths for the sake of their common shared values. McCaul had opened the door with his distasteful provocation. Levinsohn, as much of his writing testifies, relished the opportunity to challenge and undermine his opponent. His discourse of tolerance and good will surely masked his genuine need to defend Jewish interests passionately and combatively.[16]

A Jewish Critique of Christianity

In the end, Levinsohn's fictional character Mizraḥi ignores his own comments about the futility of debates, reads McCaul's work, and proceeds to undertake a powerful refutation of his arguments. He does this first and foremost by offering a rigorous critique of Christianity in both its Catholic and Protestant configurations based on an impressive knowledge of its theology, its canonical texts, and its social history. It might be divided into three primary claims: Christianity's rootedness in Judaism as well as its lack of originality and positive impact on the world; its foundation as an oral tradition no different in form from that of Judaism; and its blatant record of brutality and cruelty not only to Jews but to all peoples.

The first claim was Levinsohn's least original, as he himself acknowledged. His argument was not only based on his careful reading of Christian literature and ancient history but on the recent arguments of anti-Christian writers in his own day such as Voltaire, Montesquieu, d'Holbach, and Volney, all of whom he mentions by name, and in the case of Volney and Voltaire actually cites. He reiterates the oft-mentioned charges that Jesus never repudiated Jewish law, that he was indebted to the Pharisees in his emphasis on proper intention in observing the law, and that ancient Christianity held many superstitious, intolerant, and irrational beliefs. Such imperfections in their faith were shared equally by Catholics and Protestants. More unique was Levinsohn's claim that Christianity never succeeded in converting the millions who hold other faiths, especially the Muslims. On the contrary, the church not only failed to convince the world's majority to adopt its beliefs; it became a primary agent for spreading atheism among its own Christian community who rebelled against its authority and viewed with contempt its cultural accomplishments. This too was a point Levinsohn gleaned by reading the aforementioned Enlightenment critics of traditional Christianity.[17]

More original was Levinsohn's argument that early Christianity, like Judaism, was derived from a tradition transmitted orally, and that Christian arguments denying the validity of the Oral Law as idiosyncratic to Judaism are accordingly groundless. The rabbis never invented the notion of Oral Law as it was also found among ancients such as Solon and Lycurgus and then was adopted by the early Christians as well. This argument was so important to Levinsohn that he repeated it several times in both polemical works.[18] Recently, Eliyahu Stern has noticed the uniqueness of this claim and especially one of the key primary sources Levinsohn cited, the universal history of Christianity composed by Jacques-Bénigne (Jacob Benignus) Bossuet in its German translation with notes by Johann Andreas Cramer. For Stern, this is convincing evidence of Levinsohn's appropriation of a Catholic historian to argue against the evangelical Protestants in justifying Judaism's reliance on an oral tradition. Whereas most European Jewish enlighteners argued that Judaism could be understood through the lens of Protestantism as a religion based on faith and reason, Stern maintains, Levinsohn believed that Judaism could be understood through the lens of Catholicism and Orthodoxy as a religion based on ritual and tradition. He not only cited Bossuet/Cramer several times; he referred the reader to the index of Cramer's book, to the entry on tradition, thus reinforcing the point that Christianity's notion of tradition was parallel to that of Judaism. Stern labels Levinsohn's conception of Judaism based on this citation alone as "Catholic Judaism."[19]

No doubt Stern is correct in identifying Cramer's Bossuet as a major source of Levinsohn's argument in defending the notion of oral tradition in Judaism, but the claim that this clever tactic defined a "Catholic Judaism" is unwarranted for several reasons. In the first place, Levinsohn sometimes cited

Bossuet's text and sometimes Cramer's notes. Cramer, however, was a Protestant, and thus his German edition of Bossuet together with his animadversions was no longer a strictly Catholic history but more ecumenical in its approach and so popular it could be read profitably by Protestants and Catholics alike.[20]

In the second place, Levinsohn's reliance on the German version of Bossuet needs to be read in context, that is, together with the plethora of other sources upon which Levinsohn drew in composing his learned book—Catholic, Protestant, and secular. In this one instance regarding the oral tradition of Judaism, Levinsohn not only relied on classical precedents, as we have seen, but on two other contemporary historians: Heinrich Ehrenfried Warnekros (1752–1807) and Constantin-François de Chasseboeuf, comte de Volney (1757–1820). Warnekros was a Protestant who taught at the University of Greifswald and composed a learned work on Hebrew poetry. Levinsohn noticed how he had located the biblical roots of the notion of oral tradition.[21] Volney, in contrast, was a man of the Enlightenment, rationalist and anticlerical at his core, and a true disciple of Diderot and d'Holbach. Levinsohn cited a relatively obscure footnote from his well-known *Les Ruines, ou méditations sur les révolutions des empires*, which confirmed the claim that Christianity relied on oral traditions. Volney had read Augustine's *Answer to the Manichean Faustus*, citing Faustus's radical view that the Gospels were not written by Jesus or the apostles but by some unknown persons who sought legitimacy by assigning the false attribution. Although Volney disagreed with Faustus, he claimed that the New Testament was certainly written after the death of the apostles and must have relied on oral traditions that were then incorporated into the written text.[22] In utilizing Bossuet/Cramer, Warnekros, and Volney, Levinsohn had impressively made his scholarly case that oral traditions were not unique to Judaism and were also foundational in explaining the origins of Christianity as well. This was certainly not a view of the past seen through the lens of Catholicism but one resting on ecumenical foundations, including an Enlightenment critic of all forms of Christianity.

Finally, it needs to be stressed that Levinsohn's identifying the oral foundations of Christian tradition neither implied approval of that tradition nor suggested that it was similar in any way to its Jewish counterpart. As we shall soon see, Levinsohn was unrestrained in describing Catholicism as a fanatical, dogmatic, irrational, and intolerant religion, inflated by its own arrogance and hostile to other religious traditions, especially rabbinic Judaism. Catholicism may have originated through oral teachings, but its legacy was still one of inhumanity and cruelty. In contrast, Judaism, after the composition of the Mishnah in the second century, in Levinsohn's view, was a humane, humanly constructed, and rational tradition shaped by a creative rabbinic leadership and evolving to meet the exigencies of daily life and sensitive to the needs of its community of believers. That tradition stood in diametric opposition to the Catholic one. Levinsohn's notion of rabbinic Judaism was hardly Catholic at all![23]

Levinsohn's major emphasis in discussing Christianity in either its Catholic or Protestant iterations was its social history, its oppressive nature, and its immoral behavior through the long centuries of its existence. He recited in great detail the crimes committed in the name of Christianity, including Charlemagne's conquests, the Crusades, and the bitter wars between Catholics and Protestants in early modern Europe. He referred to the atrocities committed by the Catholic inquisitors but was equally vocal about Luther's incitement against the Jews. He also referred to more contemporary manifestations of Christian intolerance, citing simultaneously the anti-Christian poems of Voltaire in their German translation as well as the testimony of Voltaire's own critic the priest Claude-Adrien Nonnotte (1711–93). He openly mocked McCaul's efforts to paint the rabbis as sinful people because they drank on Purim, performed bizarre rituals such as *kapporet* (the custom of taking a chicken or rooster on the day before Yom Kippur and swinging it over one's head as a symbolic means of abjuring one's sins), or insisted on the absolute separation of dairy and meat products. How could one compare, he asked, the trivial nature of these with the enormity of Christian transgressions: spilling the blood of their enemies, making a mockery of the commandment to love one's neighbor, or aggrandizing wealth, especially on the part of a corrupt clergy?[24]

Most notable in this regard was Levinsohn's diatribe against contemporary Christian practices related to the slave trade. His discussion appears in a section responding to McCaul's criticisms of rabbinic attitudes toward women and slaves. After defending the latter, he pivots to describe with bitter irony how the so-called enlightened Europeans of his day dealt with slaves and subjected them to the utmost misery:

And our eyes behold how the Portuguese and the French (who pride themselves on being a wise people, lovers of enlightenment and of humanity) and the Spanish (who extol themselves on the piety of their religion) and others all trade in human beings from Africa, the

Negroes and others like them in the past and to this day, instigate
treason and evil in that land in providing money and commodities
that they bring from Europe such as brandy and other goods. They
steal and rob many human beings, tying them up in iron chains
around their neck, men, women, and children. Sometimes they kid-
nap a bride from her bridal canopy and a husband from his, and
from his father, a father from his sons, and from his wife, or a wife
from her husband and her sons. They tie up huge numbers with
ropes like animals and the courageous like dogs. These merchants
who purchase these souls follow after them with much festivity,
leaping and dancing in the company of poets and musicians while
they pay no attention to the sound of the plundered, crying and
weeping in a bitter voice. Ha! How horrible this savagery is![25]

Levinsohn added in a note how he had read a disgusting report about
the inspection of female slaves as they paraded naked before their buyers.
This he compared ironically with McCaul's singling out the Jewish refusal to
mix meat and milk as a cardinal sin. He proudly proclaimed that Jews never
trafficked in slaves, although he admitted that a few no longer living under
Jewish law had succumbed to this profit-making business. He related the
story of a Muslim leader from Sudan who stood up to the pressures of these
greedy merchants to resist the sale of slaves in his region. This information
he gleaned from the work of Johann Ernst Fabri, the well-known German
historian and geographer and his detailed descriptions of the African
continent.[26]

Levinsohn's deep sense of the horror of the slave trade is further illustrated in his recording of a conversation with a Polish priest who justified
this human trafficking by claiming that the African blacks were actually
descendants of the ancient Canaanites whom Noah had cursed with the fate of
slavery (Genesis 9:25). Levinsohn countered by pointing to the humanity
of Czar Alexander I who attempted to abolish the slave trade at the Congress
of Vienna in 1814 but could not win over the French and Spanish. He also
challenged the priest on the treatment of Polish peasants subjected to the
tyranny of Polish ministers, restrained only by the more humane Russian
leaders. Levinsohn remarked that the priest responded to him by quickly
exiting the room. Levinsohn had exposed the hypocrisy of a Christian cleric
and also had forcefully made his point to McCaul about the immorality of
the so-called Christian leaders and governments.[27]

The Moral Profile of Judaism

In striking contrast to the profile of Christians past and present was Levin-sohn's portrayal of the Jews. As instituted by the rabbis, Judaism was a highly ethical and rational religious civilization. It justly treated women, slaves, and non-Jews. It only demanded from its believers to know and fear God, to study Torah, and to embrace all of humanity, especially the rulers to whom they were beholden. Christians were never judged by Jews to be idolaters and therefore the accusations McCaul had raised regarding the injustice of rab-binic law were unjustified and inapplicable to Christians past and present. On the contrary, according to the rabbis, Christians had a place in the next world. And as Levinsohn emphasized on more than one occasion, Jews could still embrace their Christian brethren while refraining from eating their food or drinking their wine or marrying them. Whatever superstitions can be found in the long history of Judaism regarding magical practices and astrol-ogy, they were hardly unique to Jews but were equally prominent in other civilizations, including contemporary Christianity.[28]

Most dramatic of all was the contrast between the lowly life of Christian burghers in Poland and the ethics and cultural attainments of Polish Jewry:

> Go and observe those sons of the burghers among the Christians. Are they not like wild men with their evil qualities and character who never learned in their entire lives to write or read a book, and even their adults are incapable of signing their names? This is not the case of the Jews who never leave school from the age of five to fifteen. Among the young men are those outstanding and sharp in the study of the Talmud and particularly the section dealing with jurisprudence [*jure*]; others excel in the purity of the holy languages and are good and fine masters of rhetoric. Some are experts in Bible having learned without the aid of a rabbi or teacher. Sometimes they are ordained with highly prized attributes and competence in the foundations of the sciences and of logic. Each learns in alternative times from the other. Some preoccupy themselves with the study of Torah and science, toiling in the study of a foreign language or a particular science without a rabbi or teacher because they are not instructed in their schools in foreign languages and sciences. Many of them devote all of their lives to Torah and science and they are satisfied with a dried crust of bread since their Torah is their faith.[29]

After discussing the high level of Jewish education, Levinsohn shifts to a detailed description of the system of social services available within the Jewish community. He describes the altruism of men and women alike who volunteer to support the poor. He singles out especially the practice of anonymous charity where donors make their largesse invisible to the needy, describing a particular incident he personally observed in the city of Brody in 1810 where a donor simply left an envelope of money for the poor several days before Yom Kippur without revealing his identity. Levinsohn also views the *beit hamidrash* as not only a house of study with its open and accessible library but a hospitable environment offering free food and lodging. He also mentions the ransoming of prisoners in debtor prisons and the testimony of Christian judges who were astonished by the disproportionate support offered to Jews by their coreligionists, not comparable to the meager efforts of Christians, even the most affluent. Finally, he relates the story of a Jewish woman forced to pay a heavy tax on her imported merchandise who received the unsolicited support of a Jewish donor secretly paying all her expenses.[30]

After pages of testimony painting the ultimate goodness and decency of Jewish society in comparison with the Christian, Levinsohn sharpens the contrast even more with the following outpouring of anger and derision, unfettered by any need to restrain himself as a member of a beleaguered minority. He writes:

> Go and observe Jewish and Christian burghers, who among them displays more the quality of humility and who the lack of humility, even publicly? It is disgusting to me to reveal before the eyes of the reader; but go and see who among them is stricken with the French disease [syphilis]; who among them sit in taverns from early evening until late at night, sometimes until the morning in large groups together, poor, rich, men, women, young men, and young virgins in mixed company drinking until they vomit and until there is violence, and until a slumber overtakes them and they fall to the ground sleeping and lying together like animals, and especially on their Sabbath and the other days of their religious holidays? Who will then go out in mixed groups—rich and poor, men and women, young men and virgins, even young boys and girls to the small villages and the city . . . to drink? Brandy is sold cheaply there, and from their heavy drunkenness, they fall like the slain strewn across the field, some here and there. They sleep there in the forest and

field not knowing when they lay down or got up. And among the young girls who went out as virgins, some returned impregnated and sometimes some who were married had even replaced them! Or they had been taken by soldiers in their state of drunkenness, and the raped women had no idea of their lying down or rising up.[31]

Juxtaposed with this ugly and frightening portrait of Christian society is the uplifting one of its Jewish counterpart: morally upright, studious, altruistic, and modest in its dealing with all people.

On Sabbath eve close to dusk until the next day and the appearance of stars for some twenty-six consecutive hours, Jews remain in their homes; the wise ones learn what is necessary for each of them while the unlearned read the Torah and its commentaries, and those inferior to the latter read from the book of Psalms, read from the Pentateuch in Yiddish, or from another work in the same language. The women with their teenage and young girls also read the Pentateuch in Yiddish besides other books. Each father listens to his teen or younger son speak about what he learned during the week in school.

What follows is a further elaboration of the differences between Christians and Jews regarding the celebration of marriage, the modesty of Jews in the *mikvah* (ritual bath) versus the lewd practices of Christian males and females, and the distinct differences between the ways Jews care for and mourn for the dead. In sum, "All we have written until now regarding the lack of morality and humility and the like among the Christians living in Poland and Galicia [is true] with the exception of three or four percent of them."

How was it possible then, asks Levinsohn, that the Jews acquired such noble attributes lacking the cultural opportunity afforded Christian noblemen to study "in gymnasiums, lycées, or universities"?[32] It was surely due to the Talmud and the Jewish educational structures that provided their moral grounding and cultural enlightenment in a manner superior to even the best institutions of the Christian nobility.

Levinsohn's stark appraisal of the decadent culture of Christianity in comparison with that of Judaism appears to be a total reversal of his initial plea for mutual respect and toleration at the beginning of *Ahiyah*. Here the emotional intensity, the bitter contempt, and the feeling of moral and cultural superiority rose to the surface in his denunciation of his Christian contemporaries and his deep appreciation of the values and societal structures emanating out of Jewish traditional society. Levinsohn had himself called for reform of the moral and cultural life of eastern European Jews in his *Te'udah be-Yisrael*. But in this context, in responding to an abusive missionary who had threatened the very rabbinic foundations of Jewish society, he could not restrain himself from displaying his deep love and commitment to his own tradition with all of its limitations. In the light of Christian aggression, past and present, it was imperative to tell his "truth," regardless of the consequences.

To this portrait of contemporary Jewish life, Levinsohn added one more dimension: the intellectual achievements of its elites. Despite economic hardships, Jews mastered the languages of their surrounding cultures and spoke it with proper accents. Their grounding in Talmud sharpened their intellects to master new fields and languages. They grew accustomed to poverty and discrimination, but still excelled in their intellectual achievements. Such was the path of most modern Jewish intellectuals, several of whom were singled out for special mention: "Rabbi" Baruch Spinoza, Israel of Zamosh, Moses Mendelssohn, and Solomon Maimon, "among the famous who created a sensation in the world because of their wisdom." Spinoza's elevation to the top of the list is understandable given his nineteenth-century popularity among Hebrew readers, but designating him a rabbi was surely a provocative gesture on Levinsohn's part. Citing Maimon's autobiography, the story of the famous philosopher, in Levinsohn's eyes, was not atypical of many other Jewish students with the capacity to impact Christian society as a whole. Echoing a theme of his teacher Naḥman Krochmal, he claimed that other civilizations like that of the Greeks and Arabs had achieved great heights only to decline in subsequent years, while the Jews continued their cultural production without any sign of regression as professors, lawyers, doctors, and even artists and musicians.[33]

Levinsohn concludes his inventory of the virtues of his own culture with words of self-justification. He claims that his high praise is not exaggerated but is meant to counter the horrible image of his coreligionists singled out for persecution and libel for generations, including the present time. He is thankful that there still remain some good and righteous people who acknowledge the sins of the past and strive to uproot the hatred instilled over centuries. His final appeal is to the elites of Christian society who can discern truth from falsehood: "I address all the great nobles among the Christians, the distinguished honest and decent aristocrats, the elite Christian clergy, their scholars and their wise-hearted teachers who inhabit their institutions of learning, and others among them who have known me personally and who have conversed with me on more than one occasion about this matter. They should please tell [me] if they have not acknowledged fully the truthfulness [of my claims]." He sincerely hopes that other decent nobles whom he did not know personally would also recognize these truths. The majority of these people today are "lovers of truth and righteousness, not filled with hypocrisy, but raised from their youth on wisdom and science and universal morality [*Torat Adam*]." It is only from these kinds of people, Jews acknowledged, that they can learn to love the sciences and embrace the ethical life: "For in the sciences and ethics, the Christian scholars and their noblemen are our teachers and we shall try to do by their example, just as our ancient ancestors were the teachers of the Christians in religion and faith and even afterward were sometimes their instructors in certain fields."[34]

In the end, it was Levinsohn, the true maskil, who reiterated his complete faith in the cultural and political elites of his day, who, so he claimed, could never display any animosity toward the Jew nor believe in the vicious blood libels of the past. Hatred of Jews ultimately emanated from the lower classes, rooted in a lack of education in the sciences; immorality festered in the drinking taverns and in the fields, not in the academies of higher learning. Moreover, despite the atrocities of Christian history, Jews paradoxically had much to learn from these Christian elites about science and ethics. While ancient Jews were once the teachers of early Christians, the roles were now reversed, and Jews, despite their high culture just depicted in glowing terms by Levinsohn, were still in need of reform through the agency of these "good" Christians. These remarkable pages—a combustible mixture of ethnic pride in Jewish literacy and morality; bitter anger and contempt for Christian burgers; admiration and even obsequiousness toward the Christian noble class; and even a transparent sense of cultural inferiority expressed in the notion that Christians should now instruct the Jews as ancient Jews had once instructed them—encapsulate as well as any text by this author his conflicted positions vis-à-vis Christianity and his own ancestral faith.

The Chiliastic Foundation of McCaul's Beliefs

As we have seen, Levinsohn had characterized Alexander McCaul, his Christian adversary, in a variety of ways: as ill-equipped to read rabbinic texts; as deficient in the minimal linguistic and academic standards for studying ancient history and literature; as uninformed or selective in treating ancient and modern Christian thought and history; as dishonest in presenting Jewish ritual beliefs out of context or in an exaggerated or distorted manner; and as insincere in professing to love Jews while attacking the very foundations of their faith and community. Perhaps his most unusual characterization of his opponent, however, is found in *Aḥiyah Shiloni ha-ḥozeh* after a defense of some of the more fanciful Jewish beliefs found in rabbinic literature that McCaul had ridiculed for their irrational and impious nature. McCaul had singled out especially the notion of Leviathan, the biblical sea monster, and the alleged meal prepared in his honor by the rabbis. A text in the Talmud (BT Baba Batra 75a) announces that the Leviathan will be slain and its flesh served as a feast to the righteous in the next world, while its skin will be used to cover the tent where the banquet will take place. McCaul alluded to the Sukkot prayer: "May it be your will, God and God of our fathers, that just as I have fulfilled and dwelt in this sukkah, so may I merit in the coming year to dwell in the sukkah of the skin of Leviathan."[35]

Levinsohn defends, through his mouthpiece Mizraḥi, this strange Jewish custom by diminishing its significance and by pivoting to discuss a parallel manifestation of absurd belief in ancient Christianity: "Haven't you known or heard that the Christians long ago believed that in the end of days after the coming of Christ a second time (according to their opinion) to judge the entire world, the Messiah will establish a pleasurable and material world called the messianic world [*das reich Christi*] and who can relate all the hyperboles and embellishments the Christians tell about this world of pleasure in which material desires will be present in great abundance, even sexual desire."[36] Alphonso, his Christian interlocutor, meekly responds that he is correct, that the reference is to the world called "cheliasmus [*sic*]," which comes about for one thousand consecutive years immediately following the final day. Mizraḥi then offers an elaborate explanation of the ancient sources of this belief as found in the New Testament and the church fathers, underscoring the ridiculous exaggerations of material wealth associated with this fantastic epoch. But the shift from the ancient sources of this belief to modern ones is swift and intentional:

> This belief in the thousand-year period was revived with full intensity with the rise of the Lutheran sect. This belief grew stronger during the entire seventeenth century among the Lutherans and their scholars as well as among the Catholics and their wise men. So

from day to day and from hour to hour the believers stood and yearned for the coming of this last day and the beginning of the thousand-year period in which they would pleasure themselves in material delights. This hope continued until the middle of the eighteenth century (about ninety years ago) when a new group of scholars arose to study and research and to examine the Old and New Testaments and the Apocrypha in order to strengthen and firmly establish this belief.

And Alphonso adds: "There were many scholars among them including, in my estimation, the famous Johannes Albrecht Bengel."[37]

The mention of the well-known Lutheran Pietist Bengel (1687–1752), biblical scholar and editor of the Greek New Testament, in this context, is a surprise, but even more surprising is the connection Levinsohn proceeds to make between Bengel and McCaul. He first describes the academy of Christian scholars Bengel established and the intensity with which he searched for and finally determined that the precise date of Christ's second coming was June 18, 1836. Mizraḥi continues: "I will not relate here in detail all the schemes the students of Bengel concocted or their students after them because I am embarrassed to write them down because it is immoral. The famous scholars [Johann Kaspar] Lavater and [Johann Heinrich] Jung-Stilling also spoke about this thousand-year period and its pleasures."[38]

It is at this point that McCaul is linked to this well-publicized group of chiliasts:

It is a remarkable thing that precisely at the end of this period [predicted by Bengel], that is in 1836 . . . , the author of *Netivot olam* [McCaul] stood and began to make his claims in this book [the first installments of his work appeared in English in 1837], also mocking the Jews for their material meal regarding the days of the Messiah. But it appears that right before this predicted time, based on the testimony of his words that he was one of their great believers, he awaited with great anticipation this pleasurable world that was predicted to come precisely in 1836 when he would be joyous in the sight of the revenge against the Jews who would burn in fire and brimstone . . . while his body would delight in eating, drinking, and sexual activity for a long time. . . . However, when he saw that the time had expired and he feared that the Jews would make fun of

him regarding this matter [the false calculation], he proceeded to be
the first to make fun of them regarding this belief in order to reverse
his fate.[39]

Levinsohn's identification of McCaul with Bengel and German Pietism
and chiliasm is more than an interesting curiosity. To my knowledge, he is
the first Jew to locate McCaul's Christian faith within the context of evangelical Christianity and to link it directly to the messianic stream of Bengel, as
well as Lavater and Jung-Stilling. He did so in order to defend a tenuous
Jewish custom from Christian ridicule by emphasizing that Christianity had
its own ideological flaws and material fantasies even among contemporary
believers. He certainly believed he had scored points with his adversary in
raising an aspect of recent theological speculation that he deemed shameful.
Branding McCaul a chiliast and a follower of Bengel's band of false prognos-
ticators was polemically efficacious. But it was more than that. As an astute
Jewish observer of Christian theology, he had identified correctly for the first
time the deeper roots and motivations of the new Christian mission to the
Jews: an evangelical fervor, an anticipation of the return of Christ, and the
special role the Jews were expected to play in this unfolding divine drama.

Levinsohn's Motivation in Composing His Polemics

It is obvious that this discussion of five central themes in Levinsohn's two
polemical works against McCaul only scratches the surface of these two compositions, their place within Levinsohn's entire literary output, and his legacy
as the so-called "father of the eastern European Haskalah." Levinsohn was
primarily known for his *Te'udah be-Yisrael*, not for his polemical writings
against the missionaries. Despite his aspirations that *Aḥiyah Shiloni ha-ḥozeh*
would provide an accessible introduction to the larger work *Zerubavel* and
that it would be translated into English, the work appeared only in Hebrew
in a posthumous edition published in Leipzig in 1864. *Zerubavel* clearly had
a wider impact; it appeared in eight editions, first in Leipzig and then in
Warsaw and later in Vilna, between 1863 and 1910.[40] It too was never translated but clearly gained a certain degree of recognition among a highly literate
readership able to follow its elaborate discussions of the Talmud, Christian
theology, and ancient history. Given the denseness of this volume and the
degree of sophistication it required of its readers, it could not have appealed

to the uninitiated. If Montefiore had genuinely been interested in providing a reputable response to McCaul to be read by English Jews and Christians alike, he would have elected to sponsor the publication of *Aḥiyah Shiloni ha-ḥozeh*, but he declined. *Zerubavel* would have hardly satisfied his needs. In Vilna and Warsaw it obviously found a reading public who enjoyed a thorough and devastating critique of missionary arguments. Even the missionaries themselves were aware of Levinsohn's work and acknowledged it. We might recall the 1892 evaluation of McCaul's book and other publications of the London Society written by several missionaries in the field, especially that of Rev. W. Becker who claimed that "The Old Paths should be corrected with respect to the Jewish defenses, esp. Zorubabel," a clear admission that Levinsohn's book had successfully refuted McCaul's arguments.[41]

Yet by the time both of Levinsohn's polemical works had appeared, the initial alarm generated by the Hebrew publication of *Netivot olam* had long waned; almost twenty-five years had passed. We can only assume that the subsequent publications of *Zerubavel* were the result of the fame of its author and perhaps were still useful to some readers as a kind of generic handbook to refute Christian missionaries in general. When Eliezer Zweifel, a maskil who took a similar approach to that of Levinsohn (and Fuenn as well), published his response to McCaul called *Sanegor* (Advocate) in Warsaw in 1885, it was integrated into a variety of topics he treated, as well as into a variety of targets he attacked.[42] By the end of the century, McCaul's name alone apparently evoked considerably less interest among his readers.

What, in the end, motivated Isaac Baer Levinsohn to compose these two works and to devote so much time and energy to them, especially given his declining state of health? No doubt, he felt obliged to Montefiore and others to respond to the missionary; he could not have imagined that he would have so much difficulty in publishing his works during his lifetime. It would be fair to assume that he was quite aware that only a rabbinic scholar with a maskilic temperament and education such as his was capable of responding effectively to the formidable McCaul. We might recall his own enumeration of the qualifications of a real scholar of rabbinic texts discussed earlier in the chapter and the extent to which they fit him precisely—knowledgeable in Talmud, philology, ancient languages, and history. Montefiore knew well that such scholars were not to be found in London. Levinsohn could not afford to shirk his responsibility to the entire Hebrew reading public, which was inundated with numerous copies of McCaul's work distributed by the London Society throughout the continent and beyond.

Levinsohn also accepted the challenge of refuting McCaul because *Aḥi-yah Shiloni ha-ḥozeh* and *Zerubavel* were natural extensions of his life work, particularly embodied in his most important writing, *Beit Yehudah*. He had devoted his entire literary career to defending the rabbis, their exegetical traditions, their pure notion of monotheism, and their deep love of all humanity. His polemic with McCaul was simply a reiteration of the themes he had expounded throughout his career as an educator and writer. While he sought to reform Judaism from within, he also defended its integrity, its intellectual power, and its moral virtue to his fellow coreligionists who were abandoning the tradition he sought to preserve and refurbish. It was thus logical for him to regard *Zerubavel* as a genuine extension of his major defense of the rabbinic tradition. It was a sincere reflection of his life calling, which he carried out with vigor and unceasing commitment.[43]

CHAPTER 8

From Vilna to Aleppo

Two Additional Responses to McCaul's Assault

Samuel Joseph Fuenn

Samuel Joseph Fuenn (1818–90), another leading figure of the eastern European Haskalah, was thirty years younger than Isaac Baer Levinsohn, and while his scholarly accomplishments were somewhat less than those of his more prolific senior colleague, he was still highly regarded as an educator, editor, and Hebrew writer in Vilna. When Fuenn read Levinsohn's *Te'udah be-Yisrael*, the manifesto of the Haskalah, it inspired him to seek out a similar course, which he pursued with rigor and commitment. He was like his mentor not only for his enlightened views but also for his consistently strong attachment to rabbinic Judaism and to a traditional path of learning and practice. Shmuel Feiner has situated him with what he calls the camp of moderate maskilim, which included Levinsohn himself and Eliezer Zweifel (1815–88). He should also be connected ideologically to several other luminaries who preceded him or were his contemporaries, such as Naḥman Krochmal (1785–1840), Solomon Judah Loeb Rapoport (1786–1867), Heinrich Graetz (1817–91), Zacharias Frankel (1801–75), and Isaac Hirsch Weiss (1815–1905).[1]

That Fuenn also felt the need, along with Levinsohn and Zweifel, to compose a substantial rebuttal of Alexander McCaul's critique of the rabbis in *Netivot olam* suggests how threatening the missionary's work was perceived to be by the Jewish intellectual elite of eastern Europe. As in the case of

FIGURE 7. Samuel Joseph Fuenn. From the Abraham Schwadron Collection at the National Library of Israel, Jerusalem. By permission of the National Library of Israel.

Levinsohn's two books against McCaul, Fuenn's composition was stimulated in part by his interaction with Moses Montefiore whom he had met in person when the latter visited Vilna in 1846. Only three years earlier, in 1843, Fuenn, still a young man of twenty-five, had completed his manuscript *Darkhei Adonai* (The ways of God) against McCaul with the sincere expectation that Montefiore would publish it both in the original and in an English translation, as a Hebrew letter seeking Montefiore's support clearly reveals. Fuenn even opened his work with a flowery dedication to the English philanthropist in gratitude for its expected publication. We have already seen how even Levinsohn could not publish either of his books against McCaul during his lifetime; they appeared only in 1863 and 1864, long after the missionary's book had been widely disseminated across Europe and the Middle East. In the case of Fuenn, his work was never published and remains to this day in a single manuscript, part of a larger archive of his writings at the National Library in Jerusalem. Even though Montefiore was directly involved in the English publication of Levinsohn's work against the blood libel in 1840 as part of the campaign against the notorious Damascus affair, he chose not to finance the publication of Fuenn's or Levinsohn's manuscripts on McCaul despite the threat the latter posed to English Jews. And whether due to a lack of funds or the fear of the Russian censor on the part of Jewish communal leaders in Vilna, Fuenn failed to find any other path to publication. Fuenn would have later success in publishing several of his own works and earned considerable prestige as an editor of a major journal, but he seems to have abandoned this early work despite the obvious effort he had expended in preparing a finished and elegant manuscript obviously ready for submission to the publisher.[2]

Samuel Joseph Fuenn is not an unstudied figure in the history of nineteenth-century Jewish culture as a leading maskil; for his public activities on behalf of Jewish educational reform; as a teacher in the Vilna rabbinic seminary; as a historical writer; and as editor of the Hebrew weekly *Ha-Karmel*.[3] Although largely unread, *Darkhei Adonai* offers a rich testimony of his Jewish self-understanding at an early stage of his career and should be considered against the background of his later works and those of his contemporaries. My modest goal in the first section of this chapter is to offer my own initial thoughts on several aspects of the text and their potential contribution to nineteenth-century Jewish thought and Jewish-Christian polemics.[4]

A Historical Defense of the Rabbis

Darkhei Adonai, as both Shmuel Feiner and Eliyahu Stern have pointed out, is divided into roughly two equal parts. The first part offers a broad comparative history of Judaism and Christianity in their formative periods from the time of Jesus and the beginnings of rabbinic Judaism until the Middle Ages; the second turns directly to McCaul's work, presenting a detailed response to the key arguments of his polemic. The reader of both parts can well appreciate how the two sections are organically linked. Fuenn's comparative history was hardly a dispassionate and neutral retelling of the trajectories of both religions. On the contrary, it was a frontal attack on McCaul's misreading of the evolution of rabbinic Judaism and its moral assets, on the one hand, and a complete unmasking of the seemingly negative history of oppression, immorality, and internal dissension that marked the history of Christianity, a history McCaul consciously chose to suppress, on the other. Having established the larger context for judging the record of the two religions over many decades, Fuenn was then in a position to demonstrate how McCaul's denigration of Judaism and elevation of Protestant Christianity unjustly distorted the historical record. By defending the rabbinic tradition, Fuenn's major task in rebutting McCaul, he was able to fortify his individual arguments in the second part by reference to the larger context delineated in the first.

Fuenn relied on a variety of Jewish and Christian sources to construct his project of comparative history and to respond to specific points of McCaul's book. They were less numerous than those referenced by Levinsohn although still impressive. His most important source seems to have been Levinsohn's works themselves, not of course his anti-McCaul writings, which appeared in print much later, but his many other books published before 1843, especially *Beit Yehudah*, a vast repository of reflections on rabbinic Judaism. Among his other Jewish sources, Fuenn relied heavily on Isaak Markus Jost's *Geschichte der Israeliten seit der Zeit der Maccabäer*, published in nine volumes between 1820 and 1829. He was familiar with Solomon Judah Loeb Rapoport and cited several of his writings. Other contemporary Jewish authors referred to in *Darkhei Adonai* include Samuel David Luzzatto, Joseph Salvador, Mordechai Markus Friedenthal, Zevi Hirsch Katznellenbogen, Samson Bloch, David Nieto, Joel Brill, and especially Moses Mendelssohn.[5]

Besides Jost, Fuenn's primary sources for the history of Christianity were Wilhelm Traugott Krug's *Handbuch der Philosophie*, published several times in Leipzig in the 1820s, and Jacques-Bénigne Bossuet's *Einleitung in die*

Geschichte der Welt und der Religion, translated from French into German with additional critical notes by Johann Andreas Cramer (Leipzig, 1757–86). We have already encountered both authors in the previous chapter on Levinsohn. Whether or not Fuenn's first acquaintance with both standard sources came from his reading of Levinsohn, we know that he must have consulted them directly, since his references are not identical with those of his mentor.[6] I have already mentioned Eliyahu Stern's particular emphasis on the use of Bossuet/Cramer as a source of Levinsohn's and Fuenn's so-called "Catholic Judaism" and my skepticism with this interpretation. Fuenn's use of Bossuet/Cramer is not, in fact, primary to his overall discussion of either Judaism or Christianity. A rough count of the number of times Fuenn cites both Krug and Bossuet/Cramer demonstrates that both sources were equally consulted.[7] It would be more reasonable to conclude that Fuenn, like Levinsohn, was generally indifferent to the ideological background of his sources on Christianity and more interested in using both sources merely as standard guides for his subject. Indeed Krug's handbook seems no more than a kind of accessible reference tool, hardly a work of specialized knowledge. And, as Stern has already pointed out, Fuenn was capable of citing a source that appeared to contradict the view of Catholic history offered by Bossuet. I refer to Fuenn's citation of the *Kritische Geschichte der kirchlichen Unfehlbarkeit zur Beförderung einer freien Prüfung bei Katholizismus*, published anonymously but attributed to Felix Anton Blau, a strong denial of church infallibility. Fuenn, like Levinsohn, consulted such Christian authors not as primary sources in shaping his distinct point of view but merely as databases of authoritative information useful in bolstering his argument.[8] Both Jewish authors fashioned their arguments in defense of the rabbinic tradition from other sources, especially internally Jewish ones.

I cannot offer here a full and exhaustive discussion of the context and sources of *Darkhei Adonai* but instead would like to focus on a few illustrative themes Fuenn developed that might point to a broader understanding of the project as a whole, the intellectual influences from which it drew, and its own originality. My first example is from the early part of Fuenn's recitation of Jewish and Christian history. Stressing that ancient Judaism emerged in interaction with the outside world, stimulating new ideas and new reforms, "according to the spirit of the times," Fuenn chose to focus on Philo of Alexandria, whose interpretations of Judaism were based on "doctrines of reason and logic."[9] Fuenn explained that the Jews of Alexandria adopted the views of Pythagoras and Plato and merged them with the Torah.

In describing a Platonic theology fused with the sources of Judaism, Fuenn cited for his sources the work of Wilhelm Traugott Krug on Plato; the imaginary travel journal of Anacharsis the Younger in Greece written by Jean-Jacques Barthelemy; and the writings of Johann Augustus Eberhard, a German theologian and acquaintance of Mendelssohn.[10] This seemingly strange mix of sources compound the mystery of why Fuenn chose to concentrate in the first place on Philo and Alexandrian Jewry in the midst of his larger discussion on the origins of rabbinic Judaism in Palestine, the Sanhedrin, the various sects of Pharisees, Sadducees, and Essenes, Hillel and Shammai, and the early history of the tannaim. Fuenn considered "these wonderful studies" emerging among the Jews of Alexandria as quite distinct from Aristotle's materialist philosophy that separated the world from God. There was no complete system of rabbinic exegesis among Philo and his contemporaries, Fuenn admitted, but the esoteric notions of *Maaseh bereshit* (Work of Creation) and *Maaseh merkavah* (Work of the Chariot, referring to Ezekiel 1), along with thinking about the logos as an intermediary between God and the world, were developed in this stimulating environment.[11]

At first glance, it is hard to understand why this particular excursus on Philo and Neoplatonism seemingly interrupted the flow of an unbroken tradition of rabbinic leadership Fuenn reconstructed from the Second Temple period through the creation of the Palestinian and Babylonian Talmuds. The discussion seems at best an interesting digression from his main narrative on the history of rabbinic Judaism. At one point, Fuenn remarks that Philo was a contemporary of Yoḥanan Ben Zakkai,[12] the primary rabbinic leader of Palestinian Jewry after the destruction of the Temple in 70 C.E. But why was it necessary at all to include and embellish the story of Philo and his seemingly nonrabbinic version of Judaism in the history Fuenn was constructing?

The answer lies in the revival of scholarship on Philo emerging first and foremost from a group of Christian scholars in the nineteenth century who found him to be a significant forerunner of Jesus and a worthy source of inspiration in the formation of ancient Christianity. This scholarship not only revealed parallels between the spiritual worlds of Alexandria, Jesus, and his disciples but was able to construct a narrative of Christian origins independent of the rabbis altogether. In underscoring the Philonic roots of Christianity, in delineating a Philo Christianus, this scholarship was able to bypass or at least to diminish the more conventional linkage of Jesus and his Pharisaic/rabbinic background and to replace it with an alternative genealogy. In the same period Fuenn composed his response to McCaul, several other

Jewish thinkers had noticed the new Christian scholarship and felt the need to respond to it.[13]

Although Azariah dei Rossi had already recovered the Jewish roots of Philo centuries earlier, a full awareness of the stakes of this recovery in defining a modern Jewish identity emerged only in the nineteenth century. Immanuel Wolf, for example, saw Hellenism and Judaism in conflict with each other, with the former attenuating the essence of the latter. Isaak Markus Jost, on the other hand, valued Alexandria as a model of nonrabbinic diasporic culture and a universal and ethical rationalism, with an enlightened host government providing a public civic role for Jews. Opposing what he considered to be a repressive Jewish rabbinism, Jost wrote that German Jews could learn much from Philo's Jewish ideals. In contrast, Zacharias Frankel was less impressed by the Hellenistic model of Jewishness articulated by Philo and valued a Palestinian Jewish culture more authentic in its commitment to Hebraic learning and resistant to the alien cultural values attenuating the Jewish spirit. Heinrich Graetz was more ambivalent than either Jost or Frankel. He initially spoke positively about the enlightened diaspora of Alexandria but later associated Philo with a Christian sensibility, considering him as well "the father of a mystical world view," a position for which he had no liking. In other words, Jews who studied Philo in the nineteenth century were unwittingly drawn into a debate framed by Christian scholarship on the origins of early Christianity and its supposed indebtedness to Judaism. The scholarly study of Philo became a new forum for the playing out of the Jewish-Christian debate.[14]

Among these varied Jewish responses to Philo, that of Naḥman Krochmal in the twelfth gate of his *Moreh nevukhei ha-zeman* (Guide for the perplexed of this time) was central. Although Krochmal, like most of his Jewish contemporaries, had not read Philo in the original, he relied heavily on the scholarship of his two primary Christian interpreters: August F. Dähne and Johann August Wilhelm Neander, a former Jew.[15] In contrast to these two scholars, who had emphasized the affinity between Philo and Christianity, Krochmal saw "the divine Torah philosophy" of Philo and his contemporaries as a positive resource of Jewish life, an authentic product of the Jewish *Volksgeist*, and a remarkable example of the Jewish impact on the non-Jewish history of ideas. Philo for Krochmal represented the central core of Neoplatonic thought that later developed in Plotinus, in Proclus, and in kabbalah. Philonic Alexandria needed to be studied not merely as a backdrop for Christian theology but as a legitimate expression of Jewish creativity. Moreover, Philo's views were congruent with those of the rabbis; if one examined the parallels between Philonic exegesis and that of rabbinic midrash, Krochmal claimed, it was evident that Philo was rooted in Jewish religious history. Philo's reappropriation as a Jewish thinker aligned him with rabbinic Judaism, manifestly spiritual and rational at the same time, and also recast him as an enlightened Jew, a maskil in the image of Krochmal himself. From this perspective, Krochmal's reconstruction of Philo was both a response to the renewal of the Jewish-Christian debate of his own time, rooted in historicism and Hegelianism, as well as a bold attempt to expand the very definition of rabbinic civilization in order to demonstrate its rational and creative dimensions.[16]

Krochmal's essay on Philo brings into sharp focus Fuenn's positive evaluation of Philo and Alexandrian Jewry and his choice to underscore its significance in a narrative contrasting rabbinic history with that of the church. Fuenn too appreciated the fusion of pietism and rationalism in Philo's thought; he viewed it as a legitimate contribution of Jews to the history of European ideas; and by juxtaposing Alexandrian history with that of the early rabbis, he underscored the multifaceted and universal character of ancient Judaism. In the context of a polemic against Christianity, the inclusion of Philo made perfect sense.

Krochmal had died in 1840, leaving behind an unfinished and unedited manuscript that would be passed on by his children to Leopold Zunz to be edited and prepared for publication. The process went on for more than a decade and the completed manuscript was not published until 1851 in Lemberg.[17] There is no evidence that the manuscript of Krochmal's work circulated before his death, and although he was on intimate terms with several maskilim in Galicia, including Levinsohn, and conceivably shared his thoughts with them, it is hard to imagine how Fuenn would have gained access to the book prior to 1851. This is all the more intriguing because Fuenn's more mature attempt to write a comprehensive history of the Jews, the first part of *Nidḥei Yisrael*, was published only one year earlier in 1850 in Vilna. As Feiner noticed in considering this publication, "To a considerable degree, Fuenn's book prefigured some of the historical concepts that appeared soon after in Krochmal."[18]

There is no evidence whatsoever of Krochmal's direct influence on Fuenn before 1851 and certainly none as early as 1843. Still, it seems plausible to argue that Fuenn absorbed "Krochmalian" ideas about Philo and Alexandria even if he had never read Krochmal's actual words. In the first place, Azariah dei Rossi's rehabilitation of Philo was well known in maskilic circles in Fuenn's lifetime and was certainly available to Fuenn. But there were two other prominent Jewish contemporaries who were deeply invested in the study of Philo and Alexandrian Jewish culture, who were probably well known to Fuenn and were simultaneously associated with Krochmal's circle. The first was Joseph Flesch (1781–1839), the so-called "father of the Moravian Jewish Enlightenment" who had single-handedly taken on the daunting task of translating Philo from Latin to Hebrew in two collections published in the 1830s. In the preface to the second volume, which included the first Hebrew translation of *De Vita Mosis* among other works, Flesch mentioned that he had been uncertain about the reader response to his first volume, particularly because the sales were so low. But a small group who appreciated his work, especially his dear friend and soulmate the rabbi and scholar Solomon Judah Loeb Rapoport (1786–1867), strongly encouraged him to continue. Urged on by Rapoport, he persevered in bringing these precious texts to the attention of the Jewish community through his Hebrew translations.[19]

A scholar well known to Fuenn,[20] Rapoport not only played a leading role in encouraging Flesch to create a Hebrew Philo, but appreciated Philo in his own right and assigned him and Alexandrian Jewry a place in his unfinished dictionary of Hebrew and foreign terms called *Erekh milim*. Rapoport admitted that Philo often deviated from the Palestinian rabbis in many of his writings. But this he attributed to mistakes and lack of knowledge and not to willingly challenging the rabbis as in the case of the Sadducees. On the other hand, Rapoport made the following remarkable claim: "How wonderful that our master Moses Maimonides, may his memory be a blessing, who had never seen Philo's books because he did not know Greek, actually followed his path in all matters of the Torah."[21] In all likelihood, either Flesch, or Rapoport, or both were then the sources of Fuenn's own appreciative narrative regarding Philo and Alexandria; both shared and anticipated Krochmal's more developed position.[22]

Krochmal and Fuenn on the Oral Law

The prominent place afforded Philo and his cultural ambiance in the works of both Fuenn and Krochmal leads us to look for other similarities of thought between the two. I would like to offer a comparison between the two on the larger question of justifying the oral tradition of the rabbis along with the more general notion that all legal traditions, including those of Christianity, are ultimately based on oral foundations. This, of course, was particularly relevant to Jewish intellectuals seeking a cogent response to the Christian assault on rabbinic Judaism in general and to McCaul's criticisms in particular. We have considered and rejected the notion of an oral tradition in Levinsohn's work as a kind of "Catholic Judaism." In this chapter, I offer my own speculation on the general context of Fuenn's (and Levinsohn's) remarks by reference to Krochmal's well-formulated ideas.

In Jay Harris's thoughtful study of Krochmal's work, he pointed to an acute crisis facing the authority of the rabbinic tradition from the 1820s, particularly among Jewish critics of traditional Judaism. Among the most outspoken of them was the same Isaak Markus Jost who viewed the Oral Law as an act of self-aggrandizement of the rabbis or "an ideology of a guild seeking power over the people." Moreover, Jost maintained, rabbinic documents were not reliable for reconstructing Jewish history prior to the third century c.e. Harris presents a variety of other Jewish critics of the claims of rabbinic authority including Lazarus Bendavid, Edward Gans, and Michael Creizenach. Each in his own way devalued the Talmudic text and viewed it as a distortion of the original biblical religion. McCaul could not have stated it better.[23]

Facing this crisis of confidence in the Talmud by the 1830s, Krochmal attempted to use the critical methods of a particular school of legal history (*Rechtswissenschaft*) especially represented by the famous German legal historian Friedrich Karl von Savigny (1779–1861). Rejecting an idealist school of legal historians, which also included Gans, who had promoted the enactment of new progressive legislation in Germany, Savigny and his colleagues insisted that laws could not be effectively enacted through legislation; rather they developed organically, "supplied by rules communicated by writing and the word of mouth." Authentic laws emerged from "internal silently operating powers," from custom and popular faith, "not by the arbitrary will of a lawgiver."[24]

Savigny himself had little use for Jews and had even denied Gans a legal position despite his conversion to Christianity. Thus there was a touch of irony in Krochmal's justification of the rabbinic tradition and particularly its notion of "an oral law" through an appeal to Savigny's universal idea grounded in historicism and romanticism. But it perfectly suited his needs in defending the rabbis: their laws were produced over time through a slow organic process; they reflected the true spirit of the people and met their changing needs; and they were grounded in logical, rational principles.

Krochmal afforded a prominent role to the early rabbis both prior and following the editing of the Mishnah. Their reasonable exegesis derived from the biblical text; they transmitted the oral tradition faithfully through logic and reason. Due to political and economic upheavals over time, they suffered setbacks and internal controversies, but in the words of Harris, "contingent historical circumstances could not detract from the intrinsic metahistorical integrity of their system."[25] Their understanding of Jewish law was not literal but functional. They actualized the Torah, preserving both its spirituality and reasonability. In the end, Krochmal borrowed a key concept from Savigny and then bent it to his own purpose. Thus he claimed that the Jewish oral tradition was rooted in the religious consciousness of the Jewish people, a consciousness both spiritual and rational and organically evolving over time but guided and shaped by its faithful rabbinic leaders. Krochmal's apologetic defense of the rabbinic tradition left its lasting mark on Heinrich Graetz, Zacharias Frankel, and Isaac Hirsch Weiss who also sought a way of grounding the Jewish oral tradition in a historical principle universalized by Savigny for all legal cultures, including Christianity. They sought a notion of tradition based on rational concepts and reflecting the "spirit of the times," while preserving a sense of continuity with the past. Theirs was a reconstructed tradition, shaped by the exigencies of the moment, and engineered to respond to the critics of the twofold written and oral law, both within their community and beyond it. Krochmal's model well suited their simultaneous need to embrace as well as expand and restructure their own tradition. It equally matched their need to justify the oral traditions of Judaism before Christian missionaries such as McCaul. Presenting Jewish tradition as an authentic expression of a universal legal development as Krochmal and his successors had done was surely the most effective weapon both Levinsohn and Fuenn had at their disposal.

I reiterate that I can make no claims regarding the possible influence of Krochmal on Fuenn. There is no evidence that he read him or even heard of Savigny. Nevertheless, *Darkhei Adonai* offered a perspective on the oral tradition closely similar to Krochmal's. Fuenn opened the first part of his book, which he calls "Derekh emunah" (A path of faith), by stating its purpose: "It is a history of the Oral Torah [*Torah she-be-al peh*] and its holy teachings, one battle line opposite the other [*ma'arakha mul ma'arakha*] [in juxtaposition with] a history of the Christian faith, a history of its teachings and beliefs until the codification of the Jerusalem Talmud." Fuenn's title is revealing in two respects: It was not merely a comparative history of Judaism and Christianity. It was a history of the Oral Law in contrast to the history of early

Christianity, which spanned the same period; it focused directly on the essential feature of postbiblical Judaism that McCaul would not recognize as legitimate. It was also primarily a history of Palestinian Judaism, concentrating both on the same time frame and geographical location from which the two religions emerged and confronted each other.

In introducing the missionary from London and his false charges against Judaism at the beginning of his introduction, Fuenn framed McCaul's misguided mission against the Jews in the following way: "And truthfully one should forgive me for telling him this that he has no understanding of the concept of the history of any religion in general and also that of the religion of Israel. He is far from comprehending the sanctity of the history of the Jewish religion and he has not examined with the eye of a genuine scholar the branches of the science of transmission/ tradition [*Torat ha-atakah*]."[26] McCaul's limitation then was not merely his inability to understand rabbinic Judaism; it was his failure to grasp the history of religion in general and the way in which its values and beliefs were transmitted in particular. And Fuenn repeated: "We will prove that the science of transmission/tradition [*Torat ha-atakah*] is a source of living water emerging from the rock of the divine Torah."[27] In offering a truly comparative history of the two religions, their moments of contact and separation from each other, Fuenn again stressed that his opponent not only misconstrued the foundations of a written and oral tradition in Judaism but in Christianity as well and was thus deficient in understanding the history of both faiths. All religions evolve over time from the moment of their foundation, adding changes and new elements "according to the spirit of the times," like a huge sea filled with water from multiple wells and other sources that flow into each other. A scholar cannot grasp Judaism, Christianity, or Islam solely at a particular moment in time but rather must gaze over hundreds and thousands of years: "And thus a person who wants to observe from within the Jewish religion, how it rose or fell, must examine a number of generations of their passing and unfolding and the activity of each generation and their impressions."[28]

Fuenn finally articulated a clear definition of "what is called also *kabbalah* or *ha'atakah* [tradition] which is found in all religions, the Jewish, Christian, and Muslim, and without it the written law could not stand on its own. . . . These additions and explanations are transmitted from one generation to the next, from the mouth of one person to the next, not only from the mouth but from eye to eye, from act to act."[29] The tradition is valued both by the substance of what is passed down and by the quality of the one entrusted with the transmission of the message. If it has little rational basis, at least it should not contradict reason. But the tradition is as strong as those transmitting it who demonstrate moral virtue and the commitment to being faithful to the original message, and "particularly if the transmitters are rabbis, sages, and righteous people who together testify that this is truthful so that no one disagrees. Both the veracity of the message and messenger are necessary for the formation of a proper religious tradition and are consistent with the ultimate truth of Judaism rightfully called "the law of Moses from Sinai."[30]

Fuenn emphasized even more strongly the importance of proper leadership in preserving the tradition and transmitting it to each generation. These upright leaders who shape the law require the strength to understand the will and spirit of the time and the deficiencies of the people they serve, to expand and deepen an understanding of the doctrines, ethics, and rituals of the tradition, and especially "to accept change and expansion" in their interpretation of religion. Fuenn concludes: "And this phenomenon is found in every religion whether it be rabbis among the Jews, church fathers or bishops among the Christians, or muftis among the Muslims, depending on the strength of their dominion over the people."[31]

Had Fuenn conveyed the spirit of Krochmal's understanding of tradition without actually reading his book or probing his sources? I hope I have cited enough to at least suggest how closely aligned the two thinkers were in constructing their argument in favor of the rabbinic tradition. Like Krochmal, the notion of an oral tradition was common to all religions for Fuenn; it evolved gradually over time in an organic and natural way rooted in the consciousness and spirituality of a community living in the present while inspired by the memory of its collective past; and it was guided with rationality and sensitivity by a dedicated and talented leadership who upheld the highest ideals the community embodied. Fuenn had admittedly not grounded his notion of *ha'atakah* in a current theory of legal history, but he had certainly emphasized the notion of a "science" of tradition, rooted in a universal need of every religion to evolve over time and through the spirit of its people and the times in which they lived. This in fact was the gist of Krochmal's message. Just as he had displayed his enthusiasm for Philo in a manner similar to that of Krochmal, here too Fuenn had captured the spirit, if not the letter, of his powerful defense of the rabbis.[32]

The Uniqueness of Fuenn's Polemic

The affinities between Krochmal and Fuenn, however, hardly demonstrate Fuenn's lack of originality. On the contrary, if in fact he had articulated a position integrating Philo into Jewish history and argued for the universal application of a notion of an oral religious tradition eight years before Krochmal's work was published, one might argue that it was he and not Krochmal who first conceived of these ideas. Obviously lacking the intellectual tools and scholarly erudition of his older colleague, Fuenn might still deserve credit for putting into writing an argument that adumbrated Krochmal's. The irony, of course, is that Fuenn's work was lost for posterity, while Krochmal's has left its significant mark on later Jewish thought. What we might at least suggest is that a version of several of Krochmal's primary ideas was presented by a young maskil from Vilna, apparently working independently and focused primarily on responding to an outspoken missionary.

Moving beyond the question of the converging views of Fuenn and Krochmal, we might add a few additional remarks about the uniqueness of Fuenn's unpublished manuscript. In his recent essay, Eliyahu Stern found Fuenn to be most original in his remarks on Paul. In a well-crafted discussion of the indebtedness of Jesus and the apostles to Jewish beliefs and practices, Fuenn argued that even Paul's public break from Jewish law might be considered more a submission to its authority than an act of defiance against it. Had not the rabbis argued that in the time of the Messiah, all the sacrifices would cease and all other norms would be suspended and subordinated to the Messiah's authority? If indeed Paul considered Jesus the Messiah, then he was clearly acting within the normative framework of rabbinic law in suspending regularized observance while ushering in the time of the Messiah. Stern argues that Fuenn was the first to present Paul's rejection of Jewish law in its messianic context, and in this idea, he was clearly ahead of his time.[33]

I have no reason to doubt Fuenn's precocity on this or other matters mentioned above, but it might be useful to contextualize his position a bit more fully. There are an abundance of references to "the laws of the Messiah" and the suspension of conventional norms in the post-messianic era in rabbinic literature, especially pointed out by Gershom Scholem in his classic discussion of Jewish messianic thought. While no early modern Jew, to my knowledge, mentioned Paul in this context, one might usefully compare Fuenn's speculation with those of the opponents of the Sabbateans several centuries earlier. Both Jacob Sasportas in the seventeenth and Jacob Emden in the eighteenth century anticipated Fuenn's position in some ways. Sasportas did not single out Paul but referred to messianic enthusiasts in general, that is, Sabbateans, who believed that with the coming of Shabbetai Zevi, the post-halachic age had arrived. Emden spoke explicitly about Paul and his intention not to undermine the law, though he did not refer to the messianic context. In the twentieth century, of course, such historians as Hans-Joachim Schoeps and W. D. Davies, prior to Paula Fredrickson, mentioned by Stern, had articulated the notion that Paul's suspension of the law in the messianic era stemmed from rabbinic Judaism.[34]

I would add, that in addition to the interesting comments on Paul, Fuenn's fuller treatment of the history of Christianity represents one of the most conspicuous strengths of his book. Relying on Krug and Bossuet/Cramer as pointed out above, but also citing several other sources he had subsequently collected, Fuenn offered his readers a coherent and forceful portrait of the dark side of Christian history characterized by persecutions and discrimination, greed and power politics, and bitter doctrinal disputes. This stood in sharp contrast to his portrayal of rabbinic Judaism, a culture intellectually vibrant, morally sensitive, and contributing significantly to the religious ideas of early Christianity as well. The originality of his composition rests less on the specific subjects he addressed than on the general formatting of his book as a comparative history of two civilizations, one degrading and one uplifting. Of course, in these polarized and exaggerated narratives, he was following in the footsteps of Levinsohn and others who were fond of portraying Jewish saints and Christian devils.

Ultimately, in the cases of both Levinsohn and Fuenn, the exaggeration of their dichotomies was a reaction to the equally distorting representation of Judaism and the rabbis by McCaul and a long line of earlier Christian polemicists. It was also meant to remind McCaul and his acolytes that he had not only misrepresented Jewish history in his unfair depiction of rabbinic civilization but had also suppressed the entire history of the church fathers, the medieval papacy, the Crusades, the Inquisition, and much more. Fuenn, and Levinsohn were demanding a fair accounting of the past. The Protestants could not argue that their brand of Christianity was independent and un-related to Catholicism. It was in the interest of these Jewish apologists to homogenize the two into a faith of Jesus simply called Christianity and to argue that McCaul had to take responsibility for the more unenlightened and oppressive parts of this faith alongside the enlightened and spiritual dimen-sions he promoted. In the end, history would be the ultimate judge, and by presenting the full record of both civilizations side by side (*ma'araka mul ma'arakha*, as Fuenn put it above), he would set the record straight. Of course, like Krochmal and the other maskilim with historical penchants, he presented Judaism not as it was exactly but how they hoped it might more attractively appear in the form of a refurbished tradition infused by moral sensitivity and rationalism and better meeting the challenges of contemporary Jewish life. Ultimately their own historical reconstructions of Judaism were meant to preserve their ancestral faith and praxis from the extreme reproaches of Jewish and Christian critics alike. It was probably too much of a burden to place on historicism, "the faith of fallen Jews," as one twentieth-century historian once proclaimed.[35] In any case, Fuenn continued to write history, publishing an unfinished but boldly conceived universal history of the Jews in flowery maskilic Hebrew, and later a precious history of his own Jewish community in Vilna. Sadly, despite his distinguished career as writer, educator, and communal reformer, his thoughtful reflections on McCaul's recriminations and the comparative history written in his youth were completely forgotten. Nevertheless, the Hebrew manuscript that remains in Jerusalem unveils a substantial project of self-reflection as well as a gripping examination of the larger culture with which nineteenth-century Jews engaged.

Raphael Kassin

It is a testimony to the incredible reach and financial resources of the London Society for the Promotion of Christianity Amongst the Jews that numerous copies of Alexander McCaul's *Netivot olam* circulated throughout the Middle East in such cities as Istanbul, Izmir, Salonika, and Aleppo. Besides the Hebrew edition, the work was even translated into Judeo-Persian and became a conspicuous part of the new publications emerging from Christian missionary groups active in the area from the beginning of the nineteenth century and far beyond.[36]

Thanks to the extensive research of Leah Bornstein-Makovetsky, among others, we know a great deal about the operations of the Protestant missionary societies originating not only from England but from Scotland and the United States as well, which focused on potential converts among the Jewish and Muslim populations. She has meticulously documented the vast distribution of Hebrew and Ladino Bibles among Jews, the varied attempts to establish contacts between missionaries and Jews through the establishment of mission houses, classes of instruction for mothers, and preaching in hospitals and even in Jewish schools when possible. She has also carefully studied the firm opposition of rabbinic leaders to the blandishments of the missionaries, both material and spiritual. Almost without exception, the rabbis forbade any intellectual or social contact with the missionaries and displayed little knowledge of Christian doctrine other than to see its menacing nature challenging the viability of the Jewish faith. The missionaries, in fully documenting even the slightest of their accomplishments, claimed modest successes in distributing their Bibles, educating poor Jews and especially women, and offering medical support to the needy. But apart from a meager handful of individuals who converted to Christianity, the Jewish community strongly resisted the missionary efforts and no mass conversion ever took place.[37]

The rabbinic effort to address the missionary threat was almost exclusively limited to decrees discouraging or even prohibiting any social and educational interactions on the part of the Christian proselytizers with their Jewish constituencies. In most cases, this was sufficient to keep Jews at a distance from the missionaries. But there were instances where persistent Christian clergy, especially former Jews intimately familiar with Jewish traditions, were able to penetrate Jewish social space, particularly through their publications and medical services. The most important rabbinic figure Ḥayyim Palachi of Izmir was consistently critical of any formal or informal contact with missionaries despite the fact that he had welcomed Moses Margoliouth into his home and even presented him with two of his publications, as we have seen. He was also indifferent to understanding Christianity's sacred texts and cultural practices. This pattern of response was replicated by his other rabbinic colleagues.[38]

Given this dominant rabbinic consensus, the reaction of Raphael ben Elijah Kassin (1818–71) to the Christian missionaries is particularly notable for its radical divergence from the norm. Moreover, Kassin's cultural and political activities reveal a remarkably complex individual who could hardly conform to the cultural practices of his contemporaries. With the aid of Yaron Harel's previous studies of this enigmatic rabbi, I offer a broad overview of his life and thought, leading to a consideration of his highly interesting works written explicitly against Alexander McCaul's polemic.[39]

Kassin was born in Aleppo, the son of a rabbi who enjoyed the pursuit of a rigorous education in rabbinic texts. By the time his father died in 1830, he had composed three works of halachic exegesis and homiletics. He soon left Aleppo and wandered through Persia, engaging in polemics with Christian and Muslim scholars, including an appearance before the shah himself, as he himself recorded. As Harel argues, Kassin's relative isolation from centers of Torah learning and a seeming exposure to anti-Christian polemics emanating from the Shiite religious leadership most likely stimulated him to engage in intra-religious dialogue and debate. In this he was virtually unique, as we have said, among his rabbinic contemporaries.[40]

By 1846, Kassin was in Baghdad and had become embroiled in a struggle between the supporters of the *nasi* (head of Baghdad Jewry) and his chief rival Obadiah Abraham Ha-Levi, head of the rabbinical court of the Jewish community. Kassin eventually sided with the adversaries of the *nasi* and solicited leverage and support from the sultan in Istanbul for his own appointment to the new office of *ḥakham bashi* (chief rabbi) in Baghdad. With the backing of several wealthy Jews and the governmental authorities, Kassin won the appointment and returned to Baghdad in 1848 assuming his highly prized position. Acting in a domineering and arrogant manner, however, he alienated certain groups who eventually succeeded in removing him from office in 1851. From that time until 1862, he traveled to other cities, visiting Rabbi Palachi in Izmir before setting out for an extended journey to parts of Europe, Persia, and India.

Kassin's specific whereabouts during this time are unknown. Harel speculated that he was in France and possibly passed through England and Germany as well, where he plausibly might have sought out leaders of Reform Judaism. In 1862, however, he appears to have returned to Aleppo where he was named rabbi of a rival congregation challenging the authority of the *ḥakham bashi* of the city, Mordechai Ḥayyim Labaton. According to two documents written by the British acting consul at Aleppo to the British ambassador in Constantinople and discovered by Yaron Harel in the Public Records Office in London, Kassin had created a reform congregation and made himself its rabbi. The consul wrote:

> I have the honor to report to your Excellency that some excitement has been caused of late among the Jewish Community of this city by the preaching of one of the principal Rabbins who has declared himself a Religious Reformer, has denounced the precepts of the Talmud and undertaken to form a new sect of Reformed Jews.
>
> This Rabbin, who has travelled much in Europe in India and Persia, and is well versed in the Theological Literature of the Jews, has for some time been secretly expounding his views, and it is said made many converts to his cause. He has now declared his object openly and addressed letters to the Chief Rabbin of Allepo [Labaton] expatiating on the fallacies of the Talmud and arguing that its precepts are opposed to the Law of Moses, and has written to the

Christian Bishops and Mussulman Sheikhs demanding their support.[41]

The acting consul appended a public document written in Hebrew and translated into English that circulated among the Jews, apparently signed by many who bound themselves to recognizing the authority of this newly minted Reform rabbi. Labaton tried to discipline these rebels who were challenging his authority but to no avail. About to witness a riot the dissidents had seemingly fomented, Jawdat Pasha, the Muslim authority of Aleppo, intervened, ordering the rabbi to abstain from preaching and from soliciting converts to his cause. The matter was temporarily hushed up but the consul remained uncertain whether Kassin's plan would still be implemented. He was also uncertain whether the rabbi had acted out of personal ambition or out of religious conviction. The circular bound its signatories to give full rabbinic powers to Kassin, essentially undermining the authority of the *hakham bashi*. Kassin was also to be paid handsomely with a home and two servants, a lifestyle he had previously enjoyed when serving as *hakham bashi* in Baghdad, and was to be protected from any risks whether inflicted by the "Israelites" or other communities.[42]

The aftermath of this communal schism is unknown. Kassin seems to have disappeared again, perhaps silenced by the local authority and thus unable to continue his rabbinic tasks. There were also rumors of his mental illness apparently perpetuated by his adversaries. He died in 1871 with the memory of his unique religious community also buried with him.

Recently, Harel has discovered a collection of letters written by Kassin to various Jewish communities during his travels in Persia in the 1840s. The letters provide evidence that he spent several years in Palestine and functioned as an emissary while visiting various communities. In Isfahan, he engaged in debates with Muslims and Christians, claiming that he not only persuaded recent converts to return to their ancestral faith but encouraged members of other faiths to adopt Judaism. In Mashad, he comforted Jews forced to convert to Islam and fought to have them recognized as Jews by his coreligionists in Isfahan. Harel's work on these letters is still in progress.[43]

The portrait of Kassin emerging from this research is that of a highly unusual and colorful personality clearly preoccupied with theological issues such as comparative religion and religious reform, issues totally alien to his rabbinic contemporaries. I am in no position to solve the enigmas that remain regarding Kassin's rabbinic career. In now turning to his two polemical works against McCaul, which are based on a longer work never published and no longer extant, I wish to consider his responses to the missionary from the perspective of his lifelong interests. I also want to at least raise the question of how his earlier religious polemics with Christianity were related, if at all, to his later reformist tendencies. Any reader of McCaul's assault on rabbinic Judaism could not fail to have noticed the words of the acting consul in describing Kassin: "He has now declared his object openly and addressed letters to the Chief Rabbi of Allepo expatiating on the fallacies of the Talmud and arguing that its precepts are opposed to the Law of Moses." We are further told that Kassin then wrote to Christian and Muslim leaders "demanding their support."[44] McCaul, of course, had articulated the very same position in challenging the Talmud as a fallacious work opposed to Mosaic law. In seeking the support of these religious leaders, was Kassin expecting their approval of the fact that he had ultimately been convinced of the missionary's argument as well? As we shall soon see, Kassin had already established a causal relationship between McCaul's attack on the Talmud, the inability of Jewish religious leaders to answer him, and the birth of Reform Judaism. Had Kassin revisited this same causal relationship through his own life experience?

Kassin's Polemical Works

Kassin published two polemical books against Christianity in general and against McCaul's *Netivot olam* (without ever referring to the author by name) in particular: *Sefer derekh ha-ḥayyim* (The book of the path of life) in 1848 and *Sefer likkutei amrim* (The book of collections of sayings) in 1855. The first appeared in Hebrew; the second in Hebrew with a Ladino translation. Both claimed to be based on a much larger work called *Sefer derekh emet* (The book of the path of truth), which Kassin had hoped to publish but was unable to due to his fear that it might be offensive to the authorities and because of financial constraints. Kassin never adequately explained why the larger book had appeared too provocative in its arguments against Christianity, while the more modest books that were published were less offensive. In any case, he often referred to his larger polemic in a self-congratulatory manner, but also lamented the fact that it was not accessible and hoped that it might still see the light of day.

At first glance, Kassin's works appear considerably less sophisticated and learned regarding the Christian faith, ancient and modern history, and the history of the Jewish-Christian conflict than those of either of the two eastern European authors we have considered up to now. Kassin ignored many of the more detailed subjects and textual discussions raised in McCaul's large composition, although it is possible he did consider them in his larger manuscript but left them out of these shorter works. He certainly knew his New Testament and offered textual references to substantiate his points. But he had apparently read little else on Christianity nor did he refer to the tortuous history of persecution and irrationality that provided a constant theme to Levinsohn and Fuenn. In fact, Kassin, as best I can tell, did not consult any books in Western languages but relied exclusively on Hebrew sources. He cited such authors as Joseph Albo, Isaac Abravanel, Tobias Cohen, and especially Ibn Verga's *Shevet Yehudah*, using the latter especially as a source of Christian thinking and social habits.[45] His most contemporary sources were Pinḥas Hurwitz's *Sefer ha-brit* of which he used an unspecified Hebrew edition, and Israel Moses Ḥazan's *Kinat Zion* (Amsterdam, 1846). In the first case, he took exception to several of Hurwitz's arguments, especially his inadequate defense of the Oral Law. As I have pointed out elsewhere, Kassin oddly assumed that Hurwitz had composed a defense of Judaism against Christianity, which, of course, was not his intention at all and thus his criticism seems unfair and misplaced.[46] In the second case, Kassin used the recently published Ḥazan book against Reform Judaism and its approach to the Oral Law in the aftermath of a Reform Jewish synod in Braunschweig.[47] We shall return again to this source below.

Kassin's lack of sophistication and erudition in comparison to his two learned contemporaries, however, is not necessarily a proper measure of his originality. He was writing, in the first place, within a Muslim cultural context where access to European works, with the possible exception of missionary publications, was severely limited. Second, despite his often repetitive style and his rather incomplete and superficial treatment of McCaul's arguments, Kassin did approach the Jewish-Christian divide from a relatively fresh point of view. He may have been less learned than other authors we have considered, but he was not necessarily less insightful. And it is important to stress again that against the background of Jewish life in the Ottoman Empire and Persia, Kassin's discussion of Judaism and Christianity was rare and even unique.

Harel has noted that both of Kassin's books were written in dialogical form perhaps loosely imitating the framing of Judah ha-Levi's *Sefer Kuzari*. This is certainly possible, although by the nineteenth century Kassin could have found other dialogues such as those of the sixteenth-century writer Samuel Usque or the eighteenth-century David Nieto as models. In the instance of *Sefer derekh ha-ḥayyim*, Kassin tried to construct a conversation between three merchants from Babylonia who went to the desert to encounter a mysterious shepherd unaffiliated with any religion and willing to listen to their arguments against each other. The three merchants are named Jacob the Jew, who is dressed in black; Matthew the Christian, dressed in green; and Abad al Nabi, a Muslim.[48] The Muslim remains silent throughout the book with the conversation about the three religions focusing exclusively on Judaism and Christianity and primarily directed to McCaul's arguments. Perhaps Kassin had initially planned to offer a discussion of the three religions but ultimately decided a discussion of Islam was unlikely to pass muster with the authorities. In *Sefer likkutei amrim*, only Jacob and Matthew remain, indicating that Kassin's only aim at that point was to address Christian polemics with Judaism.

In *Sefer derekh ha-ḥayyim*, Kassin allows both speakers to articulate their understanding of their own faiths, to challenge the position of the other, and even to raise doubt about each's own convictions in the midst of their exchanges. Of course, Jacob the Jew, with the support of his mentor Moses, who also entered the narrative, ultimately has the upper hand in the debate and generally refutes the various arguments of *Netivot olam*. Nevertheless, Kassin gives Matthew the Christian an honest hearing and a fair depiction of the essentials of his faith.

After Jacob has concluded his opening words about the nature of the Jewish faith, the shepherd turns to Matthew to declare: "I believe in Moses and the Torah more than Jacob does."[49] Jacob challenges this assessment, questioning how the original Mosaic religion can survive the accretions of the Christian church and whether Jesus was the true messiah and the son of God. Matthew immediately takes to the offensive, challenging the very validity of Judaism and pointing out the low status of Jews among the nations, ignored by nearly all peoples and despised by many. Jacob retorts that both Christianity and Islam recognize the foundations of his faith. Matthew will have none of this. If indeed Jews were validated by the testimonies of the two other religions, how then could Jacob deem him a fool for believing in the Christian faith while still relying on his testimony to validate his own? Matthew presses further, challenging Jacob to demonstrate the integrity of Judaism based on miracles performed on behalf of Moses and the Israelites that he himself had never witnessed with his own eyes.[50]

Jacob can only answer that the Mosaic truths are not based on personal experience but on a tradition faithfully passed on by his ancestors and un-altered from generation to generation. To this Matthew confidently responds: "For we also have a heart [mind] like you and are not inferior to you in [possessing an authentic] tradition. We likewise have a tradition in our hands from our forefathers and the fathers of our fathers from the mouth of one person to the next from the first generation of the time of Jesus Christ." If this was the case, Matthew adds, how can Jacob deny that tradition of his Christian ancestors? If his own tradition is true, Christians also have one that is equally compelling and their claims are as legitimate as those of the Jews.[51] Jacob remains undaunted, acknowledging that all faith is based on tradition since no one can testify to something his eyes have not seen. With respect to Judaism, "everything goes according to the tradition but we certainly need to combine the tradition with the judgment of reason which can determine whether the tradition is true or not."[52] Based on these rational calculations, Jacob maintains, Jews have evaluated their own tradition and its founders in such a manner as to find them authentic from Joshua to Haggai, Ezra, and to the Men of the Great Assembly, the precursors of the rabbis. To this Matthew simply claims that Christians too have relied on biblical passages in the Old Testament to validate the new while relying on their own faithful witnesses such as Matthew, Luke, Mark, John, Peter, Paul, and others.[53]

Having reached an impasse over whose religious claims are ultimately valid, Jacob has no other recourse, it seems, but to refer to one Raphael Kassin, an author in his day who has written the aforementioned work *Sefer derekh emet* in which he maintained that the New Testament was neither divine nor true. This exhaustive book, still in manuscript, conclusively dem-onstrates the Jewish argument against Christianity, he claims. But Matthew parries with the following remark: "And one scholar [Alexander McCaul] from among the Christian scholars in our time was infected with a spirit of zeal for the messianic religion and wrote a book against your oral Torah and he destroyed its foundations and undermined its roots, and obliterated it with clear arguments that it wasn't divine but humanly and falsely created. He called the book *Netivot olam*, published it and disseminated it in all the land . . . not in the matter you speak in secret that you have a book *Derekh emet* in manuscript which no one has seen." Jacob acknowledges his frustra-tion that the latter book has not yet been published, lacking governmental permission and funding. Matthew again confidently responds that when the mysterious book will be printed, he would be willing to examine its arguments carefully and fittingly respond "because we also have a heart [mind] like you and we have scholars and knowledgeable people and in the place where a mistake or error [occurs] . . . we will testify to its appearance."[54]

I have summarized an essential part of this long exchange between Jew and Christian to illustrate a basic premise apparently undergirding Kassin's entire polemic against Christianity and McCaul: that despite the ultimate validity of rabbinic Judaism for Jews, the Christians also have a self-validating faith based on a tradition as authentic to them as the one embraced by the Jews. In a book intended to demolish the rival claims of Christianity over Judaism and to defend the integrity of the rabbis, Kassin appeared also to acknowledge the other side, to imply quite unexpectedly the parity of both religious traditions and the legitimacy of both to their followers, whatever the claims and counterclaims of their religious adversaries.

I offer one final example of Kassin's acknowledgment that Christianity was a positive faith for its followers. The passage to which I refer is found in a section toward the end of *Sefer derekh ha-ḥayyim* entitled "Sha'ar ha-tokhahot" (The gate of rebukes). It opens strangely with an expression of sympathy on the part of Kassin toward his religious adversary McCaul. He admits that he felt pain for "his neighbor" who followed the wrong moral path and the wrong beliefs and could not be rescued. One raised in a certain religion always thinks he is right while others are wrong; such was the fate of the author of *Netivot olam* who followed the wrong path even though he desired to help Israel.[55]

Immediately following this sentiment, Kassin shares with the reader a remnant of the dream Matthew the Christian had experienced. He was alone in a field when he met a man ready to fulfill his request to know the meaning of life. He ascended a mountain to meet a modest figure at its peak named Ben ha-adam (the son of man, Jesus). Matthew explained that his debate with a Jew and a Muslim had been suspended before the shepherd in the desert, since all the proper answers remained inaccessible in Kassin's unpublished manuscript. Matthew's divine interlocutor asked him of the whereabouts of Jacob. He was told that he had gone to an orchard to seek the path of life from Moses ben Amram, his mentor. Seemingly here as well, the Christian and the Jew, both searchers for the truth, were on parallel tracks.[56]

Kassin acknowledges that Jacob, his Jewish spokesman, was incapable of bearing "the burden" on his own and sought out his mentor Moses. However, Ben ha-adam will lighten the load for Matthew for which he is grateful.

Kassin even inserts the appropriate New Testament verses, especially Matthew 11:28: "Come to me, all who are weary and burdened, and I will give you rest." What follows is a capsule summary of Christian teaching, embellished throughout with ample references to specific verses from the Gospels. God sent Jesus his son to the world with a new covenant; his death was an atonement for sinners; and he rose from the dead to heaven and would return for his second coming. The primary commandment for Christians is to love God with all their heart and also to love their neighbors, particularly their enemies. Matthew also learns about the proper treatment of his wife and others close to him. He is admonished to be righteous both in his heart and in his public appearance. He is encouraged to pray sincerely, to not show off, and to control his passions. Matthew is inspired by Jesus's presence and message; he returns to the city to tell about the divine revelation he has witnessed, how he met Jesus face-to-face, and how he has received a New Testament, easier to bear than the Old.[57]

At this point in Kassin's narrative, prior to the fortification Jacob will receive through the words of Moses that conclude the work, the Jew appears vulnerable and ill-equipped to respond to his Christian rival. Kassin indicates that Jacob is met with hostility and even mocked for being unable to experience the glow of the divine presence that had come to Matthew. In returning to the desert, Jacob reunites with his mentor Moses and confides in him his own insecurity when witnessing Matthew's spiritual contentment while lacking his own.[58] No doubt Kassin has established this low point in Jacob's spiritual life to lift his spirit dramatically and to provide the culminating message about the essence of Jewish faith and self-realization through the commandments. We will consider this message including his direct responses to McCaul immediately below. Suffice it to underscore here Kassin's fair and even appreciative exposition of Christian faith, encapsulated in a manner to which no Christian would object. Note as well the respectful tone in which it was presented. While ultimately Kassin articulated a different path for the Jew, he never denied the Christian articles of faith for Christians, at least in this work. Finally, it is somewhat ironic that the way to Jewish self-discovery in Kassin's narrative is through the Christian. Jacob is inspired to recover his own faith in Judaism by way of the example of the Christian, secure and content in his own faith. Jacob, as we have seen, is truly jealous of his Christian rival for the inner peace he himself lacked and is spurred on to find his own. For Kassin, polemic and dialogue with the other offered the rich opportunity to locate the inner core of his own identity.

The Critique of McCaul

Jacob, of course, eventually recovers his faith and a confidence in his ancestral tradition through the intervention of Moses in the desert. While initially envious of the joy Matthew had gained through his meeting with Jesus, Jacob accepts the enormous burden imposed on him through the commandments and acknowledges the Jewish truth of immortal life. Moses offers the clinching argument in favor of the maintenance of Jewish life: It is the weight of the commandments imposed on the Jew that makes his religious experience a meaningful one, and the lack of this burden is the primary deficiency of Christianity. Being a Jew means being a faithful servant carrying out divine ordinances. One who lessened the load of the commandments as Jesus had done in Matthew 11:28, as quoted above, was teaching a false religion. The New Testament was never a divine law code prescribing positive and negative commandments, civil and criminal law necessary for the preservation of society. In its emphasis on the diminution of divine obligations, it had removed the most essential dimension of Jewish religious and spiritual life.[59]

The obligations that still remained, in Christian teaching, however, had not lightened the burden but enhanced it in an unrealistic and cruel manner. It was the utopian ethics of Jesus and his followers that irked Moses in creating a standard impossible to reach and therefore painfully unacceptable. For Moses, the ideal of loving one's enemy as opposed to simply tolerating or respecting him was beyond human grasp. It was similarly impossible to expect a grieved party to turn the other cheek. Loving one's neighbor, as the injunction in Leviticus declared, made sense in the real world only in the negative formulation of Hillel ("Do not do unto others what you would not have them do to you"). Christian expectations for priests regarding sexual abstinence enhanced sexual promiscuity rather than curbing it. Kassin was quick to point out his own observations about Christians living in contemporary Muslim society who were prone to visiting prostitutes or simply converting to Islam to ultimately relieve their sexual drives. He added how Christian men often slept with women during their menstrual cycle or when they were pregnant, thus incurring disease from impure blood "as the naturalists explain." The fate of barren Christian women unable to divorce had led to a miserable sexual life for both partners in an unhappy relationship. This was the ultimate irony: the alleged compassion of the Christian messiah who pledged to lighten the load of his followers had in the end created greater misery, that of a kind of eternal servitude stemming from a bad human relationship in marriage.[60]

Both in this final discourse of Moses and throughout *Sefer derekh ha-ḥayyim*, Kassin never forgot the major arguments of Alexander McCaul, the ultimate target of his polemic against Christianity. Kassin was less interested in most of McCaul's detailed engagements with specific rabbinic texts and rituals and passed over them in silence. What was ultimately significant to him were three themes that preoccupied him in this 1848 book: McCaul's initial hopes and later disappointments with the emergence of Reform Judaism in Germany and Great Britain; his bitter denunciation of the rabbis in their treatment of the poor and needy, as well as the non-Jew; and especially the rabbis' disrespect of and misbehavior toward women.

Kassin's comments on reform emerged from an earlier discourse of Moses on the significance of the Oral Law for Jews, clearly a general rejoinder to the thrust of McCaul's entire critique of rabbinic Judaism. At one point, Moses explicitly refers to the words of *Netivot olam* denouncing the Oral Law and to the larger response Kassin had written that still remained unpublished. He also mentions a recent work he had seen by Israel Moses Ḥazan called *Kinat Ẓion*, a collection of rabbinic opinions written in reaction to a Reform Jewish synod held in Braunschweig, already mentioned above. Ḥazan, originally stemming from Izmir and Jerusalem, had served for several years as a rabbinical emissary in western Europe, where he first noticed and reacted negatively to the emergence of Reform Judaism. He subsequently served congregations in Rome, Corfu, and Alexandria before returning to Palestine in 1862, the same year that Kassin had attempted to establish his Reform congregation in Aleppo. Ḥazan wrote several other works especially in support of the study of secular subjects by Jewish students. He was also not a foe of Christianity, having established a social relationship with the pope while serving as the Roman rabbi.[61]

It would seem, that given Ḥazan's cultural connections to Kassin's own region, his book was noticed by the latter. Perhaps in some sense, Kassin somehow identified with this local rabbi whose worldview had been shaped by his profound exposure to European Judaism. Be that as it may, Ḥazan's book triggered a response from Kassin directed not to Reform Jews per se but to McCaul. For Kassin, it was plausible to assume that there was a causal relationship between the appearance of the Hebrew version of McCaul's polemical work in 1839 and the Braunschweig conference held only five years later in 1844. Kassin related that the book defiantly attacked the Talmud and unjustly excoriated the rabbis for their treatment of the poor and women. Despite the severity of McCaul's allegations, no rabbis responded to him and their silence created the conditions by which Reform Judaism emerged. If the rabbis had responded properly in the first place, negating all of McCaul's false charges, the reformers would not have acted as they did. Yet the rabbis kept quiet perhaps because they were indifferent to their own religion, or because they could not offer a sufficient defense, or they deemed the book unworthy of any response.[62]

Kassin's observation about how McCaul had precipitated the crisis of Reform Judaism was one articulated by the missionary himself who took pride, as we have earlier seen, in the initial appearance of reform in Germany and especially in London, as a first step in undermining the grip of the rabbis over contemporary Jews. Kassin even cited the following from *Netivot olam*: "Every reflecting man must be staggered by the fact, that a strong case has been made out against the oral law—that, contemporaneously with the publication of these papers, strong symptoms of dissatisfaction with certain parts of Judaism have been manifested in one of the most respectable synagogues in London—and yet, that nothing has appeared, either in shape of defense or explanation."[63]

Kassin was certainly right in noticing a lack of serious response from the rabbis to McCaul's provocative charges. London Jews seemed generally incapable of mounting a strong counterargument, and despite Moses Montefiore's initial intervention, the major responses to McCaul from eastern European maskilim remained unpublished for many years or were never published at all.[64] How ironic it seems that Kassin ultimately appeared to adopt "the leprosy of Reform Judaism" later in his life and even appeared to critique the Talmud in a fashion reminiscent of McCaul himself, as suggested by the report of the English acting consul. One wonders how Kassin reconciled these apparently contradictory postures in justifying his own rabbinic authority in Aleppo in 1862.

Regarding McCaul's accusations that the rabbis mistreated the poor and women, Kassin had much to say, mostly about the plight of women. Kassin took note of the fact that McCaul adopted a path "of dressing oneself in the zeal for women," in arguing against McCaul's reading of the case of Ruth, who allegedly offered legal testimony in contradistinction to the prevailing rabbinic view denying female testimony. He also reacted to McCaul's accusation that the rabbis treated women as animals, that they denied their being counted in a religious quorum, and that men recited prayers that denigrate women. Women, argued Kassin, were permitted to pray especially at meal-time, although he would not contradict the other charges of the missionary. Women were indeed inferior to men and were therefore not required to perform all the commandments expected of men. While their hearts were good, he contended, they were still incapable of performing God's work as men were; their inequality before the law was thus part of the wisdom of the Creator. They had no capacity to write books, to engage in crafts or in the military.[65]

Kassin strongly denied that rabbinic legislation oppressed poor people and imposed on them decrees they could not tolerate. Ordinary Jews judged the laws of the rabbis as reasonable, and they were received willingly and lovingly. The specific legislation discussed by McCaul regarding the washing of the hands, or the laws of *eruvim*, the separation of the public and private spheres regarding Sabbath observance, were not new inventions and were even observed by Jesus and his disciples. Ordinary people, in the eyes of rabbinic Judaism, were neither fools nor wild boors but "a wise and discerning" people (Deut. 4:6) hardly deceived by their adherence to the Oral Law.[66]

In the final part of *Sefer derekh ha-ḥayyim* Kassin shifted from defending rabbinic Judaism to attacking the social practices of Christianity. Indeed, the primary argument against Christianity for Kassin was not ideological or theological but social. Kassin returned to his twin claims that Christian mores were both unrealistic and impossible to attain and, at the same time, placed so few burdens upon the believer that they encouraged laxity and sin. He again excoriated the false piety of denying a sexual life, of insisting on monogamy over bigamy (this, despite the enactment of the medieval rabbi Rabbenu Gershom against the latter), and of prohibiting divorce even in the instance when the union proved untenable to both husband and wife.[67]

Kassin ended his social critique of Christianity by emphasizing the role of public prayer, ritual, and charity in creating a religious community, qualities particularly self-evident in Judaism but sorely lacking in Christianity. Without the norms of communal legislation, individuals became lax in prayer and in social responsibilities. In this respect, Jesus's favoring of private prayer and the interiority of religious actions was to the detriment of the social welfare of the community. The moralists in both religions had emphasized the privacy of giving charity but public recognition was a primary motivating factor that the rabbis had emphasized in the shaping of normative Judaism. In the end, Judaism displayed a keen sense of social conscience and communal responsibility to a greater extent than Christianity ever had.[68]

Sefer likkutei amrim

Kassin's second polemic against McCaul, *Sefer likkutei amrim*, was published eight years later in Izmir in Hebrew with an accompanying Ladino translation. This shorter work certainly overlapped with Kassin's first book in some of its themes and concerns but also displayed several new features. It carried with it an approbation of the aforementioned Ḥayyim Palachi, an unusual gesture on the part of the rabbi who had consistently demanded a total separation between Jews and Christian missionaries and had refused to engage with them. Even more confusing was the later testimony of the American missionary Homer Morgan, who asked Palachi whether he could obtain a copy of Kassin's work; Palachi denied knowing of the book's whereabouts.[69]

In the introduction to this work, Kassin recounted his effort to respond to McCaul's polemic through the larger but still unpublished *Sefer derekh emet*. He described *Sefer derekh ha-ḥayyim* as the small book he published instead, dealing especially with the subject of women. He lamented being unable to publish the larger work and the limited circulation of the smaller one. Encouraged by friends to continue his polemic in a new dialogue, the result was this modest composition. The work was divided into three parts called "Derekh ha-sekhel" (The way of reason); "Divre nevi'im" (The words of the prophets); and "Ateret ḥakhamim" (The crown of the wise).[70]

In the first part Kassin continued the dialogue between Jacob and Matthew but this time focused on theological differences between the two religions. For the most part Matthew is put on the defensive, attempting to explain the allegedly irrational nature of the Trinity, the virgin birth, the materiality of God, and the incomprehensible nature of the miracles Jesus performed. Matthew tries to defend the rationality of these Christian dogmas, even citing Maimonides's *Guide for the Perplexed*, 1:75, argument 4, that our knowledge of a thing like the Trinity does not involve its actual existence. Jacob continues to press Matthew on these matters, concluding rather conventionally that Judaism allowed the believer to imagine a rational basis for one's beliefs; in Christianity, however, one is required to suspend reason altogether. The second part also follows familiar lines of argument pointing out certain fallacies and inconsistences in various New Testament verses regarding Immaculate Conception, the genealogy of Jesus, the private nature of Christian revelation, and more.[71]

In the third part, Kassin makes the startling admission that the rabbis actually viewed Jesus as one who had broken from their monotheistic faith and that they were responsible for his crucifixion. The decision to kill Jesus was done carefully and thoughtfully, Kassin explains. He was punished publicly because he saw himself as the son of God, elevated even above the status of the Messiah. This situation had no analogy in the evil men who threatened Jeremiah's life, as McCaul had claimed. The rabbis were attentive to the needs of the poor and women, as he had already argued, and they never demanded special honor for themselves by virtue of the title of rabbi. This did not mean, as McCaul had claimed, that they expected to be honored by their students more than the latter's parents. He also challenged McCaul's claim that the rabbis usurped the authority of the priests and Levites in interpreting the law.[72]

Kassin concluded his book with the following plea to his Christian adversaries: "We do not require you to be like us and observe the six hundred and thirteen commandments written in the Torah of Moses in order to enjoy immortal life. Rather it is sufficient for you to separate yourself from this evil and rotten faith and observe the seven Noahide commandments which you should observe in any case. But now observe them because of God's command through the hand of Moses and not from another."[73]

Kassin's conclusion was far less conciliatory and respectful of Christianity and its fundamental beliefs. His portrait of the irrationality of Christianity and its very challenge to the purity of Jewish monotheism stood in sharp contrast to Matthew's speeches in *Sefer derekh ha-ḥayyim* on the warmth and beauty Jesus conveyed to his followers. It is difficult to reconcile the difference in tone of the two works and even more difficult to respond conclusively to the question posed at the beginning of this discussion: Was there a connection between the views expressed in Kassin's polemical works against McCaul and Christianity and his later evolution as a Reform rabbi?

We have seen how Kassin himself had connected the dissemination of McCaul's attack on Judaism and the utter silence of the rabbis in responding to him with the genesis of Reform Judaism in Europe as the alleged result. But this was hardly a positive development for him; it was rather a crisis for rabbinic Judaism. That he responded so rapidly to the Christian missionary and wrote within a Muslim culture was truly exceptional; indeed, his response of 1848 appeared to be one of the earliest responses to McCaul in general.[74] As we have seen in our discussion of *Sefer derekh ha-ḥayyim*, intertwined with his repudiation of certain parts of McCaul's arguments was an apparent respect and appreciation for the Christian faith. This sentiment, however, all but vanished in *Sefer likkutei amrim*. Kassin displayed no respect for Christianity as a collective faith that he claimed should be repudiated by its followers; as individuals, former Christians could still continue to live a moral life without a religious affiliation with either Judaism or Christianity. In 1855, he appeared to fully renounce McCaul and his claims that Protestant Christianity was in fact the true Jewish faith. Only seven years later, however, back from his European travels, he had seemingly articulated McCaul's argument regarding the illegitimacy of the Oral Law without actually abdicating his Jewish faith. I cannot hazard a reasonable guess on the consistency of his views on Judaism and Christianity and on his evolution as a rabbi. Suffice it to say that Kassin's engagement with McCaul represented a special chapter in the history of Jewish-Christian entanglements and Jewish self-fashioning in nineteenth-century Europe and the Middle East.

Afterword

In 1862, a Presbyterian missionary, the Reverend Golak Nath, stationed in India, wrote the following lines based on his personal and professional experience: "The social position of a missionary, his intellectual and spiritual attainments, his highly civilized ideas, and his cultivated, refined feelings, must place him so far above his converts, generally, that there can scarcely be any fellow-feeling between them. A missionary would hardly find any loveliness in the character of his converts, to excite much kind feeling towards them. They are necessarily objects of his compassion and pity, but hardly worthy of his friendship, or capable of communion with him, except on religious subjects."[1]

Nath's remarks appear to be not only a declaration of cultural superiority or cultural imperialism but also an honest admission of the limits of the missionary's personal relationship with his subjects, his cultural alienation from them, and his inability to build fully a satisfying human relationship with them. No doubt Nath openly expressed his sense of privilege in being a European with intellectual and spiritual attainments and possessing "his highly civilized ideas" in contradistinction to the inferior and primitive ones of his converts. But perhaps he was signaling more his own disadvantage, his own limitation, in not connecting with them as a Christian should. Seeing them as "objects of his compassion and pity" was hardly the same as being their friend, expressing true Christian love and affection for them, and communing with them beyond his professional duties of focusing "on religious subjects."

How might Nath's perceptions of his relationship with the converts and the potential converts under his charge apply to McCaul's relationship with his Jewish subjects? What actually did McCaul feel toward the Jews he encountered both in Warsaw and London and toward the small number of converts he successfully led to the baptismal font? Was it an authentic expression of true Christian love or merely a posture dictated primarily by a sense of professional duty? And what about the sentiments of his Christian critics

Oxlee and Tonna, who seemingly professed an appreciation of Jews and Judaism even beyond that of McCaul in not insisting that Jews abandon their
ancestral norms and rituals? The same question might be posed about the
converts themselves. Did they perceive their conversion as a new opportunity
to embrace their fellow Christians with an intimacy previously denied them
in their former Jewish state of "unbelief"? Could they, at the same time,
sustain close relationships with relatives and friends they had left behind and
who had been a significant part of their earlier Jewish lives? Could a Christian
Jew still find common ground with his former coreligionists, somehow separating his newly found faith from his ethnic and cultural bonds with them?
Finally, could Jews in virtual combat with their Christian adversary be positively transformed or at least minimally affected by their intense encounter
with him and his ideas? Could they come away from this confrontation with
some appreciation of his position, his honest expressions of approval for
them, and even some admission that at least some of his criticisms were not
totally off the mark? Jews could not be expected to warmly embrace their
fierce Christian critic, but could they at least respect his position, his extraordinary effort to master their languages and literature, and to defend them
during the infamous blood libel of 1840? In familiarizing themselves with the
diversity of Christian approaches to Judaism and Jews, could they learn to
recognize that some Christians were more worthy of their respect than others,
and that it was even possible to build meaningful friendships with those few
who genuinely cared for their welfare?

Based on the evidence presented in this book, it might be possible to
offer some tentative answers to such questions regarding the quality of the
relationships forged by the principals of this encounter among themselves and
toward other Jews, Christians, and converts. Whether McCaul truly loved the
Jews with whom he interacted is difficult to say, even if he and his daughter
Elizabeth Finn explicitly declared this love. But what is clear is the special
relationship he developed with them in comparison with that acknowledged
by Nath regarding his Indian constituency. The Jews McCaul met engaged
the missionary from a position of greater security and pride in the literary
traditions in which they had been educated. They even displayed a clear sense
of ethical, religious, and cultural superiority when confronting McCaul and
his message. Their dialogue with him was hardly novel in their eyes but had
been shaped by hundreds of years of previous Jewish-Christian debates and a
complex relationship of subjugation and discrimination that long preceded
this present contact situation with the London Society and its distinguished

representative. At the very least, McCaul immediately perceived their formidable strengths and had to fortify himself with serious Jewish learning in order to enter into a dialogue with them. His book was impressive from the perspective of the history of Christian Hebraism but hardly passed muster with vaunted Jewish intellectuals such as Levinsohn and Fuenn who found his knowledge of rabbinics and history wanting. Such a challenge may not have elicited a deep love for his subjects, although it may have engendered a sincere respect and admiration for their high level of literacy and their intellectual accomplishments.

Margoliouth had the advantage over McCaul of familiarity and intimacy with the Jewish tradition when approaching his former coreligionists. But it is difficult to say how far this could take him when Jews discovered he was in fact an Anglican cleric. Were his fantasies of a kind of Jewish-Christian rapprochement shared by any of the Jews who encountered him during his journeys in the Middle East? He had gained entrance into synagogues and Jewish homes, if his own testimony is to be believed, but did he actually convert anyone with his intellectual arguments and did they sincerely feel a kinship to him as a former Jew who spoke their language? Margoliouth appears to have been a curiosity to his beholders and a person they should fear or suspect more than respect or admire. We might recall the fact that the famous rabbi Ḥayyim Palachi had apparently welcomed Margoliouth to his home, but this in no way altered his firm and outspoken resistance to Christian missionaries throughout his lifetime. The convert also appeared to be more fascinated with his Jewish hosts than they with him despite his efforts to present himself as their distinguished guest. Like McCaul, he made few inroads in forging warm relations with Jews, as we have seen.

Such severe limitations hampering actual intimate social bonds between missionaries, converts, and Jews, should not obscure altogether the occasional good rapport that could transpire among them. While it is hard to imagine McCaul's deep friendship with individual Jews, he no doubt admired Jewish culture and literacy; he understood and appreciated Jewish spirituality and religiosity, and he valued "authentic" Jews who did not water down their cultural values as he claimed the German Reform Jews had done. This was also the case with respect to John Oxlee and Charlotte Elizabeth Tonna, each knowledgeable of Judaism to varying degrees and each committed to allowing Jews to be Jews, to practice their traditions, and to be welcomed in all their particularity into the Christian fold. Jews doing their "Jewish thing" was an essential part of their imagined scenario of Jesus's second coming. Christians, they claimed, were dependent on Jews living out their full Jewish lives not simply by converting but by embracing Jewish rituals and laws while identifying with the faith of Christ.

Stanislaus Hoga and Moses Margoliouth could never expunge their Jewish accents and habits, their love of Jewish learning, their commitment to Jewish values, ritual, music, and collective memory; they seemed very much suspended between their Christian faiths and their Jewish selves. They were truly hyphenated figures living between the two faith communities, identifying with both but often feeling socially distant and isolated from their former and present coreligionists.

Isaac Baer Levinsohn and Samuel Joseph Fuenn were deeply committed to reform and modernization and critical of the traditionalist communities from which they came but, nevertheless, remained unwilling to throw out the baby with the bathwater. Despite their open dissent from the tradition, they still loved rabbis and rabbinic texts and they took pride in recounting the history of Jewish accomplishments and ethical behavior. They felt an intimacy with a tradition that still commanded their attention and drew them in. They also knew Christianity, its sacred texts, its complex history and its unflattering record of Jewish persecution and discrimination. At the same time, they were infatuated with German and European culture and literature and identified with the cultural elites of the Christian world. Levinsohn even acknowledged that Jews still had much to learn from educated Christians. They believed that the unsavory parts of Christianity emanated from the Catholics, not necessarily the Protestants, and from the poor and uncivilized, not the rich and educated. The persecution of the Jews was very much a matter of low class and lack of education.

The two maskilim were also suspended between a radical version of Haskalah and cultural reform and traditional Judaism. Their encounter with McCaul obliged them to embrace their tradition, but they did so by reformulating it within a European discourse, overcoming rabbinic alienation by translating it into a Christian frame of reference. Judaism in their eyes was more clearly defined, appreciated, and elevated when distinguishing its cultural formation from that of Christianity and its checkered history. Raphael Kassin too was very much a fish out of water: a Sephardic Jew enamored of European ways and the allure of Western civilization; fascinated by other religions, especially Christianity; and determined to define Judaism against the Christian and the Muslim other. In the end, he also articulated a Jewish faith shaped by his exposure to reform and maskilic values emanating from

European culture, but seemingly less familiar to a Jewish congregation rooted in Muslim and Ottoman culture. In the final analysis, the story of McCaul and each of his seven associates and their intense encounter with the other was less about mutual affection and admiration and more about the acquisition of self-knowledge through contrast and contestation, through an intense exposure to the other, leading ultimately to the construction of religious and cultural identities sometimes internally inconsistent and even conflicted.

The narrative presented in this book about an interfaith conversation of the nineteenth century is not meant to displace or diminish the importance of other well-known narratives about Jews living in Europe and the Middle East during the same era: the history of political emancipation and its challenges; the decline of Jewish communal authority; the integration and assimilation of individual Jews especially in the West; the secularization of certain segments of European Jewry; the ideological struggles between reformers and traditionalists; and the radical social, political, and economic upheavals experienced by Jews and Christians alike. My modest goal has merely been to investigate another relatively understudied dimension of Jewish-Christian relations in this era among individuals who genuinely wrestled with the meaning of their religious identity and the ways both religions affected their personal faiths and lives. Their particular Jewish-Christian debate and dialogue represented a genuine reengagement with the past and its long history of mutual recriminations, but also a novel iteration of these same old narratives and arguments in new guises and contexts. These included the presence of a new and powerful missionary organization and its bold offensive against rabbinic Judaism; a new Christian assertion of cultural superiority and aggressiveness toward the non-Christian world aligned with the expansion of European empires across the world; the emergence of a small but conspicuous community of Jewish converts to Christianity; new modes of communication through the circulation of newspapers, periodicals, and pamphlets disseminated widely across cultures and in multiple translations; as well as a creative and defiant response on the part of certain Jews confident in the value of their own culture and capable of articulating their message more clearly and more effectively through their own public forums and publications. This conversation also emerged, as we have seen, against the background of new scholarly approaches, new intellectual tools of philology, history, and social criticism, new thinking about the past, about gender relations, and about the ethical responsibility of religious traditions to the other.

Is there a legacy or afterlife of this conversation for our age, with its own concerns and challenges? Any quick Google search will reveal that Alexander McCaul's books, especially *The Old Paths*, are still being published in new editions and are still being utilized for missionary work. Missionaries continue to challenge the organized Jewish community as well as nonaffiliated Jews with their own contemporary versions of Jewish or Hebrew Christianity, missionary Judaism, and Jews for Jesus, no doubt the direct heirs of such hybrid versions of Judaism and Christianity as those articulated in the nineteenth century by Hoga, Oxlee, Tonna, and others. Modern Jewish thinkers, well into the twentieth century, as we have mentioned, strongly polemicized with Christianity in defining their own place in Western civilization, taking up the kinds of arguments articulated by Levinsohn, Fuenn, and Kassin.

What has changed is the widespread ignorance of rabbinic texts, the decline of rabbinic authority, and the irrelevance of observance and ritual for the majority of Jews. McCaul's argument rested on the assumption that the rabbis were still a force to contend with and that most Jews still valued the Talmud as the basic foundation of their Jewish identity. How effective could McCaul's critical tome be to Jewish readers with little awareness of their own sacred texts and no allegiance to their normative prescriptions? Recall again the prescient observation of R. S. Spiegel, a missionary of the London Society writing in 1892:

Most of our tracts have been written for Jews of one mind and religious thought, losing sight of the manifold and various characters (and education) of the Jews we have to deal with. To have to reckon with the orthodox Talmudicals, The Reformed or rather De-formed, the educated, the illiterate, the Chasidic-superstitious, the Socialistic, the Atheistic, the Infidel, the merely National Jew; we have to provide missionary literature for Jews who think that Judaism is more a misfortune than a religion. We have not to forget Jews who with incision think that the different religions are the same wine in glasses, differently coloured; we have to remember Jews who use certain phrases and ceremonies in an emotional way without any sanctifying influence on their lives.[2]

Over a century later, the Talmud and its authority have even less cogency for the overwhelming majority of Jews.

McCaul further assumed that evangelical Christianity, as he understood it with its basic fundamentalist assumptions, would still be viable by the second half of the nineteenth century and beyond. His desperate attempts to combat the biblical critics clearly underscored the diminution of his Christian brand. Despite his panic over the slippage of biblical literalism during the last years of his lifetime, he could have hardly anticipated the decline of Christianity in Europe and the unsustainability of a mission to European Jews based on the assumptions that informed his critique.

In the aftermath of the Holocaust and with the emergence of a Jewish state and a powerful Jewish community in North America, a heated controversy over a missionary assault on the Talmud of the mid-nineteenth century might seem increasingly remote and irrelevant to contemporary concerns. Yet, on the other hand, evangelical Christianity still flourishes in the Americas, in Africa, and in Asia; the present Israeli government garners strong political and financial support from evangelicals who fervently defend the present right-wing coalition; and increasing numbers of intermarried unions of Christians and Jews cope with the challenge of forging hybrid, nonconfessional beliefs and practices for themselves and their children. Perhaps the story of McCaul and his associates—Christians, Jews, and those in between—is not as irrelevant to our own age as it might first appear.

A Sampling of Contemporary Christian Authors Cited in Isaac Baer Levinsohn's Polemical Writings

One of the most impressive features of Isaac Baer Levinsohn's two polemical works, as we have seen, is the wide range of contemporary authors he consulted and his creative mobilization of their writing in defending Judaism against the false accusations of Alexander McCaul. This is all the more remarkable given Levinsohn's relative isolation, his lack of access to specialized libraries, and the ill health that limited his ability to travel. A complete study of his literary output would include a careful reconstruction of his bookshelf based on all of his works, a task far beyond the limitations of this study. But I offer here a brief sampling of some additional contemporary Christian authors he favored, beyond those already mentioned. By citing them, he successfully enlisted credible and up-to-date witnesses to undermine the false claims of his formidable adversary.

Levinsohn noticed the German scholar of Hebrew epigraphy Johann Joachim Bellermann (1754–1842) of Erfurt and Berlin, who had also spent time teaching in Russia. He especially singled out Bellermann's appreciative remarks on the Talmud found in his introduction to Ephraim Moses Pinner's *Compendium des Hierosolymitanischen und Babylonischen Thalmud* (Berlin, 1832). The work contained specimens of his translation of both the Palestinian and Babylonian Talmuds and an attempted biography of the Palestinian rabbi Simeon bar Yoḥai. It was published as the forerunner of his proposed translation of the Talmud, which was to have been completed in twenty-eight folio volumes, although only one appeared. Levinsohn, along with other maskilim and rabbis, had vigorously supported this project.[1]

Levinsohn was also acquainted with the work of the famous Danish writer Ludvig Holberg (1684–1754). While known primarily for his dramatic writings, especially his classical comedies, Holberg was also an author of popular histories, including one on the Jews. Levinsohn consulted the German edition of this work entitled *Jüdische Geschichte von Erschaffung der Welt bis auf gegenwärtige Zeiten* (Altona-Flensburg, 1747) on rabbinic *aggadah* and on Jesus's desire that his disciples follow Jewish law.[2]

Another Christian historian of the Jews favored by Levinsohn was Georg Bernhard Depping (1784–1853), who was born in Germany but lived in France. He composed a history in French on medieval Jewry: *Les Juifs dans le moyen âge, essai historique sur leur état civil, commercial et littéraire* (Paris, 1834). Depping submitted the work to the Royal Academy in Paris for a prize, but received only honorable mention for his effort. Levinsohn referred to the original circumstances of the French version but cited a Russian translation of the work published in 1848. He mentioned him approvingly on his distinction between gentiles and Christians, on the laws of divorce, and on the leniency of medieval French rabbis regarding wine forbidden by Jewish law.[3]

Levinsohn also cited the German Lutheran Church historian Johann Lorenz von Mosheim (1693–1755), highly acclaimed for his ecclesiastical histories translated into several languages. He discovered Mosheim through reading his animadversions on the massive biblical commentary of the Benedictine monk Antoine Augustin Calmet (1672–1757), translated into German in Bremen between 1738 and 1747. He noticed Mosheim's provocative comment comparing the Canaanites' killing of heathens with Spanish Catholics killing Jews, as well as a reference to Jewish martyrdom (*kiddush ha-shem*). As he had done in quoting the Catholic Bossuet in the version produced by the Protestant Cramer, he similarly utilized a standard Catholic commentary through the mediation of a Protestant exegete. Ideological differences between Catholics and Protestants were irrelevant in his search for reliable supports for his Jewish positions.[4]

He also liked a popular handbook of philosophy published by Wilhelm Traugott Krug (1770–1842), the German philosopher who had succeeded Kant in the chair of logic and metaphysics at the University of Königsberg before assuming a professorship at Leipzig. Krug was also a major supporter of Jewish emancipation in Germany. Levinsohn used the third edition published in 1828, taking special note of Krug's remarks that Jews hardly drink and that they are not prone to many diseases common among Christians.[5]

Levinsohn was familiar with the famous German political philosopher Samuel von Pufendorf (1632–94). He consulted his *Einleitung zu der Historie der vornehmsten Reiche und Staaten* in a later addition published in Frankfurt am Main in 1828 regarding the observance of Jewish law by Jesus.[6]

One final illustration of Levinsohn's familiarity with European literature is his mention of the German epic poem *Der Messias* of Friedrich Gottlieb Klopstock (1724–1803), as well as John Milton's *Paradise Lost and Regained,* which was apparently known to Levinsohn in its French translation. He referred to both epic works for their poetic license of exaggerating their subjects as the rabbis had done in their homiletical writings. He also noted their special praise for Christianity and their disdain for other faiths, a common practice of which McCaul had accused the rabbis.[7]

NOTES

INTRODUCTION

1. I have purposely refrained from annotating this subject and others in the introduction when they are more amply treated in subsequent chapters below with full annotation.

2. I refer especially to the works of Luigi Chiarini and Asher Temkin. On Chiarini, see Roman Marcinkowski, "Luigi Chiarini (1789–1832): An Anti-Judaistic Reformer of Judaism," *Studia Judaica* 7 (2004): 237–48. On Temkin, see Ellie R. Schainker, *Confessions of the Shtetl: Converts from Judaism in Imperial Russia, 1817–1906* (Stanford, Calif.: Stanford University Press, 2017), 60–63, 66–67.

3. Jonathan Frankel, *The Damascus Affair: "Ritual Murder," Politics, and the Jews in 1840* (Cambridge: Cambridge University Press, 1997). See as well the important supplement of David Feldman, "The Damascus Affair and the Debate on Ritual Murder in Early Victorian Britain," in *Judaism, Christianity, and Islam: Collaboration and Conflict in the Age of Diaspora*, ed. Sander L. Gilman (Hong Kong: Hong Kong University Press, 2014), 131–52.

4. Israel Jacob Yuval, *Two Nations in Your Womb: Perceptions of Jews and Christians in Late Antiquity and the Middle Ages* (Berkeley: University of California Press, 2006). Among the many other works on this theme, see Daniel Boyarin, *Border Lines: The Partition of Judaeo-Christianity* (Philadelphia: University of Pennsylvania Press, 2004); Ivan Marcus, *Rituals of Childhood: Jewish Acculturation in Medieval Europe* (New Haven, Conn.: Yale University Press, 2005); and, most recently, Annette Yoshiko Reed, *Jewish-Christianity and the History of Judaism: Collected Essays* (Tübingen: Mohr Siebeck, 2018).

5. A small sampling of the vast literature on this subject would include Susannah Heschel, *Abraham Geiger and the Jewish Jesus* (Chicago: University of Chicago Press, 1998); Fritz A. Rothschild, *Jewish Perspectives on Christianity: Leo Baeck, Martin Buber, Franz Rosenzweig, Will Herberg, and Abraham J. Heschel* (London: Continuum, 1996); Ismar Schorsch, "Editor's Introduction: Ideology and History in the Age of Emancipation," in Heinrich Graetz, *The Structure of Jewish History and Other Essays*, trans. and ed. Ismar Schorsch (New York: Ktav, 1975), 1–62; and Jay M. Harris, *Nachman Krochmal: Guiding the Perplexed of the Modern Age* (New York: New York University Press, 1991).

6. See especially Denis G. Paz, *Popular Anti-Catholicism in Mid-Victorian England* (Stanford, Calif.: Stanford University Press, 1992). David Feldman, "The Damascus Affair," discusses the significant role of anti-Catholicism in the debate over the Damascus affair among Jews and Christians. See also his "Evangelicals, Jews, and Anti-Catholicism in Britain, c. 1840–1900," *Jewish Historical Studies, Transactions of the Jewish Historical Society in England* 47 (2015):

91–104, where he traces the theme throughout the century and also argues that Jewish anti-Catholicism is an unexplored facet of Jewish history in Victorian Britain.

7. On the largest mission to the Jews in the eighteenth century, emanating from the Pietists of Halle, see Christopher M. Clark, *The Politics of Conversion: Missionary Protestantism and the Jews in Prussia, 1728–1941* (Oxford: Clarendon Press, 1995).

8. Tonna, of course, had close relationships with some English Jews, especially Jacob Franklin and Grace Aguilar; Oxlee interacted with Franklin and others as well. On this, see Chapter 5 below.

9. Andrew Porter, "An Overview," in *Missions and Empires*, ed. Norman Etherington (Oxford: Oxford University Press, 2005), 50.

10. Porter, "An Overview," 47–48.

11. In addition to the Etherington volume mentioned in note 9, see Andrew Porter "'Cultural Imperialism' and Protestant Missionary Enterprise, 1780–1914," *Journal of Imperial and Commonwealth History* 25 (1997): 367–91; Andrew Porter, *Religion Versus Empire? British Protestant Missionaries and Overseas Expansion, 1700–1914* (Manchester: Manchester University Press, 2004); Dana L. Robert, ed., *Converting Colonialism: Visions and Realities in Mission History, 1706–1914* (Grand Rapids, Mich.: William B. Eerdmans, 2008); Brian Stanley, *The Bible and the Flag: Protestant Missions and British Imperialism in the Nineteenth and Twentieth Centuries* (Leicester: Apollos, 1990); Kathleen Wilson, *The Island Race: Englishness, Empire, and Gender in the Eighteenth Century* (London: Routledge, 2003); Susan Thorne, *Congregational Missions and the Making of an Imperial Culture in Nineteenth-Century England* (Stanford, Calif.: Stanford University Press, 1999); Catherine Hall, *Civilizing Subjects: Metropole and Colony in the English Imagination, 1830–1867* (Cambridge: Cambridge University Press, 2002); Ryan Dunch, "Beyond Cultural Imperialism: Cultural Theory, Christian Missions, and Global Modernity," *History and Theory* 41 (2002): 301–25; Mary Angela Schwer, "Religious and Imperialist Discourse in Nineteenth-Century British Popular Missionary Literature" (Ph.D. diss., University of Notre Dame, 1996); and Jeffrey Cox, *The British Missionary Enterprise Since 1700* (London: Routledge, 2008).

12. See especially Lamin Sanneh, *Translating the Message: The Missionary Impact on Culture*, 2nd ed. (Maryknoll, N.Y.: Orbis Books, 2009).

13. On evangelicalism in England, see the standard works of Boyd Hilton, *The Age of Atonement: The Influence of Evangelicalism on Social and Economic Thought, 1795–1865* (Oxford: Clarendon Press, 1988); and David Bebbington, *Evangelicalism in Modern Britain* (London: Unwin Hyman, 1989). See also Nicholas M. Railton, *No North Sea: The Anglo-German Evangelical Network in the Middle of the Nineteenth Century* (London: Brill, 2000); and Donald M. Lewis, *The Origins of Christian Zionism: Lord Shaftesbury and the Evangelical Support for a Jewish Homeland* (Cambridge: Cambridge University Press, 2010).

14. Yaakov Shaḥak, "Ha-maskil ke-apologetikan: Teguvot maskilim Yehudi'im be-Mizraḥ Eropah she ha-meah ha-19 le-hatafot ha-misionaire Alexander McCaul be-sefer Netivot olam" [The maskil as an apologist: Reactions of Jewish maskilim in eastern Europe in the nineteenth century to the preachings of the missionary Alexander McCaul in the book *Netivot olam*] (master's thesis, Bar Ilan University, 1999). My thanks to Professor Shmuel Feiner for pointing me to this work.

15. W. T. Gidney, *The History of the London Society for Promoting Christianity Amongst the Jews from 1809 to 1908* (London: London Society for Promoting Christianity Amongst the Jews, 1908); Mel Scult, *Millennial Expectations and Jewish Liberties: A Study of the Efforts to Convert the Jews in Britain, up to the Mid Nineteenth Century* (Leiden: Brill, 1978).

16. Agnieszka Jagodzińska, "'For Zion's Sake I Will Not Rest': The London Society for Promoting Christianity Among the Jews and Its Nineteenth-Century Missionary Periodicals," *Church History* 82 (2013): 382–87; Agnieszka Jagodzińska, "'English Missionaries' Look at Polish Jews: The Value and Limitations of Missionary Reports as Source Material," *Polin: Studies in Polish Jewry* 27 (2015): 89–116; and Agnieszka Jagodzińska, *"Duszozbawcy"? Misje i literatura Londyńskiego Towarzystwa Krzewienia Chrześcijaństwa wśród Żydów w latach 1809–1939* [Missions and literature of the London Society for the Propagation of Christianity Amongst the Jews, 1809–1939] (Crakow: Wydawnictwo Austeria, 2017). See as well Israel Bartal, "British Missionaries in the Districts of Ḥabad" [in Hebrew], in *Ḥabad: Historia, hagut ve-dimu'i*, ed. Yonatan Meir and Gadi Sagiv (Jerusalem: Zalman Shazar Center, 2016), 145–82.

17. See Todd Endelman, *Leaving the Jewish Fold: Conversion and Radical Assimilation in Modern Jewish History* (Princeton, N.J.: Princeton University Press, 2015); and the essays in Todd Endelman, ed., *Jewish Apostasy in the Modern World* (New York: Holmes & Meier, 1987). On the earlier disdain or indifference to the study of the modern convert in Jewish historiography, see Todd Endelman, "Welcoming Ex-Jews into the Jewish Historiographical Fold," in his *Broadening Jewish History: Towards a Social History of Ordinary Jews* (Oxford: Littman Library of Jewish Civilization, 2011), 82–92. A small sampling of other recent scholarship on converts in the early modern and modern eras might include the essays and book of Jagodzińska; Schainker, *Confessions of the Shtetl*; Elisheva Carlebach, *Divided Souls: Converts from Judaism in Germany, 1500–1750* (New Haven, Conn.: Yale University Press, 2001); Deborah Hertz, *How Jews Became Germans: The History of Conversion and Assimilation in Berlin* (New Haven, Conn.: Yale University Press, 2007); and David B. Ruderman, *Connecting the Covenants: Judaism and the Search for Christian Identity in Eighteenth-Century England* (Philadelphia: University of Pennsylvania Press, 2007), which focuses on the life of one convert. For a useful overview of recent scholarly approaches to the study of converts and conversion, see Lewis R. Rambo and Charles E. Farhadian, eds. *The Oxford Handbook of Religious Conversion* (Oxford: Oxford University Press, 2014).

18. The bibliography on Tonna is cited in Chapter 5 below.

19. See especially Shmuel Feiner, *Milḥemet tarbut: Tenu'at ha-Haskalah ha-Yehudit be-me'ah ha-19* (Jerusalem: Carmel, 2010); Immanuel Etkes, ed., *Ha-dat ve-ha-ḥayyim: Tenu'at ha-Haskalah ha-Yehudit be-Mizraḥ Eropah* (Jerusalem: Zalman Shazar Center, 1993); and Mordechai Zalkin, *Ba'alot ha-shaḥar: Ha-Haskalah ha-Yehudit be-imperiyah ha-Russit be-me'ah ha-teshah esreh* (Jerusalem: Magnes Press, 2000).

20. Eliyahu Stern, "Catholic Judaism: The Political Theology of the Nineteenth-Century Russian Jewish Enlightenment," *Harvard Theological Review* 109, no. 4 (2016): 483–511; and Eliyahu Stern, "Paul in the Jerusalem of Lithuania: Samuel Joseph Fuenn's *Paths of God*," in *Talmudic Transgressions: Engaging the Work of Daniel Boyarin*, ed. Charlotte Elisheva Fonrobert et al. (Leiden: Brill, 2017), 407–17. I discuss both essays in Chapters 7 and 8 below.

CHAPTER 1

1. For a succinct biography of McCaul, see W. A. J. Archbold, "McCaul, Alexander (1799–1863)," rev. H. C. G. Matthew, *Oxford Dictionary of National Biography* (Oxford: Oxford University Press, 2004); online edition, October 2009, http://www.oxforddnb.com/view/article /17386. Other references appear below.

2. William Ayerst, ed., *The Jews of the Nineteenth Century: A Collection of Essays, Reviews, and Historical Notices, Originally Published in the "Jewish Intelligence"* (London: London Society's House, 1848).

3. William Ayerst, "The Rev. Dr. McCaul and the Jewish Mission," *Jewish Intelligence and Monthly Account of the Proceedings of the London Society for Promoting Christianity Amongst the Jews*, n.s., 4 (1864): 31–34.

4. Ayerst, "McCaul and the Jewish Mission," 35–38; the citations are on pp. 37 and 38. On Jost, see, for example, Ismar Schorch, From Wolfenbüttel to Wissenschaft: The Divergent Paths of Isaak Markus Jost and Leopold Zunz," *Leo Baeck Institute Yearbook* 22 (1977): 109–28. Jost was regularly cited in the *Jewish Intelligence* by the missionaries of the London Society as a reliable Jewish authority.

5. On Hoga, see Beth-Zion Lask Abrahams, "Stanislaus Hoga—Apostate and Penitent," *Transactions (Jewish Historical Society of England)* 15 (1939–45): 121–49; Shnayer Z. Leiman, "The Baal Teshuvah and the Emden-Eibeschuetz Controversy," *Judaic Studies* 1 (1985): 3–26; and David Ruderman, ed., *Converts of Conviction: Faith and Skepticism in Nineteenth-Century European Jewish Society* (Berlin: De Gruyter, 2017), 41–53; and see Chapter 4 below.

6. I discuss McCaul's attitude to Reform Judaism more extensively in Chapter 2.

7. Stanislaus Hoga, *Zir Ne'eman: The Faithful Missionary; A Monthly Periodical, Illustrating the Value of Judaism, with a View to Opening the Eyes of Some Deluded Christians in England to the Doings of the (So-Called) "London Society" for Promoting Christianity Among the Jews* (London: W. Brittain, 1847), 18–19.

8. Oxford Bodleian MS Eng. c. 7024, letter of Alexander McCaul to Rev. C. S. Hawtrey, 1826, fols. 137b–138a.

9. W. T. Gidney, *The History of the London Society for Promoting Christianity Amongst the Jews from 1809 to 1908* (London: London Society for Promoting Christianity Amongst the Jews, 1908).

10. Oxford Bodleian Dep. C.M.J. c. 10–24, Minute Books of the General Committees, 1821–62.

11. *Jewish Intelligence and Monthly Account of the Proceedings of the London Society for Promoting Christianity Amongst the Jews* 1–26 (1835–60); n.s., 1–4 (1861–64).

12. Elizabeth Anne Finn, *Reminiscences of Mrs. Finn, Member of the Royal Asiatic Society* (London: Marshall, Morgan and Scott, 1929).

13. McCaul's many sermons and addresses are collected in boxes in the London Society archives stored in the Bodleian Library. Most of his books, several of them cited below, are easily available online and in recently published editions.

14. The two obituaries by William Ayerst are found in *Jewish Intelligence*, n.s., 4 (1864): 2–10, 30–38. Another obituary is found in the minutes of the society for November 25, 1863, Oxford Bodleian Dep. C.M.J. c. 24, 682. See also *A Memorial Sketch of the Rev. Alexander McCaul, D.D., Rector of St. Magnus and Professor of Hebrew and Old Testament Exegesis, King's College, London, by His Eldest Son the Rev. Joseph B. McCaul, Chaplain to the Lord Bishop of Rochester, to Which Are Appended Two Funeral Sermons Preached in the Church of St. Magnus on Sunday, Nov. 22, by the Rev. Canon Jelf, D.D., Principal of King's College, and the Rev. Charles Braddy, M.A., Lecturer at St. Magnus* (London: Rivingtons, 1863).

15. Alexander McCaul, *The Old Paths; or, A Comparison of the Principles and Doctrines of Modern Judaism with the Religion of Moses and the Prophets* (London: London Society's Office, 1837).

16. Alexander McCaul, *Reasons for Believing That the Charge Lately Revived Against the Jewish People Is a Baseless Falsehood, Dedicated by Permission to Her Most Gracious Majesty the Queen* (London: Wertheim, 1840).

17. Finn, *Reminiscences*, 20–21.

18. Finn, *Reminiscences*, 22.

19. Finn, *Reminiscences*, 25. On the Jewish origins of this hymn and Leoni (Meyer Lyon), see https://hymnary.org/text/the_god_of_abraham_praise_who…reigns. Finn's reference to Hoga's Roman Catholic background is unsubstantiated to the best of my knowledge. Even if her information is correct, Hoga had certainly become a Protestant under McCaul's influence.

20. Finn, *Reminiscences*, 26. Rabbi David Woolf Marks (1811–1909) was the first religious leader of the West London Synagogue, declaring his independence from the chief rabbi of London. For more on the alleged connection between the London Society and the first English Jewish reformers, see Chapter 2.

21. Finn, *Reminiscences*, 27. Apparently it was not so unusual for educated English families in the nineteenth century to consult the German Shakespeare.

22. McCaul, *The Old Paths*, opening page entitled "Advertisement." In presenting these weekly essays as a book, McCaul's "great object was to exhibit Judaism as it appears in its practical writings." On David Levi and his translations, see David B. Ruderman, *Jewish Enlightenment in an English Key: Anglo-Jewry's Construction of Modern Jewish Thought* (Princeton, N.J.: Princeton University Press, 2000), especially 215–68.

23. Alexander McCaul, "Our Duty Towards the Jewish People," Sermon 14, *Plain Sermons on Subjects Practical and Prophetic* (London: Wertheim, 1840).

24. Alexander McCaul, *Sketches of Judaism and the Jews* (London: Wertheim, 1838).

25. *Rabbi David Kimchi's Commentary upon the Prophecies of Zechariah, Translated from the Hebrew; with Notes, and Observations on the Passages Relating to the Messiah by the Rev. A. M'Caul, A.M., of Trinity College, Dublin* (London: James Duncan, 1837).

26. McCaul, *Sketches of Judaism and the Jews*, 15–16.

27. McCaul, *The Old Paths*, 61.

28. McCaul, *The Old Paths*, 27–28.

29. McCaul, *The Old Paths*, 62–63. For more on the theme of Edom (= Esau) in rabbinic literature, see Gerson D. Cohen, "Esau as Symbol in Early Medieval Thought," in *Studies in the Variety of Rabbinic Cultures* (Philadelphia: Jewish Publication Society of America, 1991), 243–69. On the theme of rabbinic curses addressed to non-Jews, especially in medieval Ashkenazic literature, see Israel Jacob Yuval, *Two Nations in Your Womb: Perceptions of Jews and Christians in Late Antiquity and the Middle Ages* (Berkeley: University of California Press, 2006), 92–134.

30. McCaul, *The Old Paths*, 211.

31. McCaul, *The Old Paths*, 194–95.

32. McCaul, *The Old Paths*, 181–83; the citations are on p. 183.

33. McCaul, *The Old Paths*, 184.

34. McCaul, *The Old Paths*, 185–88; the citation is on p. 88. Note Raphael Kassin's response to this particular charge in Chapter 8 below.

35. *Jewish Intelligence and Monthly Account of the Proceedings of the London Society for Promoting Christianity Amongst the Jews* 5 (1839): 148; 6 (1840): 153; Oxford Bodleian Dep. C.M.J. c. 16 1840–41, 75. There is an additional reference to the issuing of two thousand more copies of *The Old Paths* in English in the Minute Books of the Society, MS Oxford Bodleian Dep. C.M.J. c. 17 1842–43, 2416. According to David Feldman, ten thousand copies of the first

edition of *The Old Paths* were distributed in the first year. See David Feldman, *Englishmen and Jews: Social Relations and Political Culture, 1840–1914* (New Haven, Conn.: Yale University Press, 1994), 55.

36. *Jewish Intelligence and Monthly Account* 12 (1846): 235.

37. *Jewish Intelligence and Monthly Account* 12 (1846): 324.

38. MS Oxford Bodleian Dep. C.M.J. d. 27 Papers 1892–1957, d. 27/3: Remarks upon the Existing Missionary Publications of the Society, Publications Sub-Committee, July 29, 1892. The three letters are dated June 23, July 1, and June 18, 1892, respectively. My gratitude to Professor Agnieszka Jagodzińska for showing me this document including the letter that follows.

39. MS Oxford Bodleian Dep. C.M.J. d. 27 Papers 1892–1957, d. 27/3. Spiegel's eight-page letter is dated June 29, 1892.

CHAPTER 2

1. The classic work on Isaac Orobio de Castro (ca. 1617–87) is by Yosef Kaplan, *From Christianity to Judaism: The Story of Isaac Orobio de Castro*, trans. Raphael Loewe (Oxford: Littman Library/Oxford University Press, 1989). Kaplan discusses all the translations of Orobio's works in an appendix, pp. 451–64, especially the French translation published in London in 1770 by a Jew named Henríquez called *Israel Vengé*, a compilation of several works including a discussion of the Messiah, Isaiah 53, and perhaps several original chapters added by the editor. This work was translated with modifications into English by Grace Aguilar, as I discuss below, and its first two chapters were retranslated by Alexander McCaul.

2. On Aguilar, see Beth-Zion Lask Abrahams, "Grace Aguilar: A Centenary Tribute," *Transactions of the Jewish Historical Society of England* 16 (1952): 137–48; Nadia Valman, *The Jewess in Nineteenth-Century British Literary Culture* (Cambridge: Cambridge University Press, 2007), 92–115; Michael Galchinsky, ed., *Grace Aguilar: Selected Writings* (Peterborough, Ontario: Broadview Press, 2003). The quote is from Michael Galchinsky, "Grace Aguilar," *Jewish Women: A Comprehensive Historical Encyclopedia*, February 27, 2009, Jewish Women's Archive, http://jwa.org/encyclopedia/article/aguilar-grace.

3. Grace Aguilar, *Israel Defended; or, The Jewish Exposition of the Hebrew Prophecies Applied by the Christians to Their Messiah by Isaac Orobio, Translated from the French; and Printed Expressly for the Use of Young Persons of the Jewish Faith* (London: Printed by John Wertheimer and Co., 1838). Note that the edition was printed for private circulation. The citation is from p. vii of the translator's preface. Aguilar's role as a translator, as Iris Idelson-Shein reminded me, was common among Christian and Jewish women, especially in England. See, for example, Deborah Uman, *Women as Translators in Early Modern England* (Newark: University of Delaware Press, 2012); and Caroline Bland and Hilary Brown, "Women as Cultural Mediators and Translators," *Oxford German Studies* 42 (2013): 111–18. On the literacy of Jewish women, especially in reading western European languages, see Iris Parush, *Reading Jewish Women: Marginality and Modernization in Nineteenth-Century Eastern European Society* (Waltham, Mass.: Brandeis University Press, 2004).

4. For Tonna's relationship to Aguilar, see Hilary L. Rubenstein, "A Pioneering Philosemite: Charlotte Elizabeth Tonna (1790–1846) and the Jews," *Jewish Historical Studies* [published by the Jewish Historical Society of England] 35 (1996–98): 103–18. I treat Tonna comprehensively in Chapter 5 below.

5. Galchinsky, "Grace Aguilar."

6. I examined a copy at the Katz Center library of the University of Pennsylvania in Philadelphia owned by the physician Joshua Cohen of Baltimore, who added comments in the margins. His entire library was given to Dropsie College Library (now the core collection of the Katz library), along with that of Isaac Leeser, yet another close associate of Aguilar and her publisher in the United States. The book was presented to him personally by Moses Mocatta (1768–1857), a patron of the works of Grace Aguilar, a translator himself, and most likely a person who played a role in encouraging Aguilar to publish the English Orobio. Mocatta's *Faith Strengthened* (1851) was a translation from the Hebrew of the famous *Ḥizzuḳ Emunah* of Isaac ben Abraham of Troki, the famous Karaite polemicist. His other translation, entitled *The Inquisition and Judaism* (1845), was a sermon on Isaiah 42:22 addressed to Jewish martyrs on the occasion of an auto-da-fé at Lisbon in 1705.

Joshua Cohen wrote the following on the title page of his copy, dated August 6, 1853:

> Given me by Mr. Mocatta, terrible and insincere Jew. [He apparently refers to Orobio here!] There is subtlety in some points and great fallacies in others, particularly in the argument on the immutability of the law being given by God to Moses. Fundamentally different in that no mention whatever is made of the miracles which prove that Christianity could not be so important. The strongest part is that Jesus could not be the messiah of the Jews because more of the prophecies of him as concerning them are fulfilled, but [the argument that] the messiah that the Jews still expect the fulfillment of Isaiah's and Jeremiah's prophecies concerning them after 3000 years . . . is lastly fallacious. But the argument concerning Shiloh . . . is strong.

Joshua I. Cohen (1801–70) was president of the medical and chirurgical faculty of the University of Maryland and owned one of the finest Judaica collections in the United States. His collection was donated by his heirs to Dropsie College in 1915. My thanks to Dr. Arthur Kiron for this information.

7. The citation is from Aguilar, *Israel Defended*, vi. She added: "The cruelties inflicted on Orobio; the awful bigotry of the Catholics of Spain, in which nation he drew breath, and lived in continued fear of his Jewish descent being discovered; the very different light in which we were regarded in the seventeenth century to that of the nineteenth; all these facts may well excuse the violence in which some parts of the original are written, pervading the whole, indeed, to a degree, which without altering the sense could not be entirely eradicated."

8. Alexander McCaul, *Israel Avenged by Don Isaac Orobio: Translated and Answered*, 3 parts (London: Wertheim, 1839–40). The citation is from the preface, p. i. He continued: "She wishes for our conversion, she prays for it, and teaches the Jewish youth to join in the prayer; consistency would lead her to hold up the light to our view. In her heart and prayers she is a convert-maker, and it is upon the heart that God looks. If convert-making be a practice repugnant to Jewish principles, she is verily guilty before the Searcher of hearts" (iii).

9. Johann Andreas Eisenmenger (1654–1704) was the author of *Entdecktes Judenthum*, a highly critical treatment of Judaism. On him, see Jacob Katz, *From Prejudice to Destruction: Anti-Semitism, 1700–1933* (Cambridge, Mass.: Harvard University Press, 1984), 13–22. The Reverend William Ayerst, one of McCaul's colleagues at the London Society, in his eulogy of McCaul in 1863, strongly contrasted the loving spirit of McCaul toward Jews and Judaism with the caustic and destructive approach of Eisenmenger, as we have seen. See Chapter 1 above.

10. McCaul, *Israel Avenged*, 14, where he cited from the *Exemplar humanae vitae* (Gouda, 1687), 347. On da Costa, see Uriel da Costa, *Examination of Pharisaic Traditions*, ed. and trans. H. P. Salomon and I. S. D. Sassoon (Leiden: Brill, 1993), introduction. McCaul mentioned Thomas de Pinedo in *Israel Avenged*, 23. Pinedo was known primarily as a scholar of ancient Greek, who, in contrast to Orobio, spoke positively of Christianity. His most important publication was his Latin edition of Stephen of Byzantium's geographical work published in Amsterdam in 1678.

11. McCaul, *Israel Avenged*, 24–33. He referred to several examples of Jewish prayers on 33–34.

12. McCaul, *Israel Avenged*, 88–111. On Albo, see the useful synthesis of Dror Erlich in the Stanford Encyclopedia of Philosophy, http://plato.stanford.edu/entries/albo-joseph/, especially his observation: "Remaining faithful to the dogmatic method, Albo argues that in Mosaic Law, and in divine law in general, changes in the details of the commandments may take place, but their fundamental principles cannot change." McCaul drew heavily from Albo, *Sefer Ha-Ikkarim*, treatise 3, chapters 13–22, especially 14 and 16.

13. McCaul, *Israel Avenged*, 115–27.

14. McCaul, *Israel Avenged*, 129–31, especially 129: "Orobio speaks all the way through as if he and his colleagues were really keeping the law, and yet he and they had nothing but a counterfeit, a caricature dishonouring to God and uncharitable to man, the worst feature of which, its intolerance, appears to be that part of it most easily apprehended and best understood by this nursling of inquisitorial cruelty."

15. McCaul, *Israel Avenged*, 171.

16. McCaul, *Israel Avenged*, 148–70, where these English clerics are cited. Note especially McCaul's negative position regarding Jewish civic emancipation and cultural integration on 148–49:

> In some other countries all hope of the Messiah's advent has been given up. An attempt is making to identify the Jews as part and parcel of the nations amongst whom they reside, and a desire expressed to strike out of the prayer-book all the petitions for restoration to the land of Israel. In fact the enlighteners there wish to shake off altogether their holy nationality—to sink their privileges as Jews—and to be incorporated into the Gentile body politic. The reprint of Orobio's book shows that the respectable persons concerned in it are far from sharing these Infidel opinions—they are looking themselves and teaching their brethren to look for the total extermination of the nations amongst whom they dwell, rather than their own amalgamation with the Gentiles by any so-called act of emancipation.

17. McCaul, *Israel Avenged*, 195.

18. *Jewish Intelligence and Monthly Account of the Proceedings of the London Society for Promoting Christianity Amongst the Jews* 5 (1839): 104–6; 6 (1840): 388, 392.

19. See Chapters 7 and 8 below.

20. Alexander McCaul, *The Old Paths; or, A Comparison of the Principles and Doctrines of Modern Judaism*, 2nd ed. (London: London Society's Office, 1846), vii–viii.

21. The best treatment of McCaul and his connections with the English Jewish reformers is David Feldman, *Englishmen and Jews: Social Relations and Political Culture, 1840–1914* (New Haven, Conn.: Yale University Press, 1994), chap. 2, called "Rabbinism, Popery, and Reform."

22. Alexander McCaul, *Sketches of Judaism and the Jews* (London: Wertheim, 1838), 44–46.

23. McCaul, *Sketches of Judaism*, 49–52.

24. McCaul, *Sketches of Judaism*, 67–68.

25. McCaul, *Sketches of Judaism*, 122.

26. Alexander Behr, *Lehrbuch der mosaischen Religion* (Munich: Carl Wolf, 1826), https://books.google.com/books?id = uKpBAAAAYAAJ. Bing (1752–1841) was an Orthodox rabbi and a student of Nathan Adler. Despite his involvement in this particular catechism, he appeared an unlikely candidate for reformist positions.

27. J. Johlson, *Die Lehren der Mosaischen Religion*, 3rd ed. (Frankfurt a. M.: Andreäischen, 1829), https://books.google.de/books?id = k4ZLAAAAIAAJ.

28. McCaul, *Sketches of Judaism*, 123, 131–32.

29. On this work, see Jay Berkovitz, *Rites and Passages: The Beginnings of Modern Jewish Culture in France, 1650–1860* (Philadelphia: University of Pennsylvania Press, 2010), 220–21. See, more generally, Jacob Petuchowski, "Manuals and Catechisms of the Jewish Religion in the Early Period of Emancipation," in *Studies in Nineteenth-Century Jewish Intellectual History*, ed. Alexander Altmann (Cambridge, Mass.: Harvard University Press, 1964), 47–64.

30. McCaul, *Sketches of Judaism*, 152.

31. McCaul, *Sketches of Judaism*, 91.

32. McCaul, *Sketches of Judaism*, 92–94.

33. McCaul, *Sketches of Judaism*, 97–99. McCaul had translated into English the prayer of Sarah more than 150 years before that of Chava Weissler in her *Voices of the Matriarchs: Listening to the Prayers of Early Modern Jewish Women* (Boston: Beacon Press, 1998), 130–33.

34. McCaul, *Sketches of Judaism*, 107, 114.

35. McCaul, *Sketches of Judaism*, 4–6.

36. See especially Valman, *The Jewess in Nineteenth-Century British Literary Culture*, 51–84; Kathryn Gleadle, "Charlotte Elizabeth Tonna and the Mobilization of Tory Women in Early Victorian England," *Historical Journal* 50 (2007): 97–117; and Miriam Elizabeth Burstein, "Protestants Against the Jewish and Catholic Family, c. 1829 to c. 1860," *Victorian Literature and Culture* 31 (2003): 333–57. See also Julie Melnyk, ed., *Women's Theology in Nineteenth-Century Britain: Transfiguring the Faith of Their Fathers* (New York: Garland, 1998); and Sue Morgan and Jacqueline deVries, eds., *Women, Gender and Religious Cultures in Britain, 1800–1940* (London: Routledge, 2010), especially the essays by Julie Melnyk ("Women, Writing and the Creation of Theological Cultures," 32–53) and Pamela J. Walker ("'With Fear and Trembling': Women, Preaching and Spiritual Authority," 94–116).

37. Valman, *The Jewess*, 53.

38. Valman, *The Jewess*, 84.

39. On the parallels as well as differences between the evangelical critiques of rabbinic Judaism and Roman Catholicism, see especially the essay of Burstein, "Protestants Against the Jewish and Catholic Family."

40. Valman, *The Jewess*, 227 n. 35.

41. Valman, *The Jewess*, 83.

42. Nadia Valman, "Bad Jew/Good Jewess: Gender and Semitic Discourse in Nineteenth-Century England," in *Philosemitism in History*, ed. Jonathan Karp and Adam Sutcliffe (Cambridge: Cambridge University Press, 2011), 149–69.

CHAPTER 3

1. Joseph B. McCaul, "A Voice from the Tomb," reprinted from the *Morning Post*, October 4, 1866. The letter of Alexander McCaul that follows was sent from Rectory London Bridge and is dated April 1855.

2. "A Voice from the Tomb," *Morning Post*, October 4, 1866.

3. *Jerusalem: Its Bishop, Its Missionaries, and Its Converts; Being a Series of Letters Addressed to the Editor of the "Daily News" in the Year 1858, by the Late Rev. Alexander McCaul, D.D., with Other Letters, &c., Illustrative Thereof, Collected and Edited by His Son, Samuel McCaul, B.C.L, of St. John's College, Oxford* (London: Trübner, 1866). I first located the work in the archives of the London Society, Oxford Bodleian Dep. C.M.J. d. 149, 1861–68.

4. The standard works that competently review this history include Nicholas M. Railton, *No North Sea: The Anglo-German Evangelical Network in the Middle of the Nineteenth Century* (Leiden: Brill, 2000); Yaron Perry, *British Mission to the Jews in Nineteenth-Century Palestine* (London: Frank Cass, 2003); and Donald M. Lewis, *The Origins of Christian Zionism: Lord Shaftesbury and the Evangelical Support for a Jewish Homeland* (Cambridge: Cambridge University Press, 2010). See also Sarah Kochav, "Beginning at Jerusalem: The Mission to the Jews and English Evangelical Eschatology," in *Jerusalem in the Mind of the Western World*, ed. Yehoshua Ben-Arieh and Moshe Davis (Westport, Conn.: Praeger, 1997), 91–107; Franz Kobler, *The Vision Was There: A History of the British Movement for the Restoration of the Jews to Palestine* (London: Lincolns-Prager, 1956); and Sherman Lieber, *Mystics and Missionaries: The Jews in Palestine 1799–1840* (Salt Lake City: University of Utah Press, 1992). Railton cites McCaul on pp. 224–25.

5. Gobat's appointment and his activities and Finn's opposition to him are well discussed in the works mentioned in the previous note, especially Railton, *No North Sea*, 219–38 (the Finn citation is on p. 232); Perry, *British Mission*, 92–103; and Lewis, *Origins of Christian Zionism*, 299–307.

6. On Nicolayson, see especially Lewis, *Origins of Christian Zionism*, 220–22.

7. The sequence of events summarized in the last paragraphs is easily constructed from a variety of pamphlets written at the height of the controversy. I list here a sampling of those I have consulted either in the Bodleian Library, Oxford, or the British Library, London: *The History of Simeon Rosenthal*, 4 pages, no date; James Finn, *Bishop Gobat and the English Consul at Jerusalem*, a letter reprinted from the *Daily News* in reply to Bishop Gobat's speech at Weston-Super-Mare (London, 1858); James Finn, *The Rosenthal Case*, letters to the *Morning Herald, Standard*, and *Guardian* (London, 1866 and 1867); Amelia Hanna Rosenthal, *Mrs. Rosenthal's Story: or, A Narrative of Events in Jerusalem*, with a preface by Joseph B. McCaul (London, 1865); Wildon Charles Simeon Rosenthal, *The History of Simeon Rosenthal: His Conversion; and His Subsequent Persecution and Imprisonment by Bishop Gobat*, compiled by Dr. H. Bonar (Printed for private circulation in Gloucester, 1858); Joseph Cotton Wigram et al., *Report of the Conference upon the Rosenthal Case, Held with the Representatives of the Committee of the London Society for Promoting Christianity Amongst the Jews . . . with an Appendix Containing the Bishop of Rochester's Refutation of the Charges Brought Against Him by the Earl of Shaftesbury in His Recent Pamphlet* (London, 1866); W. D. Veitch et al., *A Reply to Two Pamphlets by James Graham and W. Holman Hunt Respectively Concerning Jerusalem: Its Bishop, Missions etc. Containing an Authorized Statement of Bishop Gobat; Compiled by Order of the Committee of the Jerusalem Diocesan Fund* (London, 1858); and William Holman Hunt, *Jerusalem: Bishop Gobat*

in re Hanna Hadoub; with Original Documents Detailing the Case (London, 1858). In addition, see Perry, *Origins of Christian Zionism*, 122 n. 26.

8. *Jerusalem: Its Bishop, Its Missionaries, and Its Converts*, 3.

9. *Jerusalem: Its Bishop, Its Missionaries, and Its Converts*, 13.

10. *Jerusalem: Its Bishop, Its Missionaries, and Its Converts*, 32–54; the quotation is on p. 54.

11. *Jerusalem: Its Bishop, Its Missionaries, and Its Converts*, 66, 68.

12. *Essays and Reviews* (London: John W. Parker, 1860); *Essays and Reviews: The 1860 Text and Its Reading*, ed. Victor Shea and William Whitla (Charlottesville: University Press of Virginia, 2000). See also Josef L. Altholz, "The Mind of Victorian Orthodoxy: Responses to 'Essays and Reviews,' 1860–1864," *Church History* 51 (1982): 186–97.

13. The following works written by Alexander McCaul in the last years of his life are listed here and discussed chronologically in the remainder of this chapter: *Some Notes on the First Chapter of Genesis with Reference to Statements to "Essays and Reviews"* (London: Wertheim, Macintosh, and Hunt, 1861); *Rationalism and Deistic Infidelity: Three Letters to the Editor of "The Record" Newspaper* (London: Wertheim, Macintosh and Hunt, 1861); *Testimonies to the Divine Authority and Inspiration of the Holy Scriptures as Taught by the Church of England in Reply to the Statements of Mr. James Fitzjames Stephen* (London: Rivingtons, 1862); *An Examination of Bp. Colenso's Difficulties with Regard to the Pentateuch and Some Reasons for Believing in Its Authenticity and Divine Origin* (London: Rivingtons, 1863); J. Field Johnston, *M'Caul v. Colenso: Libel: Report of the Trial in M'Caul v. Colenso, in the Court of Proper Pleas, Dublin, Before a Special Jury* (Dublin: Hodges, Smith, 1863); and *Canon Stanley's "Lectures on the History of the Jewish Church," Reviewed, and Their True Character Exposed* (London: 'Record' Office, 1863). McCaul did not write *M'Caul v. Colenso*, but it does reflect his thinking, as I argue below.

14. McCaul, *Some Notes on the First Chapter of Genesis*, 8.

15. McCaul, *Some Notes on the First Chapter of Genesis*, 9.

16. McCaul, *Some Notes on the First Chapter of Genesis*, 46–48.

17. McCaul, *Rationalism and Deistic Infidelity*, 3–22.

18. McCaul, *Rationalism and Deistic Infidelity*, 23–30. The citations are on 29–30.

19. Leslie Stephen, *The Life of Sir James Fitzjames Stephen, Bart., K.C.S.I.: A Judge of the High Court of Justice* (London: Smith, Elder, 1895), 184–203, especially 185–86. See also James C. Livingston, "The Religious Creed and Criticism of Sir James Fitzjames Stephen," *Victorian Studies* 17 (1974): 279–300; and James A. Colaiaco, *James Fitzjames Stephen and the Crisis of Victorian Thought* (London: Macmillan, 1983). On Rowland Williams, see Keith Robbins, "Williams, Rowland (1817–1870)," *Oxford Dictionary of National Biography*, https://doi.org/10.1093/ref:odnb/29545.

20. McCaul, *Testimonies to the Divine Authority*, 2–3, 23.

21. McCaul, *Testimonies to the Divine Authority*, 37.

22. McCaul, *Testimonies to the Divine Authority*, 142–43.

23. On Colenso, see Jonathan A. Draper, ed., *The Eye of the Storm: Bishop John William Colenso and the Crisis of Biblical Interpretation* (London: Bloomsbury, 2003), especially the article of Timothy Larsen, "Bishop Colenso and His Critics: The Strange Emergence of Biblical Criticism in Victorian Britain, 42–63.

24. See Joseph McCaul, *Bishop Colenso's Criticism Criticised in a Series of Ten Letters Addressed to the Editor of the "Record" Newspaper with Notes and a Postscript* (London: Wertheim, Macintosh, and Hunt, 1863). The postscript includes comments of learned Jews against Colenso, including Hermann Adler.

25. I am indebted to Jerry Singerman in helping me clarify this point. I acknowledge that the authorship and context of this curious text requires more elucidation than I can offer in this chapter.

26. Johnston, *M'Caul v. Colenso*, 3.

27. Johnston, *M'Caul v. Colenso*, 6.

28. Johnston, *M'Caul v. Colenso*, 7.

29. Johnston, *M'Caul v. Colenso*, 8.

30. Johnston, *M'Caul v. Colenso*, 9.

31. Johnston, *M'Caul v. Colenso*, 23–24, 40.

32. Johnston, *M'Caul v. Colenso*, 41–42, 48.

33. Johnston, *M'Caul v. Colenso*, 51.

34. Johnston, *M'Caul v. Colenso*, 64. 67.

35. Johnston, *M'Caul v. Colenso*, 71.

36. McCaul, *Canon Stanley's "Lectures on the History of the Jewish Church,"* 4. On Stanley, see Simon Goldhill, "What Has Alexandria to Do with Jerusalem? Writing the History of the Jews in the Nineteenth Century," *Historical Journal* 59 (2016): 125–51, especially note 66 on earlier scholarship. See also P. C. Hammond, "Stanley, Arthur Penrhyn (1815–1881)," *Oxford Dictionary of National Biography*, https://doi.org/10.1093/ref:odnb/26259.

37. McCaul, *Canon Stanley's "Lectures on the History of the Jewish Church,"* 29–30.

38. In addition to the eulogy of William Ayerst discussed in Chapter 1 above, see *A Memorial Sketch of the Rev. Alexander McCaul, D.D., Rector of St. Magnus and Professor of Hebrew and Old Testament Exegesis, King's College, London, by His Eldest Son, the Rev. Joseph B. McCaul, Chaplain to the Lord Bishop of Rochester to Which Are Appended Two Funeral Sermons Preached in the Church of St. Magnus on Sunday, Nov. 22, by the Rev. Canon Jelf, D.D., Principal of King's College, and the Rev. Charles Braddy, M.A., Lecturer at St. Magnus* (London: Rivingtons, 1863). See also the eulogy contained in the minute books of the London Society for the Promotion of Christianity Amongst the Jews, Oxford Bodleian Dep. C.M.J. c. 24 (November 25, 1863), 682.

CHAPTER 4

1. Stanislaus Hoga, *Eldad and Medad: A Dialogue Between a Converted Jew and a Modern Jew* (London: B. Wertheim, 1843). For earlier scholarship on Hoga, see below.

2. Hoga, *Eldad and Medad*, 4.

3. Hoga, *Eldad and Medad*, 7.

4. Beth-Zion Lask Abrahams, "Stanislaus Hoga—Apostate and Penitent," *Transactions (Jewish Historical Society of England)* 15 (1939–45), 121–49; and Shnayer Z. Leiman, "The Baal Teshuvah and the Emden-Eibeschuetz Controversy," *Judaic Studies* 1 (1985): 3–26.

5. Much of this information comes from the aforementioned essay by Abrahams, which relies heavily on Ezriel Frenk, *Meshumodim in Pojlen in 19-ten johr-hundert* (Warsaw: Freyd, 1923), 38–110. Frenk's research has been challenged and refined by later scholars. See, for example, Marcin Wodziński, *Haskalah and Hasidism in the Kingdom of Poland: A History of Conflict* (Oxford: Littman Library of Jewish Civilization, 2005); and by the same author, *Hasidism and Politics: The Kingdom of Poland, 1815–1864* (Oxford: Littman Library of Jewish Civilization, 2013); Glenn Dynner, *Men of Silk: The Hasidic Conquest of Polish Jewish Society* (Oxford: Oxford University Press, 2006), 109–113, 162, 216. I was able to gain a general impression of

Hoga's Polish work *Tu Chazy czyli Rozmowa o Zydach* (Warsaw: Bayckiego, 1830) with the gracious help of Professor Agnieszka Jagodzińska who translated parts for me. What is clear is that this early work, written in dialogue form, offers striking parallels to *Eldad and Medad* and needs to be compared with it along with Hoga's later English writings. This is a task for future scholarship.

6. For more on McCaul's relationship with Hoga, see David Ruderman, "Towards a Preliminary Portrait of an Evangelical Missionary to the Jews: The Many Faces of Alexander McCaul (1799–1863)," *Jewish Historical Studies: Transactions of the Jewish Historical Society of England* 47 (2015): 48–69; and Chapter 1 above.

7. Hoga, *Eldad and Medad*, 24.

8. Hoga, *Eldad and Medad*, 15.

9. I have seen only the second enlarged edition: Stanislau Hoga, *The Controversy of Zion: A Meditation on Judaism and Christianity*, 2nd ed., enl. (London: Wertheim, 1845); citations refer to this edition.

10. Hoga, *The Controversy of Zion*, viii.

11. Hoga, *The Controversy of Zion*, xvii.

12. Hoga, *The Controversy of Zion*, xviii.

13. Hoga, *The Controversy of Zion*, xxv, xxx.

14. Hoga, *The Controversy of Zion*, 59. I refer to Moses Margoliouth, *The Fundamental Principles of Modern Judaism Investigated: Together with a Memoir of the Author and an Introduction . . . Dedicated by Permission to the Rev. Alexander McCaul*, preface by Rev. Henry Raikes, A.M. (London: B. Wertheim, 1843); and see Chapter 6 below. Hoga mentions phylacteries and fringes as Margoliouth had done, but substitutes circumcision for *mezuzah*. Agnieszka Jagodzińska reminded me of the interesting parallel between Hoga and Abraham Jacob Schwartzenberg (1762–1843), another famous convert associated with the London Society, who insisted on wearing his phylacteries, fringes, and beard, and generally dressing as a Jew even after he converted. Schwartzenberg was also baptized by Alexander McCaul in 1828. On him, see W. T. Gidney, *The History of the London Society for Promoting Christianity Amongst the Jews from 1809 to 1908* (London: London Society for Promoting Christianity Amongst the Jews, 1908), 221–22.

15. Hoga, *The Controversy of Zion*, 56.

16. Stanislaus Hoga, *Zir Ne'eman: The Faithful Missionary; A Monthly Periodical, Illustrating the Value of Judaism, with a View to Opening the Eyes of Some Deluded Christians in England to the Doings of the (So-Called) "London Society" for Promoting Christianity Among the Jews* (London: W. Brittain, 1847), 3–5.

17. Hoga, *Zir Ne'eman*, 10–19.

18. Hoga, *Zir Ne'eman*, 34–48.

19. Abrahams, "Stanislaus Hoga—Apostate and Penitent," 129.

20. Leiman, "The Baal Teshuvah and the Emden-Eibeschuetz Controversy," 13.

21. Tobias Theodores, review of *Three More Letters to His Grace the Lord Archbishop of Canterbury on the Culpability and Unauthorized Presumption of the Gentile Christian Church in Requiring the Jew to Forsake the Law of Moses*, by John Oxlee, *Jewish Chronicle*, May 16, 1845, 164. On Theodores, also a founder of the Reform congregation in Manchester, see Michael Meyer, *Response to Modernity: A History of the Reform Movement in Judaism* (Oxford: Oxford University Press, 1988), 177; and Bill Williams, *The Making of Manchester Jewry* (Manchester: University of Manchester Press, 1976). On John Oxlee and Charlotte Elizabeth Tonna, see Chapter 5 below, where both Oxlee and Tonna are treated in depth.

22. *Jewish Chronicle*, March 19, 1847, 98–99. Theodores briefly responded to Hoga on March 26, 1847, 111–12, followed by Hoga's extensive responses on May 28, 1847, 144–46, and June 11, 1847, 155–57.

23. *Jewish Chronicle*, August 20, 1847, 227–28. The citation is on p. 228.

24. *Jewish Chronicle*, September 3, 1847, 230–31, 238–39, entitled "Jewish Emancipation and the Conversion Society."

25. *Jewish Chronicle*, November 12, 1847, 309, entitled "Moses and Plato." Hoga was responding to what Oxlee had written on October 22, 1847, 282, denying the claim of any connection between Moses, Plato, and Pythagoras.

26. *Jewish Chronicle*, November 19, 1847, 317–18; December 3, 1847, 336. The citation is from p. 336.

27. *Voice of Israel*, September 1, 1845, 167–68. On Herschell, see Michael R. Darby, *The Emergence of the Hebrew-Christian Movement in Nineteenth-Century Britain* (Leiden: Brill, 2010), 124–33; and Nicholas M. Railton, *No North Sea: The Anglo-German Evangelical Network in the Middle of the Nineteenth Century* (Leiden: Brill, 2000), 207–10.

28. *Voice of Jacob* 2 (August 1843): 215 (Franklin's brief notice of *Eldad and Medad*); 3 (February 1844): 95 and 103; the citation is from p. 95.

29. *Voice of Jacob* 3 (February 1844): 95 and 103; and see note 14 above. On Margoliouth, see Chapter 6 below.

30. Abrahams, "Stanislaus Hoga—Apostate and Penitent," 146. I can now add that Hoga was buried in Highgate Cemetery, London, grave number 10092, square 50, Western Cemetery. My effort to secure a picture of the headstone on the grave was hampered by the fact that another person was later buried in the same plot and his gravestone is the only one extant.

31. Abrahams, "Stanislaus Hoga—Apostate and Penitent," 145–46, 149. The reference by Elizabeth Finn to Hoga's scientific attainments is in *Reminiscences of Mrs. Finn, Member of the Royal Asiatic Society* (London: Marshall, Morgan, and Scott, 1929), 25. For other references to Hoga as an inventor, see *Inventors' Gazette*, June 15, 1857, 276, https://books.google.com/books?id=VkcEAAAAQAAJ; *Commissioners of Patents' Journal*, August 21, 1857, no. 1547, https://books.google.com/books?id=fZJGAQAAMAAJ; *Repertory of Patent Inventions and Other Discoveries* 30 (1857): 261, https://books.google.com/books?id=eKwoAQAAMAAJ; and *Repertory of Patent Inventions* 21 (1853): 318, https://books.google.com/books?id=roc EAAAAQAAJ.

32. Hoga, *The Controversy of Zion*, xi.

CHAPTER 5

1. See Chapter 4 at n. 21.

2. Michael R. Darby, *The Emergence of the Hebrew-Christian Movement in Nineteenth-Century Britain* (Leiden: Brill, 2010).

3. See G. C. Boase, "Oxlee, John (1779–1854)," rev. John D. Haigh, *Oxford Dictionary of National Biography* (Oxford: Oxford University Press, 2004), http://www.oxforddnb.com/view/article/21059. This essay heavily relies on Gideon Smales, *Whitby Authors and Their Publications, with the Titles of All the Books Printed in Whitby* (Whitby: Horne and Son, 1867), 105–11. See also the obituary in the *Gentleman's Magazine and Historical Review* (London), February 1855, 203–4. In addition to Oxlee's writing discussed in this chapter, Oxlee penned seven letters to a Jew referred to as S. M. (not J. M. as in the Boase

article), all published in the London Society publication the *Jewish Repository* 2 (1814): 148–53, 183–90, 295–305; 3 (1815): 99–107, 144–48, 222–32, 258–70, 294–97, 348–57, 457–65. Boase also mentions that Oxlee corresponded from 1842 to 1854 with a Jewish scholar named Mr. Peynado. I could not locate these letters but can easily identify the Jew as Joseph Rodriques Peynado, a Sephardic merchant and member of the Bevis Marks congregation in London. He was also a regular correspondent and close associate of Isaac Leeser of Philadelphia, writing regularly on matters relating to Jewish-Christian relations in Leeser's *Occident and American Jewish Advocate*. Of particular relevance are two essays he wrote: "An Examination of Bishop Pearson's Exposition of the Apostle's Creed," *Occident* 5 (1847): 496–99; and "A Letter to the Rev. A. M'Caul," *Occident* 7 (1849): 25–31. In June 1843, a year after its publication, he sent Leeser a copy of Oxlee's *Three Letters* as mentioned in "Literary Notices," *Occident* 1, no. 3 (1843); and see below.

    4. John Oxlee, *The Christian Doctrines of the Trinity and Incarnation Considered and Maintained on the Principles of Judaism*, 3 vols. (London, 1815, 1820, 1850). It is interesting that the first volume was published by the London Society, while the other two volumes were published by commercial publishers.

    5. Oxlee, *Christian Doctrines*, 1:7.

    6. Oxlee, *Christian Doctrines*, 1:13.

    7. Oxlee, *Christian Doctrines*, 3:270.

    8. Oxlee, *Christian Doctrines*, 3:311–12.

    9. Oxlee, *Christian Doctrines*, 3:333–34.

    10. Oxlee, *Christian Doctrines*, 3:334–38, mentioning a Bishop Burgess (probably Thomas Burgess [1756–1837]), Bishop Heber (probably Reginald Heber [1783–1826]), Rev. Dr. Vicesimus Knox, headmaster of the Tunbridge Grammar School, and Rev. Dr. Mill, the Hebrew professor at Cambridge who learned of Oxlee's work from Bishop Middleton. This was William Hodge Mill (1792–1853), the first principal of Bishop's College, Calcutta, and later regius professor of Hebrew at Cambridge; and his predecessor, the founder of the Bishop's College in Calcutta, Thomas Fanshawe Middleton (1769–1822). According to Oxlee, Mill reviewed the first volume but had reservations about it.

    11. Oxlee referred to Coleridge in *The Christian Doctrines*, 3:338. See Samuel Taylor Coleridge, *Notes on English Divines*, ed. Derwent Coleridge, in 2 vols. (London: Edward Moxon, 1853), 2:255–65; the citation is on p. 260.

    12. John Oxlee [the Elder], *The Mysterious Stranger; or, Dialogues on Doctrine; Dialogue the First, Between the Jew Rabbi and the Stranger*, ed. John Oxlee [Oxlee's son] (London: Joseph Masters, 1859), 3–6; the citation is on p. 3.

    13. Oxlee, *Mysterious Stranger*, 7, 13.

    14. Oxlee, *Mysterious Stranger*, 23, 24.

    15. John Oxlee, *Three Letters Humbly Submitted to the Consideration of His Grace the Most Reverend the Lord Archbishop of Canterbury, Primate of All England, and Metropolitan, on the Inexpediency and Futility of Any Attempt to Convert the Jews to the Christian Faith, in the Way and Manner Hitherto Practised, Being a General Discussion of the Whole Jewish Question* (London: Sold by Hatchard and Son, 1842), 3 (mentioning his relationship to the London Society), 5–24.

    16. Oxlee, *Three Letters*, 24–25.

    17. Oxlee, *Three Letters*, 25–27.

    18. Oxlee, *Three Letters*, 32–35; the citation is on p. 34.

    19. Oxlee, *Three Letters*, 56–60; the citation is on p. 56.

    20. Oxlee, *Three Letters*, 83–84.

21. Jacob Franklin, review of *Three Letters*, by John Oxlee, *Voice of Jacob* 2 (March 31, 1843): 142. On Franklin and his editorship of this journal, see Chapter 4; on his relationship to Charlotte Elizabeth Tonna, see below. Franklin's personal papers are located in the library of the University of Southampton and certainly deserve further scrutiny. See http://www .southampton.ac.uk/archives/cataloguedatabases/webguidemss120.page.

22. Franklin, review of *Three Letters*, 142.

23. Franklin, review of *Three Letters*,142.

24. John Oxlee, *Three More Letters Humbly Submitted to the Consideration of His Grace the Most Reverend the Lord Archbishop of Canterbury, Primate of All England, and Metropolitan, on the Culpability and Unauthorised Presumption of the Gentile Christian Church in Requiring the Jew to Forsake the Law of Moses Before He Can Be Allowed Publicly to Embrace the Gospel of Christ; Containing, also, Metaphysical Disquisitions on the Godhead; and a Confutation of the Diabolarchy* (London: Sold by Hatchard and Son, 1845), 3.

25. Oxlee, *Three More Letters*, 4.

26. Oxlee, *Three More Letters*, 5.

27. Oxlee, *Three More Letters*, 52, 66, 68, and 75, respectively.

28. Oxlee, *Three More Letters*, 102.

29. Oxlee, *Three More Letters*, 120–21.

30. Oxlee, *Three More Letters*, 127–35; the citations are on pp. 127, 130, and 132, respectively. On Michael Solomon Alexander, the bishop of Jerusalem, see Yaron Perry, "Alexander, Michael Solomon (1799–1845)," *Oxford Dictionary of National Biography* (Oxford: Oxford University Press, 2004), http://www.oxforddnb.com/view/article/334; and the additional bibliography, especially Yaron Perry, *British Mission to the Jews in Nineteenth-Century Palestine* (London: Frank Cass, 2003). For more on the bishopric of Jerusalem, see Chapter 3 above, especially note 4.

31. Tobias Theodores, review of *Three More Letters to His Grace the Lord Archbishop of Canterbury on the Culpability and Unauthorized Presumption of the Gentile Christian Church in Requiring the Jew to Forsake the Law of Moses*, by John Oxlee, *Jewish Chronicle*, May 16, 1845, 165. On Theodores, also a founder of the Reform congregation in Manchester, see Chapter 4, especially note 21.

32. Theodores, review of *Three More Letters*, 165. On Modena's work and its nineteenth-century publication, see Yaacob Dweck, *The Scandal of Kabbalah: Leon Modena, Jewish Mysticism, Early Modern Venice* (Princeton, N.J.: Princeton University Press, 2011), especially 216–21.

33. Theodores, review of *Three More Letters*, 166. On Galatinus (1460–1540), see Saverio Campanini, "Pietro Galatino und seine Verteidigung der christlichen Kabbala," in *Reuchlins Freunde und Gegner: Kommunikative Konstellationen eines frühneuzeitlichen Medienereignisses*, ed. Wilhelm Kühlmann, Pforzheimer Reuchlinschriften 12 (Ostfildern: Jan Thorbecke Verlag, 2010), 69–88. Theodores also refers to other Christian mystics and kabbalists such as Raymond Lull, Pico della Mirandola, Johannes Reuchlin, Cornelius Agrippa, and Paracelsus.

34. Theodores, review of John Oxlee, *Jewish Chronicle*, June 27, 1845, 191–92, and July 11, 1845, 202–3; the citation is on p. 202.

35. Theodores, review of John Oxlee, July 11, 1845, 203.

36. See note 3 above.

37. "Biography of the Rev. John Oxlee," *Jewish Messenger*, December 18, 1857, 102.

38. *Jewish Chronicle and Hebrew Observer* (London), January 29, 1858, obituary of John Oxlee with biographical notice abridged from a lecture by John Dowson, M.D. (taken from the *Whitby Gazette*, December 19, 1857).

39. Hilary L.Rubenstein, "A Pioneering Philosemite: Charlotte Elizabeth Tonna (1790–1846) and the Jews," *Jewish Historical Studies* [published by the Jewish Historical Society of England] 35 (1996–98): 103–18; Mary Lenard, "Tonna, Charlotte Elizabeth (1790–1846)," *Oxford Dictionary of National Biography* (Oxford: Oxford University Press, 2004), http://www.oxforddnb.com/view/article/27537. See also Margaret Beetham, *A Magazine of Her Own? Domesticity and Desire in the Woman's Magazine, 1800–1914* (London: Routledge, 1996); Joseph A. Kestner, *Protest and Reform: The British Social Narrative by Women, 1827–1867* (Madison: University of Wisconsin Press, 1985); Christine L. Krueger, *The Reader's Repentance: Women Preachers, Women Writers, and Nineteenth-Century Social Discourse* (Chicago: University of Chicago Press, 1992); and Mary Lenard, "Deathbeds and Didacticism: Charlotte Elizabeth Tonna and Victorian Social Reform Literature," in *Silent Voices: Forgotten Novels by Victorian Women Writers*, ed. Brenda Ayres (Westport, Conn.: Praeger, 2003). Also important is the discussion of Tonna in Donald M. Lewis, *The Origins of Christian Zionism: Lord Shaftesbury and the Evangelical Support for a Jewish Homeland* (Cambridge: Cambridge University Press, 2010), 189–96.

40. *Christian Lady's Magazine* 19 (June 1843): 558.

41. Charlotte Elizabeth Tonna, "Oxlee's Letters," *Christian Ladies Magazine* 23 (1845): 446–50. The citation is on p. 446.

42. Tonna, "Oxlee's Letters," 447–48.

43. Tonna, "Oxlee's Letters," 448–49.

44. Tonna, "Oxlee's Letters," 450.

45. Charlotte Elizabeth Tonna, "Fringes and Phylacteries," *Christian Lady's Magazine* 19 (January 1843): 63–68. The citations are from 64, 66, and 67, respectively.

46. Jacob Franklin, "To the Editor of the Christian Lady's Magazine," *Christian Lady's Magazine* 19 (May 1843): 438–40; Tonna's response follows on pp. 440–47.

47. Lewis, *Origins of Christian Zionism*, 190. Tonna's panegyric is found in *Christian Lady's Magazine* 19 (April 1843): 352–56. On McNeile, see John Wolffe, "McNeile, Hugh Boyd (1795–1879)," *Oxford Dictionary of National Biography* (Oxford: Oxford University Press, 2004), http://www.oxforddnb.com/view/article/17711.

48. *Christian Lady's Magazine* 19 (May 1843): 441–42.

49. Hugh M'Neile, *Popular Lectures on the Prophecies Relative to the Jewish Nation*, 3rd ed. (London: J. Hatchard and Son, 1840).

50. Hugh M'Neile, "To the Correspondent of the Editor of the Christian Lady's Magazine Who Signs Himself 'Jacob,'" *Christian Lady's Magazine* 19 (June 1843): 539–45, 546–55. The citations are found on pp. 544, 551, and 552, respectively.

51. *Christian Lady's Magazine* 19 (June 1843): 555–60.

52. See note 30 above as well as Chapter 3. In addition, see the useful works of Nicholas Railton, *No North Sea: The Anglo-German Evangelical Network in the Middle of the Nineteenth Century* (Leiden: Brill, 2000); and Lewis, *Origins of Christian Zionism*, especially 287–98. On the Jewish community of Jerusalem, see Yehoshua Ben-Arieh, *Jerusalem in the Nineteenth Century: The Old City* (Jerusalem: Yad Ben Zvi; and New York: St. Martin's Press, 1984).

53. Charlotte Elizabeth [Tonna], *Israel's Ordinances: A Few Thoughts on Their Perpetuity Respectfully Suggested in a Letter to the Right Rev. the Bishop of Jerusalem* (London: Seeley, Burnside, and Seeley, 1843), 4–5.

54. Tonna, *Israel's Ordinances*, 17.

55. Tonna, *Israel's Ordinances*, 35.

56. Moses Margoliouth, *The Fundamental Principles of Modern Judaism Investigated: Together with a Memoir of the Author and an Introduction . . . Dedicated by Permission to the Rev. Alexander McCaul*, preface by Rev. Henry Raikes, A.M. (London B. Wertheim, 1843); Margoliouth, *Israel's Ordinances Examined: A Reply to Charlotte Elizabeth's Letter to the Right Rev. the Bishop of Jerusalem* (London: B. Wertheim, 1844).

57. Charlotte Elizabeth Tonna, "A Vindication," *Christian Lady's Magazine* 20 (November 1843): 443–54. The citation is on p. 444. She is referring to Margoliouth, *The Fundamental Principles*, 82–83.

58. Tonna, "A Vindication," 448.

59. Tonna, "A Vindication," 451.

60. Jacob Franklin also responded to Margoliouth's attack in the *Voice of Jacob* 3 (October 1843): 26–28. Besides offering a vigorous defense of the three rituals Margoliouth had singled out for mockery, Franklin also praised the honest convictions of Tonna in her "Vindication" against "this rancorous apostate."

61. Margoliouth, *Israel's Ordinances Examined*, 1–7. The last citation is on p. 7. It is interesting to note that Margoliouth eventually modified his view regarding the claims of Hebrew Christians to the actual land of Israel. Writing in 1878, only three years before his death, he strongly denied the rights of unbaptized Jews to the land but boldly claimed that Jewish converts to Christianity were fully entitled and encouraged to reside there. See Moses Margoliouth, *The Destinies of Israel and the Claims of Hebrew Christians upon the Sitting Congress, Inscribed to the Plentipotentiaries at the Berlin Congress and Other Diplomatists* (London: Elliot Stock, 1878). On pp. 22–23, he writes:

We consider ourselves, therefore, the legitimate claimants of the above named City and Land. We long to enjoy our right to the cultivation of the myriads of acres of the waste places in that Land. Let the great Christian Powers, now ruling by the Providence of the King of kings and Lord of lords, guarantee to us autonomy and we shall be ready to enter upon our inheritance and take possession of it, either by allotment, or by any other arrangement according to the circumstances. . . . Such an event . . . must precede the national penitence and restoration of Israel. It is vain to talk of the restoration of the Jewish nation to the Land of Israel, whilst the nation continues to reject Jesus as the Messiah. The whole tenor of prophecy, in the Old and New Testaments, militates against such a theory. The Jewish people, as a nation, were cast out of the Land because of unbelief. . . . But the rightful claims of Hebrew Christians, the "remnant according to the election of grace," to the repossession of and autonomy in the Holy Land, must be admitted by every intelligent student of "the Oracles of God" as well as owned by the Christian potentates of the world, and by the expounders of Divine and human legislation.

62. There are many instances of warm exchange between Tonna and Franklin in both their respective periodicals discussed already by Hillary Rubinstein in her aforementioned article. His mention of negative references to him in Tonna's own periodical might surely refer to her "Vindication" among others.

63. Margoliouth, *Israel's Ordinances Examined*, 9.

64. Margoliouth, *Israel's Ordinances Examined*, 43–57. The description of the prayer for Montefiore is on pp. 56–57.

65. *Voice of Jacob*, July 31, 1846, 172–75.

66. *Voice of Jacob*, July 31, 1846, 174.

67. *Voice of Jacob*, July 31, 1846, 174

68. *Voice of Jacob*, July 31, 1846, 175.

CHAPTER 6

1. This is discussed in Chapter 5 above.

2. Peter Jones devoted an entire monograph to the life of Moses Margoliouth entitled *Moses: A Short Account of the Life of Reverend Moses Margoliouth* (London: Minerva Press, 1999). The book offers able summaries of Margoliouth's principal works, a useful description of the English and Irish parishes that Margoliouth served, and important background on the primary Christian associates and patrons in his life. Jones is weaker on Margoliouth's Jewish background and scholarly achievements and particularly frustrates this reader by not offering adequate documentation of the sources he uses. David S. Katz, "Margoliouth, Moses (1815–1881)," *Oxford Dictionary of National Biography* (Oxford: Oxford University Press, 2004), http://www.oxford dnb.com/view/article/18055, relies heavily on Jones's work. There are brief discussions of Margoliouth in Michael R. Darby, *The Emergence of the Hebrew Christian Movement in Nineteenth-Century Britain* (Leiden: Brill, 2010); and in Todd Endelman, *Leaving the Jewish Fold: Conversion and Radical Assimilation in Modern Jewish History* (Princeton, N.J.: Princeton University Press, 2015). Most recently, Jill Golub has written a most competent undergraduate honors' thesis at the University of Pennsylvania, Department of History, in 2017, entitled "Between Judaism and Christianity: The Intellectual Journey of Moses Margoliouth." Among the many strengths of her work is the discovery of a cache of unpublished letters written by or about Margoliouth in the Lambeth Palace Library, London. I am indebted to her for making these letters available to me, letters that even the thorough Jones seems to have missed in his own treatment.

3. The date of his birth is usually given as 1820, but Peter Jones, *Moses*, 17, corrects this date and suggests 1815, which David Katz follows. Both seem to have ignored the date supplied by Margoliouth himself in the beginning of *The Fundamental Principles of Modern Judaism Investigated: Together with a Memoir of the Author and an Introduction . . . Dedicated by Permission to the Rev. Alexander McCaul*, preface by Rev. Henry Raikes, A.M. (London: B. Wertheim, 1843), i, which I have adopted. On the Jewish history of Suwałki, see "Suwałki," *YIVO Encyclopedia of Jews in Eastern Europe*, http://www.yivoencyclopedia.org/article.aspx/Suwalki; and Yehuda Alroi and Yosef Chrust, eds., *Jewish Community Book Suwalk and Vicinity (Suwałki, Poland)*, partial English translation of *Sefer kehilat Suvalk u-benotehah* (Tel Aviv: Yair-Abraham Stern, 1989), https://www.jewishgen.org/Yizkor/Suwalki/Suwalki.html#TOCE9.

4. On Raikes, see G. C. Boase, "Raikes, Henry (1782–1854)," rev. Simon Harrison, *Oxford Dictionary of National Biography* (Oxford: Oxford University Press, 2004), http://www.oxford dnb.com/view/article/23014.

5. Bergfeldt's involvement in distributing missionary Bibles was well documented in the London Society's publications. See, for example, *Children's Jewish Advocate* 5 (February 1859): 45–47; Gidney, *The History of the London Society for Promoting Christianity Amongst the Jews from 1809 to 1908* (London: London Society for Promoting Christianity Amongst the Jews, 1908), 228; and *Missionary Register* 21 (1833): 48.

6. Margoliouth, *The Fundamental Principles*, "Memoir," i–x; the citation is on p. i.

7. Margoliouth, *The Fundamental Principles*, 1–117; the citations are on pp. 6, 108, 71, and 65, respectively.

8. Margoliouth, *The Fundamental Principles*, 82.

9. Margoliouth, *The Fundamental Principles*, 82–83; and see the discussion of McNeile, Tonna, and Margoliouth in Chapter 5 above.

10. Margoliouth, *The Fundamental Principles*, 84–89; the citations are on pp. 87, 86, and 89, respectively.

11. Margoliouth, *The Fundamental Principles*, 115–93; the citation is on p. 117.

12. Margoliouth, *The Fundamental Principles*, 193–220. The string of citations is on p. 193.

13. Margoliouth, *The Fundamental Principles*, 220–21. On Rabbi Moses, see David Assaf, *Untold Tales of the Hasidim: Crisis and Discontent in the History of Hasidism* (Waltham, Mass.: Brandeis University Press, 2010), 29–96. Margoliouth's source on the missionary Mr. Cohen is the periodical of the London Society *Jewish Intelligence and Monthly Report* 9 (1843): 100.

14. Margoliouth, *The Fundamental Principles*, 222, 223.

15. Margoliouth, *The Fundamental Principles*, 225, 226.

16. Margoliouth, *The Fundamental Principles*, 227.

17. Margoliouth, *The Fundamental Principles*, 228–41; the citation is on p. 238.

18. Margoliouth, *The Fundamental Principles*, 242–47; the citation on Wessely is on p. 247. Margoliouth was fond of referring to Wessely's poem. See, for example, Moses Margoliouth, *The Poetry of the Hebrew Pentateuch: Being Four Essays on Moses and the Mosaic Age* (London: Samuel Bagster and Sons, 1871), 96; and his *A Pilgrimage to the Land of My Fathers*, 2 vols. (London: Richard Bentley, 1850), 1:25.

19. Margoliouth, *The Fundamental Principles*, 251–59; the citation is on p. 258.

20. See note 2 above.

21. I briefly discuss these letters later in the chapter; see below.

22. Margoliouth, *A Pilgrimage*, 1:27 (letter 6), 62 (letter 7), 65 (letter 8), and 70 (letter 9).

23. Margoliouth, *A Pilgrimage*, 1:89 (letter 9). On Tobias Cohen and his medical textbook, see David B. Ruderman, *Jewish Thought and Scientific Discovery in Early Modern Europe* (New Haven, Conn.: Yale University Press, 1995), 229–55.

24. Margoliouth, *A Pilgrimage*, 1:89–90 (letter 9).

25. Margoliouth, *The Fundamental Principles*, vii; Jones, *Moses*, 31.

26. On George Margoliouth, scholar of Hebrew and Semitic languages and librarian of the British Museum, see the obituary from the *Times*, May 17, 1924, reproduced in Jones, *Moses*, 185–87.

27. Margoliouth, *The Fundamental Principles*, vii; Jones, *Moses*, 31.

28. On Margoliouth's financial situation and his dependence on his father, I rely on Jones, *Moses*, 25, 32–34. On his Russian trip, see Jones, *Moses*, 123–29.

29. Margoliouth, *A Pilgrimage*, 1:30–31 (letter 6). The reference to Rashi, based on *Midrash Tanhuma*, reads as follows: "Thus, too, you will find that in the case of the ten generations from Adam to Noah it states 'So-and-so begat so-and-so,' but when it reaches Noah it deals with him at length. Similarly, of the ten generations from Noah to Abraham it gives but a brief account, but when it comes to Abraham it speaks of him more fully. It may be compared to the case of a jewel that falls into the sand: a man searches in the sand, sifts it in a sieve until he finds the jewel. When he has found it he throws away the pebbles and keeps the jewel."

30. Margoliouth, *A Pilgrimage*, 1:31–32 (letter 6).

31. Margoliouth, *A Pilgrimage*, 1:33–58 (letter 6).

32. Margoliouth, *A Pilgrimage*, 1:94–98 (letter 11); the citations are on pp. 94, 95, and 98, respectively.

33. Margoliouth, *A Pilgrimage*, 1:108–10 (letter 11). On Obadiah in the house of Jezebel, see 1 Kings 18:3–4.

34. Margoliouth, *A Pilgrimage*, 1:143–47 (letter 14); the citation is on pp. 146–47. On Benisch, see Sidney Lee, "Benisch, Abraham (1811–1878)," rev. Roger T. Stearn, *Oxford Dictionary of National Biography* (Oxford: Oxford University Press, 2004), http://www.oxforddnb.com/view/article/2095.

35. Margoliouth, *A Pilgrimage*, 1:344–58 (letter 29); the citations are on pp. 347 and 357.

36. Margoliouth, *A Pilgrimage*, 1:361–63 (letter 29); the citations are on p. 362. His reference to Jewish composers is taken from Benjamin Disraeli's *Coningsby*. Sander Gilman well summarizes his view: "Benjamin Disraeli, novelist and politician manqué, had countered that view in his novel *Coningsby* (1844) in which Sidonie, the embodiment of all that is positive among the Jews, forcefully declares that 'musical Europe is ours!' for every time a Christian listens to a [Gioacchino] Rossini [1792–1868] or a [Giacomo] Meyerbeer [1791–1864] or is 'thrilled into raptures at the notes of an aria by a [Giuditta] Pasta [1798–1865] or a [Giulia] Grisi [1811–1869], little do they suspect that they are offering their homage to "the sweet singers of Israel!" " The Jews are endowed 'with the almost exclusive privilege of music.'" See Benjamin Disraeli, *Coningsby; or, The New Generation* (Harmondsworth, England: Penguin Books, 1983), 271; and Sander L. Gilman, "Are Jews Musical? Historical Notes on the Question of Jewish Modernism and Nationalism," *Modern Judaism* 28 (2008): 239–56; the citation is on p. 241. Disraeli's unique claim that Rossini was Jewish was incorrect. On this, see Gilman, "Are Jews Musical?," 253 n. 4.

Margoliouth's fascination with Jewish music, liturgy, and Hebrew poetry is a constant theme not only in *A Pilgrimage* but in several of his other works. Besides *The Fundamental Principles* described above and *The Curates of Riversdale* described below, see his *The Poetry of the Hebrew Pentateuch; Sacred Minstrelsy: A Lecture on Biblical and Post-Biblical Hebrew Music* (London, 1860); and *The Star of Jacob* (Dublin, 1847), 21–40, 118–40.

37. Margoliouth, *A Pilgrimage*, 2:142–47 (letter 15); the citation is on p. 146.

38. Margoliouth, *A Pilgrimage*, 2:357–63 (letter 3); see also 2:278 (letter 27).

39. Margoliouth, *A Pilgrimage*, 2:216 (letter 20).

40. Margoliouth, *A Pilgrimage*, 2:245–48 (letter 23); the citation is on pp. 247–48. On the history and present location of the Damascus Keter, see http://web.nli.org.il/sites/NLI/English/collections/treasures/shapell_manuscripts/mikra/damasc/Pages/default.aspx. On Palachi, see Yaron Ben Naeh, "Pallache, Ḥayyim," in *Encyclopedia of Jews in the Islamic World*, online ed., 2010, ed. Norman A. Stillman, and see below, Chapter 8.

41. Margoliouth, *A Pilgrimage*, 2:83 (letter 8) and 91–98 (letter 9).

42. Margoliouth, *A Pilgrimage*, 2:166–76 (letter 16); the citation is on p. 175.

43. Margoliouth, *A Pilgrimage*, vol. 2, letters 30–34. The citations are from pp. 302, 324, and 333–34, respectively.

44. The documents defending Margoliouth in this affair are collected in Moses Margoliouth, *Farewell Address to the Parishioners of Wybunbury on His Retiring from the Office of Curate of the Above Parish* (Manchester: Cave and Sever, 1855).

45. The letters describing the Burney affair in 1860 including Margoliouth's self-defense are found in the Archbishop's Papers Collection at the Lambeth Palace Library, MS Tait 116, fols. 363–73; Tait 117, fols. 9–17, including a letter of support from Alexander McCaul, who claimed he had not been in recent contact with him.

46. During this same period of time, Margoliouth attempted to alleviate his horrible economic situation by applying to the Royal Literary Fund for relief. MS British Museum 1552 contains his application for March 28, 1861. In it, he mentions his birth in Poland forty-three

years ago, that he is married with three children and has recently suffered economic loss and ill health. He received a letter from Joseph McCaul, the son of Alexander. He was granted forty pounds and submitted a letter of thanks. He applied again on January 5, 1863, and similarly wrote a moving letter regarding his economic plight, mentioning his project of an annotated Hebrew Old Testament and his work on Hebrew poetry. This time Alexander McCaul wrote a brief letter of support on his behalf, literally months before he died. This time he received a grant of twenty-five pounds. Once more on July 3, 1871, "crushed in health and spirit," he applied again to the same fund and was rewarded with forty pounds.

47. The letters from and about Chaja Margoliouth are found in the same Lambeth Palace Library collection, MS Tait 124, fols. 1–10. I offer a small sampling of Margoliouth's long, detailed, and intimate letter about the state of his marriage (fols. 2–3):

> She lived with me about two years; she did eat and drink of the same as I did without any simple questions of conscience. However, she found the quiet existence of a Christian minister intolerable, and after a series of outrages, which would have killed many a man, a separation was arranged and she was henceforth to receive an allowance from me, on condition that she remained to live at Berlin, and to forfeit that allowance as soon as she quitted the German capital, that was in 1845. I was then Incumbent of Glasnevin near Dublin, examining chaplain and private secretary to the late Bishop of Kildare. To my indescribable consternation, some months after she left Ireland, she returned to Dublin enceinte and wished to force herself upon my living with her. She remained in Dublin till she was confined and then by the help of some unprincipled Jews commenced a most systematic process of persecution against me and at last instituted proceedings against me, in the provocative Court, for the restoration of conjugal rights, which were thrown out of the Court, at the very first step, as had no means of proving the marriage, which took place in Poland, when both were minors. So much for the assertion that she does not live with me on account of my having embraced Christianity. However, the annoyance and trouble which the woman caused me impaired my health very much, I was obliged to give up my post in Ireland, and accepted a mission to the East; that was in 1847. As soon as I quitted Glasnevin, the unhappy woman spread a report through England, Ireland, and Scotland, that I had eloped with a young lady.

48. *The Curates of Riversdale: Recollections in the Life of a Clergyman; Written by Himself* [a novel by Moses Margoliouth] (London: Hurst and Blackett, 1860), title page. He obviously refers to Arthur Wellesley, 1st Duke of Wellington (1769–1852), one of the leading military and political figures of nineteenth-century England.

49. The reference is to Benjamin Kennicott (1718–83), the English churchman and biblical scholar who attempted to establish a new authoritative text of the Old Testament based on all extant manuscripts. There is indeed a Kennicott Scholarship that is administered at Oxford until this day. See http://www.orinst.ox.ac.uk/administration/trust_funds/kennicott_fund .html. On Kennicott, see David B. Ruderman, *Jewish Enlightenment in an English Key: Anglo-Jewry's Construction of Modern Jewish Thought* (Princeton, N.J.: Princeton University Press, 2000).

50. Margoliouth, *The Curates of Riversdale*, 30.

51. Margoliouth, *The Curates of Riversdale*, 40.

52. Margoliouth, *The Curates of Riversdale*, 86.

53. Margoliouth, *The Curates of Riversdale*, 216–17.

54. Margoliouth, *The Curates of Riversdale*, 217, 225, respectively.

55. Margoliouth, *The Curates of Riversdale*, 235, 228, 246, respectively.

56. Archbishop's Papers Collection of the Lambeth Palace Library, MS Tait 116, fols. 365, 368.

57. See Chapter 4 above.

58. Moses Margoliouth, *The History of the Jews in Great Britain*, 3 vols. (London: Richard Bentley, 1851), 2:228–29.

59. "London Society for Promoting Christianity Amongst the Jews," *Star of Jacob* [ed. M. Margoliouth] 1 (1847): 155–67; the citations are on pp. 155, 156, and 157, respectively.

60. *The Anglo-Hebrews: Their Past Wrongs and Present Grievances; Two Epistles (with a Postscript), Written for All Classes of the British Public, by a Clergyman of the Church of England* (London: L. Booth, 1856). The author cites Margoliouth's *History of the Jews in Great Britain* on pp. 39 and 55. In the first instance, he declares: "The writer made ample use of that work whilst preparing these letters for the British public." See Endelman, *Leaving the Jewish Fold*, 398 n. 27.

61. [Margoliouth], *The Anglo-Hebrews*, 70.

62. [Margoliouth], *The Anglo-Hebrews*, 70–71.

63. [Margoliouth], *The Anglo-Hebrews*, 72–73.

64. [Margoliouth], *The Anglo-Hebrews*, 73.

65. [Margoliouth], *The Anglo-Hebrews*, 120.

CHAPTER 7

1. The principal responses (besides those of Levinsohn discussed below) include Abraham Benisch, *The Principal Charges of Dr. M'Caul's Old Paths . . . Considered and Answered* (London, 1858); Naftali Hertz Bernstein, *Adar ḥakhamim* (Odessa, 1868); Judah Loeb Chari, *Sefer kol Yehudah . . . neged ha-meḥaber Sefer netivot olam* (Vienna, 1864); Samuel Joseph Fuenn, *Darkei Adonai*, MS Heb. 8390, National Library of Israel; Raphael Kassin, *Sefer derekh ha-ḥayyim* (Constantinople, 1848); Raphael Kassin, *Sefer likkutei amrim* (Izmir, 1855); Judah Yudal Middleman, *Sefer netivot emet . . . ve-hu neged ha-ḥibbur Netivot olam* (London, 1847); Meir Yechiel Yanishkar, *Even shoham*, MS Heb. 8375, National Library of Israel; and Eliezer Zweifel, *Sanegor* (Warsaw, 1885).

2. See the concise recent summary of his life and writings by Mordechai Zalkin, "Levinzon, Yitsḥak Ber," *YIVO Encyclopedia of Jews in Eastern Europe*, http://www.yivoencyclopedia .org/article.aspx/Levinzon_Yitshak_Ber.

3. Immanuel Etkes, Hebrew introduction to Isaac Baer Levinsohn, *Te'udah be-Yisrael* (Vilna, 1828; facsimile ed., Jerusalem: Zalman Shazar Center, 1977); Michael Stanislawski, *Tsar Nicholas I and the Jews: The Transformation of Jewish Society in Russia, 1823–1833* (Philadelphia: Jewish Publication Society of America, 1983); Eli Lederhendler, *The Road to Modern Jewish Politics: Political Tradition and Political Reconstruction in the Jewish Community of Tsarist Russia* (Oxford: Oxford University Press, 1989); and Eliyahu Stern, "Catholic Judaism: The Political Theology of the Nineteenth-Century Russian Jewish Enlightenment," *Harvard Theological Review* 109, no. 4 (2016): 483–511. My thanks to Professor Stern for allowing me to read several drafts of this article prior to publication, which focuses more directly on Levinsohn's polemical

writings. Stern argues that McCaul's anti-Talmudic work was primarily written to challenge the granting of political rights to Jews unless they converted, and, furthermore, Levinsohn's strong response to McCaul was really a veiled attack against the Russian government and its anti-rabbinic policies. See my additional comments on Stern's essay below.

4. See David Ber Nathanson, *Sefer ha-zikhronot: Divrei ḥayyei yemei Ribal* (Warsaw, 1899); Louis S. Greenberg, *Isaac Baer Levinsohn: A Critical Investigation of the Works of Rabbi Isaac Baer Levinsohn (Ribal)* (New York: Bloch, 1930); Menaham Zohori, *Mishnato ha-le'umit shel Yizḥak Baer (Dov) Levinsohn* (Jerusalem: Ha-histadrut ha-Ẓionit ha-olamit, 2002); Israel Zinberg, *A History of Jewish Literature* (Cincinnati: Hebrew Union College Press, 1978), 11:21–94; Joseph Klausner, *Historia shel ha-sifrut ha-Ivrit ha-ḥadasha* (Jerusalem: Aḥiasaf, 1960), 3:33–115.

5. Eliezer Schweid, *A History of Modern Jewish Religious Philosophy*, trans. Leonard Levin (Leiden: Brill, 2015), 2:111–18; Shmuel Feiner, *Haskalah and History: The Emergence of a Modern Jewish Historical Consciousness*, trans. Chaya Naor and Sondra Silverston (Oxford: Littman Library of Jewish Civilization, 2002), 178–92.

6. My citations are from the seventh edition of Isaac Baer Levinsohn, *Zerubavel . . . [neged] da'at rosh mastineinu . . . be-sifro Netivot olam* (Vilna: Isaac Funk, 1901), in 4 parts.

7. I have used the first edition entitled *Aḥiyah Shiloni ha-ḥozeh: Kolel bittul ta'anotov shel Sefer netivot olam* (Leipzig: Vollrath, 1864), published after the author's death by Jacob Israel Levinsohn. The intended English translation is mentioned in a note at the beginning of the volume. Stern, "Catholic Judaism," 496, incorrectly describes *Aḥiyah* as a play for popular consumption. It was neither a play nor were its profound arguments meant for "popular consumption."

8. Levinsohn, *Zerubavel*, 1:6

9. Levinsohn, *Zerubavel*, 1: 6.

10. Levinsohn, *Zerubavel*, 1: 7–11.

11. Levinsohn, *Aḥiyah Shiloni ha-ḥozeh*, 5–7.

12. Levinsohn, *Aḥiyah Shiloni ha-ḥozeh*, 8–9.

13. Levinsohn, *Aḥiyah Shiloni ha-ḥozeh*, 9–10.

14. Levinsohn, *Aḥiyah Shiloni ha-ḥozeh*, 11.

15. Perhaps the one exception to this tentative generalization is Solomon Ibn Verga's *Shevet Yehudah*, as persuasively presented by Jeremy Cohen in *A Historian in Exile: Solomon ibn Verga, "Shevet Yehudah," and the Jewish-Christian Encounter* (Philadelphia: University of Pennsylvania Press, 2017). Levinsohn, of course, was familiar with Ibn Verga's work and even cites him, among many other authors, in the midst of his remarks on the futility of disputations. See *Aḥiyah Shiloni ha-ḥozeh*, 8. But also see the following note.

16. Compare Cohen's words on Ibn Verga, *A Historian in Exile*, 203 n. 39: "*Shevet Yehudah*, we have seen, does aspire to a post-polemical age, a period of new, mutual toleration and respect between Christians and Jews, at the same time as it vehemently expressed the will to maintain Jewish difference in that Christian world."

17. Levinsohn, *Aḥiyah Shiloni ha-ḥozeh*, 18–19 (the argument concerning Islam and other religions), 21 (the list of anti-Christian writers), 28–31 (for the general argument and throughout the book).

18. Levinsohn, *Aḥiyah Shiloni ha-ḥozeh*, 75; Levinsohn, *Zerubavel*, 1:95, 103.

19. Stern, "Catholic Judaism." Levinsohn consulted Jacques-Bénigne Bossuet, *Einleitung in die Geschichte der Welt und der Religion*, trans. Johann Andreas Cramer (Leipzig, 1757–86).

On Bossuet (1627–1704), see Owen Chadwick, *From Bossuet to Newman* (Cambridge: Cambridge University Press, 1987); the older study of Ella K. Sanders, *Jacques Bénigne Bossuet: A Study* (New York: Society for Promoting Christian Knowledge, 1921); and Richard Costigan, *The Consensus of the Church and Papal Infallibility* (Washington, D.C.: Catholic University Press, 2005), chap. 2. On Johann Andreas Cramer, see the entry on him in *The Oxford Companion to German Literature*, 3rd ed., ed. Henry Garland and Mary Garland (Oxford: Oxford University Press, 2005); and Eberhard Reichmann. "Johann Andreas Cramer und die deutsche Geschichtsprosa der Aufklärung," *Monatshefte* 54, no. 2 (February 1962): 59–67.

20. Levinsohn also cited Bossuet/Cramer in *Zerubavel*, 1:20, 64, 133; 2:21; 4:42; *Aḥiyah Shiloni ha-ḥozeh*, 31, 89; *Efes damim* (Warsaw, 1879), 74–75; *Yemin ẓidki* (Warsaw, 1881), 60–61; *Beit Yehudah* (Warsaw, 1878), 73. Stern further claims that Levinsohn's "Catholic Judaism" was the source of a similar notion of Samuel Joseph Fuenn and the foundation of the political theology of the eastern European Jewish Enlightenment. On Fuenn, see Chapter 8 below.

21. Levinsohn cited from Warnekros's work on Hebrew antiquities, *Entwurf der hebräischen Alterthümer* (Weimar, 1832) in *Zerubavel*, 1:68 and 111 and 3:100 and 103; in *Te'udah be-Yisrael*, 74; in *Yemin ẓidki*, 10, 100; and in *Beit Yehudah*, 1:23

22. Volney was best known for his *Les Ruines, ou méditations sur les révolutions des empires*, an essay on the philosophy of history containing a vision of the final union of all religions by the recognition of the common truth underlying them all. Thomas Jefferson translated the invocation plus the first twenty chapters of the 1802 Paris edition of Volney's *Les Ruines*. On Volney, see François Furstenberg, *When the United States Spoke French: Five Refugees Who Shaped a Nation* (New York: Penguin, 2014); Jean Gaulmier, *L'Idéologue Volney (1757–1820): Contribution à l'histoire de l'Orientalisme* (Beyrouth: Impr. Catholique, 1951); and *Encyclopedia of the Enlightenment*, ed. Alan Charles Kors (Oxford: Oxford University Press, 2005), s.v. "Volney, Constantin-François de Chasseboeuf." The text Levinsohn cited is found conveniently in the online edition Constantin-François Chasseboeuf, Marquis de Volney, *The Ruins; or, A Survey of the Revolutions of Empires* (1789), http://oll.libertyfund.org/titles/volney-the-ruins-or -a-survery-of-the-revolutions-of-empires, 209 n. 37. Levinsohn cited Volney in *Aḥiyah Shiloni ha-ḥozeh*, 32 and earlier on 21.

23. Compare Stern, "Catholic Judaism," especially 500–502. Stern's focus on tradition as a process rather than a specific content, constantly changing in light of the encounter between reason and doctrine (502), surely reflects how Levinsohn viewed the rabbinic tradition but hardly the Catholic one.

24. Levinsohn, *Aḥiyah Shiloni ha-ḥozeh*, 45–55; he referred to the German translation of Voltaire's epic poem *Henriade*, first published in 1723, on pp. 47, 49. On this work, see Voltaire, *La Henriade*, ed. O. R. Taylor, 2 vols. (Geneva: Institut et Musée Voltaire, 1965). See *Aḥiyah*, 48, where Levinsohn cites Nonnotte, also in German translation, from his *Les Erreurs de Voltaire*. I have used the edition published in Amsterdam, 1766, vol. 2, chap. 27, pp. 287–94. On Nonnotte, see John Christian Laursen and María José Villaverde, eds., *Paradoxes of Religious Toleration in Early Modern Political Thought* (Plymouth, U.K.: Lexington Books, 2012), especially Jonathan Israel, "Tolerance and Intolerance in the Writings of the French *Antiphilosophes*," 193–206. Levinsohn also cited Voltaire and Nonnotte in *Te'udah be-Yisrael*, 110, and *Beit Yehudah*, 36–37. On other nineteenth-century Jewish expressions of moral superiority vis-à-vis Christian society, see Richard I. Cohen, " 'Jewish Contribution to Civilization' and Its Implications for Notions of 'Jewish Superiority' in the Modern Period," in *The Jewish Contribution to Civilization: Reassessing an Idea*, ed. Jeremy Cohen and Richard I. Cohen (Oxford: Littman Library of Jewish Civilization, 2008), 11–23.

25. Levinsohn, *Zerubavel*, 2:71. Levinsohn's description of slavery needs to be read in the context of other maskilic discussions of slavery in the eighteenth and nineteenth centuries, such as those of Judah Horowitz, Samuel Romanelli, and Samson Bloch, intelligently discussed by Iris Idelson-Shein, *Difference of a Different Kind: Jewish Constructions of Race During the Long Eighteenth Century* (Philadelphia: University of Pennsylvania Press, 2014), 81–89. What appears somewhat different to me about Levinsohn's discussion of the slave trade is its location in the midst of a critique of Christian civilization, demonstrating the superiority of Jewish over Christian ethics. He was not merely identifying with the norms of good Enlightenment discourse in these passages; he was attacking the very hypocrisy and double standards of Christian European society in general. Bloch similarly waxed eloquently about the plight of slaves, but Levinsohn did more than depict their horrible plight. He used the slave trade as a polemical sword against Christian values directed at both Catholics and Protestants.

26. Levinsohn, *Zerubavel*, 2:72. His reference is to Johann Ernst Fabri (1755–1825), the noted German geographer and statistician. Levinsohn consulted Fabri's *Kurzer Abriss der Geographie,* (Halle: Verlag des Waisenhauses, 1785); I have used the 1812 edition where the reference is on p. 215. On Fabri, see Han F. Vermeulen, *Before Boas: The Genesis of Ethnography and Ethnology in the German Enlightenment* (Lincoln: University of Nebraska Press, 2015), 341–42, 445–46.

27. Levinsohn, *Zerubavel*, 2:72–73.

28. These comments appear throughout his works, but see especially Levinsohn, *Zerubavel*, 2:3–70, 74–107; on loving Christians without marrying them, see 4:116.

29. Levinsohn, *Ahiyah Shiloni ha-hozeh*, 117–18.

30. Levinsohn, *Ahiyah Shiloni ha-hozeh*, 118–20.

31. Levinsohn, *Ahiyah Shiloni ha-hozeh*, 121.

32. Levinsohn, *Ahiyah Shiloni ha-hozeh*, 123.

33. Levinsohn, *Ahiyah Shiloni ha-hozeh*, 124–26.

34. Levinsohn, *Ahiyah Shiloni ha-hozeh*, 128.

35. Levinsohn, *Ahiyah Shiloni ha-hozeh*, 68.

36. Levinsohn, *Ahiyah Shiloni ha-hozeh*, 69.

37. Levinsohn, *Ahiyah Shiloni ha-hozeh*, 70.

38. Levinsohn, *Ahiyah Shiloni ha-hozeh*, 71. On Bengel, see Henning Graf Reventlow, *History of Biblical Interpretation*, vol. 4, *From the Enlightenment to the Twentieth Century* (Atlanta: Society of Biblical Literature, 2010), 77–82; Jonathan Sheehan, *The Enlightenment Bible: Translation, Scholarship, Culture* (Princeton, N.J.: Princeton University Press, 2005), 93–117; and Jaroslav Pelikan, "In Memoriam: Johann Albrecht Bengel, June 24, 1687, to November 2, 1752," *Concordia Theological Monthly* 23 (1952): 785–96. On his eschatological calculations, see especially Mark D. Isaacs, "The End-Time Calculation of Johann Albrecht Bengel," *Journal of Unification Studies* 11 (2010), http://www.tparents.org/Library/Unification/Publications/JUS-11-2010/JUS-11-07.htm. On Jung-Stilling (1740–1817), see E. H. B. Neff, "Jung-Stilling, Johann Heinrich," *The Mennonite Encyclopedia* (Scottdale, Pa.: Mennonite Publishing House, 1957), 3:127–28. On Lavater (1741–1801), see Ellis Shookman, ed., *The Faces of Physiognomy: Interdisciplinary Approaches to Johann Caspar Lavater* (Columbia, S.C.: Camden House, 1993); Horse Weigelt, *Johann Kaspar Lavater: Leben, Werk, und Wirkung* (Göttingen: Vandenhoeck & Ruprecht, 1991).

39. Levinsohn, *Ahiyah Shiloni ha-hozeh*, 71.

40. Leipzig, 1863; Warsaw, 1870, 1875, 1878, 1890, 1893; and Vilna, 1901, 1910.

41. See Chapter 1 above, especially note 37.

42. On Zweifel and his ideological affinities with Levinsohn and Fuenn, see Shmuel Feiner, *Milḥemet tarbut: Tenu'at ha-Haskalah ha-Yehudit be-me'ah ha-19* (Jerusalem: Carmel, 2010), 150–80.

43. I have included a sampling of some of the contemporary Christian sources Levinsohn used in composing his two polemical works in an appendix to this book.

CHAPTER 8

1. Most of my information is based on Feiner's studies. See especially Shmuel Feiner, *Milḥemet tarbut: Tenu'at ha-Haskalah ha-Yehudit be-me'ah ha-19* (Jerusalem: Carmel, 2010), 181–230; Shmuel Feiner, *Rashi (Samuel Joseph) Fuenn: Me-Haskalah loḥemet Le-Haskalah mishmeret* (Jerusalem: Merkaz Dinur, 1993) (an anthology of some of Fuenn's Hebrew writings; Feiner's introduction here is identical with the essay in the previous volume); Shmuel Feiner, *Haskalah ve-historia: Toledoteha shel hakarat he-avar Yehudit modernit* (Jerusalem: Machon Zalman Shazar, 1995), 262–72; and Shmuel Feiner, "Fuenn, Shemu'el Yosef," *YIVO Encyclopedia of Jews in Eastern Europe*, www.yivoencyclopedia.org/article.aspx/Fuenn_Shemuel_Yosef. See as well Michael Stanislawski, *Tsar Nicholas I and the Jews: The Transformation of Jewish Society in Russia, 1825–1855* (Philadelphia: Jewish Publication Society of America, 1983); Mordechai Zalkin, *Ba'alot ha-shaḥar: Ha-Haskalah ha-Yehudit be-imperiyah ha-Russit be-me'ah ha-tesha esreh* (Jerusalem: Magnes Press, 2000); and Chanan Gafni, *Peshuta shel Mishnah: Iyyunim be-ḥeker sifrut Ḥazal be-et ha-ḥadasha* (Tel Aviv: Ha-Kibbutz ha-Meuchad, 2011), 73–89.

2. The circumstances leading to the failure of publication of Fuenn's book are described in Feiner, *Milḥemet tarbut*, 202–3. Fuenn's letter to Montefiore was published by Feiner in *Me-Haskalah loḥemet*, 187–88, and compare as well 194–96. Additional details are discussed by Eliyahu Stern in the two essays mentioned in note 4 below. The manuscript of *Darkhei Adonai* is listed as MS Heb. 8390 of the National Library of Israel and is part of the Fuenn archive housed in the library. My sincere thanks to Professor Stern who reproduced for me his copy of the manuscript.

3. See the references in note 1 above.

4. See Eliyahu Stern, "Catholic Judaism: The Political Theology of the Nineteenth-Century Russian Jewish Enlightenment," *Harvard Theological Review* 109, no. 4 (2106): 483–511; and Stern's essay on Fuenn alone, "Paul in the Jerusalem of Lithuania: Samuel Joseph Fuenn's *Paths of God*," in *Talmudic Transgressions: Engaging the Work of Daniel Boyarin*, ed. Charlotte Elisheva Fonrobert et al. (Leiden: Brill, 2017), 407–17.

5. For example, Fuenn cited Levinsohn's *Beit Yehudah* in *Darkhei Adonai*, 1:51. He also cites his *Efes damim* on 1:84 and his *Leḥem shamayim* in 2:61. Jost's history is cited on 1:21, 79, and 93; Rapoport is cited from an essay published in *Bikkurei ha-itim* on the Essenes (1:19) and from a letter published in Ḥayyim Slonimski's *Sefer toledot ha-shamayim* from the first edition of 1838 (1:37). Fuenn cites Luzzatto's *Ohev ger* (Vienna, 1830), a guide to Targum Onkeles on 1:68. He mentions Joseph Salvador's *Histoire des institutions de Mosie et du people Hebreu*, 1828, in 2:33 and 62; Mordechai Markus Friedenthal, *Yesodei ha-dat ikkarei ha-emunah* (Breslau, 1816–18), in 2:51; Ẓevi Hirsch Katznellenbogen [Fuenn relates that Katznellenbogen had shown him a particular responsum of Solomon Ben Adret] in 2:57; Samson Bloch from *Kerem ḥemed* 1 (1833), letter 34, in 2:60; David Nieto from his *Mateh Dan*, 3:16, in 2:111; Joel Brill citing Moses Mendelssohn, in 2:138; and Moses Mendelssohn's *Jerusalem* as well as his introduction

to Menasseh Ben Israel's *Teshu'at Yisrael* mentioned explicitly in 2:70 and 138, but clearly a primary influence on Fuenn in general.

6. Besides these two authors whom Fuenn cites multiple times, he also refers to Christoph Wilhelm Hufeland's *Microbiotica*, a standard medical reference, mentioned by Levinsohn in *Zerubavel*, 7th ed. (Vilna: Isaac Funk, 1901), 22; Fuenn refers to the book in *Darkhei Adonai*, 2:48.

7. Krug is cited by Fuenn in *Darkhei Adonai*, 1:23, 27, 48, 49, 61, 105; 2:21–22. Bossuet/Kramer is cited on 1:78, 80, 82, 115, 118, 119; 2:27. Krug was not a Catholic historian and was also a primary source for Levinsohn. Cramer, for that matter, was not a Catholic either, as discussed in Chapter 7.

8. The *Kritische Geschichte* was first published by Philipp Wilhelm Eichenberg in Frankfurt am Main in 1791. Felix Anton Blau was a professor of theology at Mainz prior to his premature death in 1798. On him, see Jörg Schweigard, *Felix Anton Blau: Frühdemokrat, Theologe, Menschenfreund* (Obernburg am Main: Logo-Verlag, 2007). Other Christian writers cited by Fuenn include Johann Augustus Eberhard (1739–1809) from his *Neue vermischte Schriften* (Halle, 1786) (*Darkhei Adonai*, 1:27); Friedrich Schiller (1759–1805), from his famous aesthetic letters, *Über die ästhetische Erziehung des Menschen in einer Reihe von Briefen*, first published in 1794 (cited in *Darkhei Adonai*, 1:105 and 2:22); Jean-Jacques Rousseau's *Emile*, book 5, first published in 1762 (cited in *Darkhei Adonai*, 2:23); Ludwig Wachler (1767–1838), probably referring to his *Grundriss einer Encyklopädie der theologischen Wissenschaften*, published in 1795 and also cited by Levinsohn in *Ahiyah ha-Shiloni ha-hozeh* (Leipzig: Vollrath, 1864), 115 (cited in *Darkhei Adonai*, 2:55); and Cassiodorus Epiphanius, *Historia Ecclesiastica Triparita* (Frankfurt am Main, 1572), book 5, p. 299 (cited in *Darkhei Adonai*, 2:90). There are a few other Christian sources mentioned very briefly in passing by Fuenn in *Darkhei Adonai*, 2:55–56, when referring to the oppressive history of Christianity, which I cannot yet identify.

9. Fuenn, *Darkhei Adonai*, 1:8.

10. I have already referred to Krug and Eberhard above in the text and in note 8. Jean-Jacques Barthelemy (1716–95), a Jesuit and classical scholar, published his imaginary travel guide in 1788, which had a major impact on the revival of Hellenism in nineteenth-century France and beyond. The French work was soon translated into English and German. Fuenn cited Krug, Barthelemy (in French), and Eberhard in a note on 1:27 of *Darkhei Adonai*.

11. Fuenn, *Darkhei Adonai*, 1:26–30.

12. Fuenn, *Darkhei Adonai*, 1:30.

13. For general background, see Arnaldo Momigliano, "Prologue in Germany," in *Novo contributo alla storia degli classici e del mondo antico* (Rome: Edizioni storia e letteratura, 1992), 543–62; and by the same author, "J. G. Droysen Between Greeks and Jews (1970)," in *Studies in Modern Scholarship*, ed. G. W. Bowersock and T. J. Cornell (Berkeley: University of California Press, 1994), 147–61. See as well the more recent essay of Simon Goldhill, "What Has Alexandria to Do with Jerusalem? Writing the History of the Jews in the Nineteenth Century," *Historical Journal* 59 (2016): 125–51. For the beginning of interest in Philo among sixteenth-century Jews, see Joanna Weinberg, "The Quest for Philo in Sixteenth-Century Jewish Historiography," in *Jewish History: Essays in Honour of Chimen Abramsky*, ed. Ada Rapoport-Albert and Steven Zipperstein (London: Halban, 1988), 163–87.

14. The entire paragraph relies on the essay of Maren R. Niehoff, "Alexandrian Judaism in Nineteenth-Century Wissenschaft des Judentums: Between Christianity and Modernization," in *Jüdische Geschichte in hellenistisch-römanischer Zeit*, ed. Aharon Oppenheimer (Munich: R. Oldenbourg, 1999), 9–28. See also Yaakov Shavit, *Athens in Jerusalem: Classical*

Antiquity and Hellenism in the Making of the Modern Secular Jew (London: Littman Library of Jewish Civilization, 1997); and Deborah Rose Sills, "Re-inventing the Past: Philo and the Historiography of Jewish Identity" (Ph.D. diss., University of California at Santa Barbara, 1984). My thanks to Dr. Ze'ev Strauss for these references.

15. On the latter, see Annette Yoshiko Reed, *Jewish-Christianity and the History of Judaism: Collected Essays* (Tübingen: Mohr Siebeck, 2018), 377–86.

16. This briefly summarizes a draft of the first part of Ze'ev Strauss's forthcoming book *Rabbi Jedidja ha-Alexandri und die Maskilim: Die Wiederentdeckung der Religionsphilosophie des Philon von Alexandria in der osteuropäischen Haskala*, Jewish Thought, Philosophy and Religion 7 (Berlin: De Gruyter, forthcoming 2020). My thanks to Dr. Strauss for allowing me to read this still unpublished work and see below, note 22.

17. See especially Ismar Schorsch, "The Production of a Classic: Zunz as Krochmal's Editor," *Leo Baeck Institute Yearbook* 31 (1986): 281–315. Four brief excerpts of the work were published a year after Krochmal's death in 1841. See *Kerem ḥemed* 5 (1841): 51–98.

18. Shmuel Feiner, "Nineteenth-Century Jewish Historiography: The Second Track," in *Reshaping the Past: Jewish History and the Historians*, ed. Jonathan Frankel, Studies in Contemporary Jewry 10 (Oxford: Oxford University Press, 1994), 30.

19. On Flesch, see Michael L. Miller, *Rabbis and Revolution: The Jews of Moravia in the Age of Revolution* (Stanford, Calif.: Stanford University Press, 2011); and the earlier essay of Leopold Löw, "Abraham und Josef Flesch und ihre Zeit: Ein Beitrag zur neuern Geschichte der Jeschiboth und der jüdischen studien," *Ben Chananya: Monatsschrift für jüdische Theologie* 1 (1858): 409–14, 482–94, 537–50. Flesch's first volume entitled *Min Ha-yoresh divrei elohim* was published by Moses Landau in Prague in 1830. The second volume entitled *Ḥayyei Moshe*, appeared in 1838 from the same publisher. The reference to Rapoport appears on the second page of the author's introduction to the latter work (there is no pagination).

20. See note 5 above. On Rapoport, see Isaac Barzilay, *Shlomo Yehudah Rapoport (Shir) (1790–1867) and His Contemporaries* (Jerusalem: Masada Press, 1969).

21. *Erekh milim* was published by Moses Landau in Prague in 1852. Only the first volume covering the letter "aleph" appeared in the author's lifetime. The entry on Alexandria is found on pp. 98–103; the citation is on p. 101. Of course, this volume appeared after Fuenn had composed his own work. Yet Rapoport's interest in Philo and Alexandria emerged much earlier as his support of Flesch indicates.

22. I am again indebted to Dr. Ze'ev Strauss for discussing his insights with me regarding Flesch and Rapoport, the subject of a soon-to-be-completed chapter of his forthcoming book mentioned above in note 16, which I have not yet read.

23. Jay M. Harris, *Nachman Krochmal: Guiding the Perplexed of the Modern Age* (New York: New York University Press, 1991), especially 206–25. Besides the Harris book, I have consulted the following works in writing this section: Simon Rawidowicz, *Kitvei Rabbi Naḥman Krochmal*, 2nd enl. ed. (London: Ararat, 1961); Yehoyada Amir, "The Perplexity of Our Time: Nachman Krochmal and Modern Jewish Existence," *Modern Judaism* 23 (October 2003): 264–301; Andreas Lehnardt, "Die Entwicklung von Halakha in der Geschichtsphilosophie Nachman Krochmals," *Frankfurter judaistische Beiträge* 29 (2002): 105–26; Andreas Lehnardt, "Nachman Krochmal and Leopold Zunz: On the Influence of the *Moreh nevukhe ha-zeman* on the *Wissenschaft des Judentums*," *European Journal of Jewish Studies* 7 (2013): 171–85. I have not yet seen Yehoyada Amir's new book *Sha'arim le-emunah zerufah: Hithadshut ha-ḥayyim ha-Yehudi'im be-mishnato shel Naḥman Krochmal* (Jerusalem: Magnes Press, 2018).

24. Harris, *Nachman Krochmal*, 225–34; the citation is on p. 228. The best discussion of Savigny's work is by Frederick C. Beiser, "Savigny and the Historical School of Law," in *The German Historicist Tradition* (Oxford: Oxford University Press, 2011), chap. 5. See also Donald R. Kelley, *Historians and the Law in Postrevolutionary France* (Princeton, N.J.: Princeton University Press, 1984). Note also the cogent remarks of Olga Litvak, *Haskalah: The Romantic Movement in Judaism* (New Brunswick, N.J.: Rutgers University Press, 2012), 38–39, on Savigny and Jacob Grimm. On the possible impact of Savigny on Zacharias Frankel, the leader of Conservative Judaism, see Andreas Brämer, *Rabbiner Zacharias Frankel: Wissenschaft des Judentums und konservative Reform im 19. Jahrhundert* (Hildesheim: Olms, 2000), 258–61.

25. Harris, *Nachman Krochmal*, 244, and generally 235–49.

26. Fuenn, *Darkhei Adonai*, 1:2

27. Fuenn, *Darkhei Adonai*, 1:3.

28. Fuenn, *Darkhei Adonai*, 1:4.

29. Fuenn, *Darkhei Adonai*, 1:5–6.

30. Fuenn, *Darkhei Adonai*, 1:6.

31. Fuenn, *Darkhei Adonai*, 1: 8.

32. One other possible parallel between Fuenn and Krochmal's defenses of the rabbinic tradition may be found in their respective treatments of the *aggadah*, the nonlegal, homiletical portions of rabbinic literature. Fuenn, in *Darkhei Adonai*, 1:100–102, offered an analysis of this genre by classifying it within seven distinct categories. Krochmal presented a similar classification but limited it to four categories. As Harris argued, Krochmal's discussion of *aggadah* seems to have left its impression on Rapoport, Weiss, and even Levinsohn. See Harris, *Nachman Krochmal*, 286–95.

33. Stern, "Paul in the Jerusalem of Lithuania"; see note 4 above.

34. See Gershom Scholem, *The Messianic Idea in Judaism and Other Essays on Jewish Spirituality* (New York: Schocken, 1971), especially the first three chapters, pp. 1–77, and the sources he lists. On Sasportas's view, see *Sefer zizit novel Zevi*, ed. Isaiah Tishby (Jerusalem: Mossad Bialik, 1954), 131. On Emden's position, see Leah Gottleib, "*Resen mateh* of R. Jacob Emden: Early and Late Editions" [in Hebrew], in *Be-darkhei shalom: Iyyunim be-hagut Yehudit mugashim le-Shalom Rosenberg*, ed. Benjamin Ish-Shalom (Jerusalem: Beit Morasha, 2006), 302–3. My thanks to Dr. Maoz Kahana for these references. On the modern thinkers, see Hans-Joachim Schoeps, *Paul: The Theology of the Apostle in Light of Jewish Religious History*, trans. H. Knight (Cambridge: Cambridge University Press, 2002); and W. D. Davies, *Torah in the Messianic Age and/or the World to Come* (Philadelphia: Society of Biblical Literature, 1952).

35. David M. Myers and Alexander Kaye, eds., *The Faith of Fallen Jews: Yosef Hayim Yerushalmi and the Writing of Jewish History* (Waltham, Mass.: Brandeis University Press, 2014).

36. On the circulation of McCaul's book throughout the Middle East, see the many references in Leah Bornstein-Makovetsky, "Evangelism," chapter 4 of her forthcoming book on Christian missionary societies and Middle Eastern Jewry. My sincere thanks to her for allowing me to read an unpublished version of this chapter. On the Judeo-Persian translation of *Sefer netivot olam*, see Yaron Harel, "Likkutei amrim in Ladino: On the Polemical Literature of Rabbi Raphael Kassin" [in Hebrew], in *Languages and Literatures of Sephardic and Oriental Jews: Proceedings of the Sixth International Congress for Research on the Sephardi and Oriental Jewish Heritage* (Jerusalem: Bialik Institute, 2009), 110.

37. See Leah Bornstein-Makovetsky, "Evangelism," as well as the following unpublished and published essays written by her: "The Confrontation of the Community of Izmir with the

Phenomena of Modernization and Secularization in the Nineteenth Century," Hebrew typescript; "Jewish Converts to Islam and Christianity in the Ottoman Empire in the Nineteenth Century," in *The Last Ottoman Century and Beyond: The Jews in Turkey and the Balkans, 1808– 1945*, ed. Mina Rozen (Tel Aviv: Tel Aviv University Press, 2002), 83–128; "The Activities of the American Mission Among the Jews of Istanbul, Salonika, Izmir" [in Hebrew], in *Yemei ha-sahar: Perakim be-toledot ha-Yehudim ba-imperiyah ha-Otmanit*, ed. Mina Rozen (Tel Aviv: Tel Aviv University Press, 1996), 273–311; "Protestant Mission Societies and the Jews of Izmir in the Nineteenth Century" [in Hebrew], in *Ha-imperiyah ha-Otmanit: Kovez meḥkarim*, ed. Shaul Regev and Jacob J. Spiegel (Ramat Gan: Bar Ilan University Press, in press); "The Rulings of the Rabbis of Istanbul, Salonika, Izmir Regarding Missionary Protestant Activity in the Nineteenth Century," Hebrew typescript; and the Hebrew typescript of her lecture "The Means of Struggle of the Rabbis of Istanbul, Salonika, and Izmir with the Christian Mission," delivered at a conference in honor of Zvi Zohar, at Bar Ilan University, January 2018. My sincere gratitude to Professor Borstein-Makovetsky for allowing me to read all of these works invaluable in understanding the context of Kassin's own polemics.

38. Palachi is mentioned often in the essays of Bornstein-Makovetsky cited in the previous note, especially "Evangelism," where she previously noticed his meeting with Margoliouth, discussed by me in Chapter 6 above, and in her "The Rulings of the Rabbis." See also Simon Eckstein, *Toledot ha-Ḥabif: Toledot ḥayyav u-fo'alo shel Rabbeinu Ḥayyim Palachi* (Jerusalem: Hoẓa'at ha-Leviyyim, 1999).

39. In addition to the essay mentioned above in note 36, I consulted the following works of Yaron Harel, *Intrigue and Revolution: Chief Rabbis in Aleppo, Baghdad, and Damascus, 1744– 1914*, trans. Jonathan Chipman (Oxford: Littman Library of Jewish Civilization, 2015), chap. 3; "A Spiritual Agitation in the East: The Founding of a Reform Community in Aleppo in 1862" [in Hebrew], *Hebrew Union College Annual* 63 (1992): 19–35; and his Hebrew Lecture on Raphael Kassin in Persia delivered at a conference at Bar Ilan University in honor of Zvi Zohar, January 2018. I want to thank Professor Harel for his kindness in allowing me to read this talk and for providing me with a list of all his publications on Kassin. I have adopted the spelling "Kassin" at the suggestion of Professor Harel.

40. See Harel, "Likkutei amrim," 107, which relies on the essay of Daniel Tsadik, "Nineteenth-Century Shi'i Anti-Christian Polemics and the Jewish Aramaic Nevu'at ha-Yeled," *Iranian Studies* 35 (2004): 5–15.

41. Harel, "Spiritual Agitation in the East," 32–33.

42. Harel, "Spiritual Agitation in the East," 33–35.

43. See note 40 above.

44. Harel, "Spiritual Agitation in the East," 32–33.

45. See, for example Raphael Kassin, *Sefer derekh ha-ḥayyim* (Constantinople, 1848), 34b, 46a.

46. David B. Ruderman, *A Best-Selling Hebrew Book of the Modern Era: The Book of the Covenant of Pinhas Hurwitz and Its Remarkable Legacy* (Seattle: University of Washington Press, 2014), 108–9.

47. Kassin, *Sefer derekh ha-ḥayyim*, 14b–15b.

48. Kassin, *Sefer derekh ha-ḥayyim*, 2b–3b.

49. Kassin, *Sefer derekh ha-ḥayyim*, 6a.

50. Kassin, *Sefer derekh ha-ḥayyim*, 6b–7b.

51. Kassin, *Sefer derekh ha-ḥayyim*, 8a.

52. Kassin, *Sefer derekh ha-ḥayyim*, 8b.

53. Kassin, *Sefer derekh ha-ḥayyim*, 9a–b.

54. Kassin, *Sefer derekh ha-ḥayyim*, 10a–11b.

55. Kassin, *Sefer derekh ha-ḥayyim*, 42b.

56. Kassin, *Sefer derekh ha-ḥayyim*, 43a–b.

57. Kassin, *Sefer derekh ha-ḥayyim*, 44a–45b.

58. Kassin, *Sefer derekh ha-ḥayyim*, 46a.

59. Kassin, *Sefer derekh ha-ḥayyim*, 46b–47b.

60. Kassin, *Sefer derekh ha-ḥayyim*, 48a–50a; the reference to Christian conversions to Islam is on 49b.

61. On Ḥazan, see Zvi Zohar, *Rabbinic Creativity in the Modern Middle East* (London: Bloomsbury, 2013); 203–32; Robert Bonfil, "Al memoriale dell'Università Israelitica di Roma sopra il soggiorno romano di Rabbi Israel Mosè Hazan (1847–1852)," *Annuario di Studi Ebraici* 10 (1984): 29–64; and Jose Faur Ha-Levi, *Ha-Rav Yisrael Moshe Ḥazan: Ha-ish ve-mishnato* (Haifa: Arbel, 1978).

62. Kassin, *Sefer derekh ha-ḥayyim*, 14b–16a.

63. I cite from the original English version of Alexander McCaul, *The Old Paths*, Friday, February 24, 1837. The Hebrew translation of this text is in Kassin, *Sefer derekh ha-ḥayyim*, 16b.

64. The major Jewish responses to McCaul's book are listed above in Chapter 7, note 1.

65. Kassin, *Sefer derekh ha-ḥayyim*, 20b–21b.

66. Kassin, *Sefer derekh ha-ḥayyim*, 27b–28b.

67. Kassin, *Sefer derekh ha-ḥayyim*, 48a–50a, 52a–55b.

68. Kassin, *Sefer derekh ha-ḥayyim*, 59b–61a.

69. See Bornstein-Makovetsky, "Activities of the American Mission," 304–5.

70. Raphael Kassin, *Sefer likkutei amrim* (Izmir, 1855), 4b–6b.

71. Kassin, *Sefer likkutei amrim*, 7b–30b, 31b–64b.

72. Kassin, *Sefer likkutei amrim*, 65b–91b.

73. Kassin, *Sefer likkutei amrim*, 92b.

74. Among the main Jewish responses, listed above in Chapter 7, note 1, only one book preceded Kassin's and only one year earlier: Judah Yudal Middleman, *Sefer netivot emet . . . ve-hu neged ha-ḥibbur Netivot olam* (London, 1847).

AFTERWORD

1. Cited from Jeffrey Cox, *The British Missionary Enterprise Since 1700* (London: Routledge, 2008), 19.

2. See Chapter 1, note 38, above.

APPENDIX

1. On Bellermann, see Michael Meyer, *Judaism Within Modernity: Essays on Jewish History and Religion* (Detroit: Wayne State University Press, 2001), 171–72, 179. Levinsohn cited him in *Zerubavel*, 7th ed. (Vilna: Isaac Funk, 1901), 1:47, 68, 71

2. On Holberg, see Sven Hakon Rossel, ed., *Ludvig Holberg: A European Writer; A Study in Influence and Reception* (Amsterdam: Rodopi, 1994); and Nils Roemer, *Jewish Scholarship and Culture in Nineteenth-Century Germany: Between History and Faith* (Madison: University

of Wisconsin Press, 2005), 17. Levinsohn cited him in *Zerubavel*, 1:20, 48; *Aḥiyah Shiloni ha-ḥozeh* (Leipzig: Vollrath, 1864), 73; *Beit Yehudah* (Warsaw, 1878), 75; *Yemin ẓidki* (Warsaw, 1881), 55.

3. Levinsohn cited Depping in *Zerubavel*, 2:7 and 4:78, 116. On Depping's Jewish history, see Gotthard Deutsch and Max Schloessinger, "Depping, Georges Bernard," *Jewish Encyclopedia*, http://www.jewishencyclopedia.com/articles/5094-depping-georges-bernard.

4. On Mosheim, see J. G. A. Pocock, *Barbarism and Religion*, vol. 5, *Religion: The First Triumph* (Cambridge: Cambridge University Press, 2010), 163–212. Levinsohn cites him in *Zerubavel*, 2:116, 3:10, 51, and 4:130; *Te'udah be-Yisrael* (Vilna, 1828; facsimile ed., Jerusalem: Zalman Shazar Center, 1977), 47.

5. Levinsohn cited Krug in *Zerubavel*, 2:117; *Aḥiyah Shiloni ha-ḥozeh*, 92; *Efes damim* (Warsaw, 1879), 74, 87; and *Beit Yehudah*, 2:8. He referred to Krug's *Handbuch der Philosophie*, 3rd ed. (Leipzig, 1828), 27–29. On Krug and the Jews, see Uwe Backes, "Der Philosoph Wilhelm Traugott Krug: Sein Stellung im volmärzlichen Liberalismus und sein Wirken für die Judenemanzipation in Sachsen," in *Bausteine einer jüdischen Geschichte der Universität*, ed. Stephan Wendehorst (Leipzig: Simon Dubnow Institute, 2006), 483–504.

6. He cited from Samuel von Pufendorf, *Einleitung zu der Historie der vornehmsten Reiche und Staaten, so itziger Zeit in Europa sich befinden* (Frankfurt am Main, 1828), 2:34. On Pufendorf, see Craig L. Carr, ed., *The Political Writings of Samuel Pufendorf* (Oxford: Oxford University Press, 1994); Peter Reill, *The German Enlightenment and the Rise of Historicism* (Berkeley: University of California Press, 1975), 15–22; and Michael Seidler, "Pufendorf's Moral and Political Philosophy," *Stanford Encyclopedia of Philosophy* (2010; rev. 2018), http://plato.stanford .edu/entries/pufendorf-moral/. Levinsohn also cited Pufendorf in *Efes damim*, 73.

7. Levinsohn cited them in *Zerubavel*, 3:68 and 4:38. On Klopstock as a Hebraist, see Ofri Ilany, "Is Judah Indeed the Teutonic Fatherland? The Debate over the Hebrew Legacy at the Turn of the Eighteenth Century," *Naharaim* 8, no. 1 (2014): 34–37.

INDEX

Abrahams, Rachel Beth-Zion Lask, 33, 68, 74, 79
Abravanel, Isaac, 36, 118, 185
Aguilar, Grace, 32–38
Aḥiyah Shiloni ha-ḥozeh, 144, 146, 148–50, 157, 160, 163, 164. *See also* Levinsohn, Isaac Baer
Albo, Joseph, 35–36, 145, 185
Aleppo, 2, 142, 180, 181–83, 192
Alexander, Michael Solomon, 50–51, 92, 102–4, 106
Alexander I, Czar, 154
Alexandria. *See* Philo of Alexandria
Al-Ḥarizi, Judah, 118
American Hebrew and Jewish Messenger, 94
Amsterdam, 118; conversos, 32, 34–35, 124
Astruc, Jean, 56
Augustine of Hippo, *Answer to the Manichean Faustus*, 152
Ayerst, William, 13, 15–16, 22, 28

Bachert, S. J., 29
Baeck, Leo, 6
Bauer, Bruno, 57
Bagdad, 2, 142, 182, 183
Bartal, Israel, 11
Barthelemy, Jean-Jaques, 170
Becker, W., 29, 163
Behr, Alexander, 41
Beit Yehudah, 144, 146, 164, 168. *See also* Levinsohn, Isaac Baer
Bellerman, Johann Joachim, 205
Bendavid, Lazarus, 174
Bengel, Johannes Albrecht, 161–62
Benisch, Abraham. 126–27
Bergfeldt, J. G., 113
Bible, criticism versus inerrancy, 54–66
Bing, Abraham, 41
Blau, Felix Anton, 169

Blayney, Benjamin, 37
Bloch, Samson, 168
Block, Isaac, 53
Bonsen, Baron von, 64
Bornstein-Makovetsky, Leah, 180
Bossuet, Jacques-Bénigne, 151–52, 168–69, 179, 206
Brill, Joel, 168
brit milah (circumcision), 72, 103, 104
Burney, Charles, 130, 135
Burstein, Miriam Elizabeth, 45
Butler, Joseph, 37
Buxtorf, Johannes, 95

Cabbala and Cabbalists, 84–85, 93
Cahen, Samuel, 42
Calmet, Antoine Augustin, 206
Castro, Isaac Orobio de, 32–38
catechisms. *See* Reform Judaism
Catholic-Protestant divide, 7
Charlemagne, 153
Chiarini, Luigi, 69
Chizzuk Emunah. See Troki, Isaac of
Christian-Jews, 122–26
Christian Lady's Magazine, 2, 96, 98, 106. *See also* Tonna, Charlotte Elizabeth
Cohen, missionary to Jews of Smyrna, 116
Cohen, Tobias, 120–21, 185
Colenso, John William, 59–64, 65
Coleridge, Samuel Taylor, 84
Costa, Uriel da, 34–35
Coverdale, Myles, 135
Cramer, Johann Andreas, 151–52, 168, 179, 206
Creizenach, Michael, 174
Czartoryski, Adam, 68

Dähne, August, F., 171
Dalman, G. H., 29

Damascus blood libel, 4–5, 19, 22, 142, 144, 146, 167, 198
Damascus Keter, 128
Danowski, Yozeph, 129. *See also* Suwalki, Poland
Darkhei Adonai. See Fuenn, Samuel Joseph
Darwin, Charles, 55
Davies, W. D., 179
Davis, Nathan, 140
Depping, Georg Bernhard, 206
D'Holbach, Paul-Henri Thiry, Baron, 150, 152
Diderot, Denis, 152
Disraeli, Benjamin, 30, 127, 229n36
Dowson, John, 96
Dublin, 1, 19, 60, 101, 112, 119, 132, 133

Eberhard, Johann Augustus, 170
Eisenmenger, Johann Andreas, 15, 34
Emden, Jacob, 178–79
Endelman, Todd, 11
Essays and Reviews, 55, 57, 61, 64
Etkes, Immanuel, 11, 145
Ewald, Ferdinand Christian, 102, 107, 129

Fabri, Johann Ernst, 154
Feiner, Shmuel, 11, 145, 168, 172
Feuerbach, Ludwig, 57
Finn, Elizabeth, 18, 19, 20–22, 79, 198
Finn, James, 19, 20, 50–54, 117
Flesch, Joseph, 173
Frankel, Jonathan, 4
Frankel, Zacharias, 165, 171, 175
Franklin, Jacob, 78–79, 88–91, 100–101, 110; his relationship with Charlotte Elizabeth Tonna, 96, 101–9, 136
Fredrickson, Paula, 179
Frey, Joseph, 7
Friedenthal, Mordechai Markus, 168
fringes. *See zizit*
Fuenn, Samuel Joseph, 2, 3, 142, 165–80, 199, 202; the parallels to Naḥman Krochmal on the oral law, 171–77; on Philo of Alexandria, 169–73
Fürst, Julius, 37, 93

Galatinus, Petrus, 93
Galchinsky, Michael, 32, 33
Gans, Edward, 174
Geiger, Abraham, 6, 145
Gersonides, Moses, 118

Gesenius, Wilhelm, 36
Gidney, W. T., 11, 14, 18
Gill, John, 15
Gleadle, Kathryn, 45
Gobat, Samuel, 50–54, 129, 132
Goldberg (Margoliouth), Chaja, 112, 120, 131, 230n47
Goethe, Johann Wolfgang, 57
Graetz, Heinrich, 6, 165, 171, 175
Graham, James, 52

Hadoud, Hanna, 53
Ha-Karmel. See Fuenn, Samuel Joseph
Ha-Levi, Judah, 118, 129, 185
Ha-Levi, Obadiah Abraham, 182
Ha-Nagid, Samuel, 118
Harel, Yaron, 181, 182, 183
Harkavy, Abraham, 128
Harris, Jay, 174–75
Hawtrey, C. S., 17
Ḥazzan, Israel Moses, 185, 191
Hebraism, Christian, 18, 199
Hengstenberg, Ernst Wilhelm, 135
Herschell, Ridley Haim, 77–78
Hertz Ben Pinchas, 77
Hoga, Stanislaus, 1, 3, 4, 16–17, 21–22, 38, 67–80, 81, 88, 92, 100, 136, 200, 202; his *Controversy of Zion*, 71–73, 77–79, 80; his *Eldad and Medad*, 67–68, 71, 78; his *Ẓir Ne'eman: The Faithful Missionary*, 73–75, 76; and Jewish emancipation, 76–77
Holberg, Ludvig, 206
Holdsworth, George, 132–34
Horsley, Samuel, 37
Hunt, Holman, 52
Hurwitz, Jacob Isaac, the *hozeh* of Lublin, 69
Hurwitz, Pinḥas, 185

Ibn Ezra, Abraham, 35, 118
Ibn Gabirol, Solomon, 118
Ibn Ḥasdai, Abraham, 118
Ibn Verga, Solomon, 17, 86, 185

Jagodzińska, Agnieszka, 11
Jerusalem, debate over mission to Jewish-Christians in, 47–54, 66, 91–92, 102–3
Jewish-Christian debate, in the nineteenth century, 5–8, 12
Jewish Chronicle, 70, 74, 75, 78, 95
Jewish Intelligence and Monthly Account, 18, 28, 37, 88, 90

Jewish music, 127–28, 135–36, 229n36
Jewish women, 26–28, 34, 42–46, 192–93; in
   comparison with Christian women, 45–46
Johlson, Joseph, 41
Jones, Peter, 119
Josephus, Flavius, 58, 118
Jost, Isaak Markus, 16, 29, 37, 168, 171, 174
Jowett, Benjamin, 55
Jung-Stilling, Johann Heinrich, 161–62

Kabbala Denudata. See Rosenroth, Christian
   Knorr von
Karo, Joseph, 40
Kassin, Raphael, 2, 3, 8, 142, 180–96,
   200–201, 202; his critique of McCaul,
   190–93; his polemical work Sefer derekh ha-
   ḥayyim, 184–93, 195; his polemical work
   Sefer likkutei amrim, 184, 186, 194–96; and
   Reform Judaism, 191–92
Katznellenbogen, Ẓevi Hirsch, 168
Kidder, Richard, 15
Kimḥi, David, 22, 25, 35, 40, 41, 118
Klopstock, Friedrich Gottlieb, 207
Kook, Abraham Isaac ha-Cohen, 68
Kremenetz, 2, 144
Krochmal, Na-77, 179
Krug, Wilhelm Traugott, 168, 169, 170, 179,
   206–7

Labaton, Mordechai Ḥayyim, 182, 183
La Mettrie, Julien Offray de, 149
Lavater, Joyhann Kaspar, 161–62
Lederhendler, Eli, 145
Lee, Samuel, 75
Leeser, Isaac, 94
Leiman, Shnayer Z., 68, 74
Lessing, Gotthold, 57
Levi, David, 22
Levinsohn, Isaac Baer, 2, 3, 29, 142–64, 165,
   167, 168, 179, 199, 200, 202; the chiliastic
   view of McCaul, 159–62; his critique of
   Christianity, 150–54; his critique of slavery,
   153–54, 234n25; on the futility of religious
   polemic, 148–50; on the morality of
   Judaism, 155–59; on the qualifications of a
   rabbinic scholar, 146–48; his use of
   contemporary Christian authors, 205–7.
   See also Zerubavel
Lightfoot, John, 15
Limborch, Philipp van, 15
Liverpool, 90, 100, 112, 113, 119

London, 1, 16, 17, 20, 26, 33, 42, 43, 70, 73,
   84, 90, 91, 107, 113, 131, 163, 192
London Society for the Promotion of Christianity Amongst the Jews, 1, 7, 18, 45,
   48–50, 52–54, 65, 74, 76, 85, 86, 87, 91–92,
   99, 102, 109, 113, 118, 198; Moses Margoliouth's attitude toward, 131, 136–41; its
   opposition to Jewish emancipation, 76–77;
   Stanislaus Hoga's attitude toward, 73–74,
   76–77
Luther, Martin, and Lutherans, 135, 153,
   160–61
Luzzatto, Moses Ḥayyim, 118
Luzzatto, Samuel David, 168

Macgowan, Edward, 51
Maimon, Solomon, 158
Maimonides, Moses, 27, 35, 118, 126, 173, 194
Margoliouth, Chaja. See Goldberg, Chaja
Margoliouth, Moses, 1, 3, 8, 72, 78, 100, 102,
   107, 110–41, 181, 199, 200; his The Anglo-
   Hebrews: Their Past Wrongs and Present
   Grievances, 138–40; his attitude toward the
   London Society for the Promotion of
   Christianity Amongst the Jews, 136–40; his
   connections with family, 120–22; his The
   Curates of Riversdale, 131–36, 138; his The
   Destinies of Israel and the Claims of Hebrew
   Christians upon the Sitting Congress,
   226n61; his The Fundamental Principles of
   Modern Judaism Investigated, 78–79,
   112–19, 136; his love of Jewish music and
   liturgy, 127–28, 135–36, 229n36; his A
   Pilgrimage to the Land of My Fathers,
   119–30
Marks, David Woolf, 21, 39. See also Reform
   Judaism
McCaul, Alexander, 1, 3, 4, 8, 13–66, 102, 104,
   110, 116–17, 137, 142, 147, 150, 153, 163, 167,
   168, 176, 179–80, 184, 187, 189, 192, 196,
   207; author of The Old Paths, 4, 22–28;
   author of Sketches of Judaism and the Jews,
   23, 39–43; being labeled a chiliast, 159–62;
   Isaac Orobio de Castro's polemic, 32–38;
   against emancipation and integration of
   Jews, 36–37, 216n16; his defense of the
   inerrancy of the Bible, 54–66; his denunciation of the rabbis, 23–28; his literalist
   reading of the Old Testament, 10, 54–66;
   his praise of Jewish culture and learning,
   23; his relationships with his subjects,

McCaul, Alexander (*continued*)
   197–201; his relationship with Stanislaus
   Hoga, 68, 74; his wife Mary Clarke Crosth-
   waite, 19; on Jewish-Christians in
   Jerusalem, 47–54; Jewish detractors of, 2; as
   missionary, 10–11
McCaul, Joseph, 49–50, 60, 230n46
McCaul, Samuel, 50, 52–53
McNeile, Hugh, 100–102, 104–5, 114
Mendelssohn, Felix, 127
Mendelssohn, Moses, 3, 39–40, 135, 144, 145,
   149, 158, 168
Metz, 120–21
Meyerbeer, Giacomo, 127, 228n
mezuzah (container holding biblical verses
   affixed to the doorpost), 78, 106, 114
Mezzofanti, Giuseppe Caspar, 132
Milton, John, 207
Mirabeau, Marquis de, 149
missionary: as cultural imperialist, 8–11; his
   personal relations with his subjects,
   197–201
Modena, Leon, 93
Montefiore, Moses, 102, 107, 145, 146, 163,
   167, 191
Monteleone, Benedict, 132–36
Montesquieu, Charles-Louis de Secondat,
   Baron de, 150
Morgan, Homer, 194
Morgan, Thomas, 56
Moses, son of Shneyer Zalman of Lyady, 116
Mosheim, Johann Lorenz von, 206

Nath, Golak, 197
Nathanson, David Ber, 145
Neander, Johann August Wilhelm, 132, 171
Netivot olam, 4, 70, 144, 148, 163, 165, 180,
   184, 186, 187, 191. *See also* Hoga, Stanislaus;
   McCaul, Alexander; *Old Paths*
Newman, John Henry, 53
Newton, Thomas, 37
Nicolayson, John, 51
Nidhei Yisrael. See Fuenn, Samuel Joseph
Nieto, David, 168, 186
Nonnotte, Claude-Adrien, 153

Old Paths, 4, 16, 17, 19, 21, 22–31, 38, 39, 42,
   58, 70, 73, 76, 116, 202; its impact, 28–31;
   on the rabbinic treatment of non-Jews,
   23–25; on the rabbinic treatment of the
   poor, 23, 25–26; on the rabbinic treatment

of women, 26–28. *See also* McCaul,
   Alexander
oral law, tradition: Fuenn and Krochmal's
   defense of, 173–77; Levinsohn's sources of,
   151–53; McCaul's view of rabbinism, 39
Oxlee, John, 2, 3, 75, 76, 77, 81–96, 98–99,
   103–4, 107, 198, 199, 202; his attitude to
   the London Society, 86–96; his *The
   Christian Doctrines of the Trinity and Incarnation*, 82, 84; his *The Mysterious Stranger*,
   84–86; his *Three Letters Humbly Submitted
   to . . . the Lord Archbishop of Canterbury*,
   85–90; his *Three More Letters Humbly
   Submitted to . . . the Lord Archbishop of
   Canterbury*, 85, 90–94, 98

Palachi, Hayyim, 128, 181, 182, 194
Paul, 106, 113 (Saul of Tarsus), 187; suspension
   of halakha in post-messianic era, 178–79
Pearson, John, 15
Peynado, Joseph Rodrigues, 94, 223n3
Philo of Alexandria, 118, 169–73, 178; and his
   central place in Judaism, 170–73; and the
   roots of Christianity, 170. *See also* Fuenn,
   Samuel Joseph
phylacteries. *See tefillin*
Pietism. *See* Bengel, Johannes Albrecht
Pinedo, Thomas de, 35
Pinner, Ephraim Moses, 205
Plato. *See* Fuenn, Samuel Joseph; Philo of
   Alexandria
Porter, Andrew, 9–10
premillennialism, 10
Pufendorf, Samuel von, 207
Pusey, Edward, 53, 132

Rabbenu Gershom, on polygamy, 27, 193
Raikes, Henry, 112–13
Rapoport, Solomon Judah Loeb, 165, 168, 173
Rashi, 118, 124
Reggio, Isaac Samuel, 126
Reform Judaism, 16–17, 21, 22, 38–42, 73, 137,
   182, 184, 185, 191–92, 195; catechisms of,
   41–42. *See also* Marks, David Woolf
Riqueti, Victor de, 149
Rose, Henry, 19
Rosenroth, Christian Knorr von, 17
Rosenthal, Simeon, 51–54
Rosicrucians, and Swedenborgians, 93
Rossi, Azaria dei, 171, 172–73

Rossini, Gioacchino, 127, 229n
Rubenstein, Hilary L., 96

Saadia Gaon, 118, 149
Sabbateans, 178
Said, Edward, 9
Salvador, Joseph, 168
Sanegor. See Zwiefel, Eliezer
Sasportas, Jacob, 178
Savigny, Friedrich Karl von, 174
Schainker, Ellie, 11
Schiller, Friedrich, 57
Schoeps, Hans-Joachim, 179
Scholem, Gershom, 178
Schweid, Eliezer, 145
Scult, Mel, 11
Sefer derekh emet, 184, 187, 194. See also
    Kassin, Raphael
Sefer derekh ha-ḥayyim. See Kassin, Raphael
Sefer likkutei amrim. See Kassin Raphael
Shaḥak, Yaakov, 11
Shevet Jehudah. See Ibn Verga, Solomon
Sketches of Judaism and the Jews, 39–48. See
    also McCaul, Alexander
Spener, Philipp, 57
Spiegel, R. S., 30, 202
Spinoza, Barukh, 158
Stanislawski, Michael, 145
Stanley, Dean Arthur, 64–65
Star of Jacob, 137–38. See also Margoliouth,
    Moses
Stephen, James Fitzjames, 57–59
Stephen, Leslie, 57–58
Stern, Abraham Jacob, 69
Stern, Eliyahu, 11–12, 145, 151–53, 168, 169,
    178, 179
Stockfeld, J., 28–29
Strauss, David Friedich, 57
Suwalki, Poland, 112, 122, 129

Talmud, McCaul's assault on, 4, 22–28. See
    also oral law, tradition
tefillin (phylacteries), 72, 100, 114, 115
teḥinah, 43–44
Te'udah be-Yisrael, 144, 145, 162, 165. See also
    Levinsohn, Isaac Baer
Theodores, Tobias, 75, 76, 81, 92–94, 96
Tindal, Matthew, 56
Toland, John, 56

Tonna, Charlotte Elisabeth, 2, 3, 33, 75, 76,
    81, 92, 96–109, 114, 133, 198, 199, 202; her
    correspondence with Moses Margoliouth,
    104–7, 110; her letter to Michael Alexander,
    102–4; her relationship with Jacob
    Franklin, 100–109; her view of John Oxlee,
    98–99
Tractarianism, accusations of, 53
Tremellius, Immanuel, 135
Troki, Isaac of, 18
Tugenhold, Jacob, 69

Usque, Samuel, 186

Valman, Nadia, 33, 45–46
Vega, Joseph Penso de la, 118
Vilna, 2, 162, 163, 165, 167, 178, 180
Voice of Jacob, 75, 78, 88, 90, 96, 106, 110, 126,
    136, 138. See also Franklin, Jacob
Voice of Israel, 77
Volney, Constantin François de Chassebœuf,
    comte de, 150, 152
Voltaire (François-Marie Arouet), 149, 150, 153

Wagenseil, Johann Christoph, 15
Warmekros, Heinrich Ehrenfried, 152
Warsaw, 1, 16, 17, 19, 20, 43, 69, 70, 162, 163
Weiss, Isaac Hirsch, 165, 175
Wessely, Naphtali, 40, 118
Whatley, Richard, 132
Wieland, Christoph Martin, 57
Williams, Rowland, 57–58, 64
Wolf, Immanuel, 171

Yellin, Avinoam, 128
Yoḥanan Ben Zakkai, 170
Yuval, Israel, 5

Zalkin, Mordechai, 11
Zamosh, Israel of, 158
Zante, Abraham Ha-Cohen of, 135
Zbytkower, Berek, 69
Ze'enah u Re'enah, 44
Zerubavel, 29, 144, 146–48, 162, 163, 164. See
    also Levinsohn, Isaac Baer
Zir Ne'eman: The Faithful Missionary, 16–17.
    See also Hoga, Stanislaus
ziẓit (fringes), 72, 100, 104, 105, 106, 114, 115
Zunz, Leopold, 135, 172
Zwiefel, Eliezer, 142, 163, 165

ACKNOWLEDGMENTS

This book emerged serendipitously and unintentionally from my interest in following up a curious footnote reference in a previous book of mine. When I eventually identified Alexander McCaul and his associates, I became quickly engaged in a subject way beyond my usual chronological reach as a historian, but closely connected to two of my long-held interests: the history of Jewish-Christian relations and the study of those individuals with multiple religious loyalties whom I had previously labeled as those with "mingled identities." It is my hope that, despite my limitations as a historian of the nineteenth century, I have done justice to my subject in drawing from my larger perspective as a historian of Jewish-Christian encounters in earlier centuries. It has been, no doubt, an enriching experience for me to probe the lives and thoughts of the individuals I have uncovered and to link them in a broad conversation across faiths, time periods, and regions.

As in the past I have incurred many debts. I began to think seriously about the subject of this book during my semester fellowship at the Institute for Advanced Study of the Central European University, Budapest, in the spring of 2015. From Budapest, I went to London to take up residency for a month as the first Scholar-in-Residence of the Jewish Historical Society of England. During that time I was able to work regularly in the wonderful archives of the London Society for the Promotion of Christianity Amongst the Jews at the Bodleian Library at Oxford and at the British Library in London; and thanks to the remarkable initiative of Professor Piet Van Boxel, then president of the Jewish Historical Society, I also participated in a conference on converts and missionaries in nineteenth-century England organized by the society. This led to my first publication on McCaul, in *Jewish Historical Studies: Transactions of the Jewish Historical Society of England*.

I continued to work on this project during spring research leaves from the University of Pennsylvania while serving as an Alexander van Humboldt

Research Award Recipient at Goethe University, Frankfurt am Main, Germany (2016–19). I am most grateful to the Humboldt Foundation for its generous support of my work. My sincere thanks as well to my gracious hosts at Goethe University: Professors Christian Wiese, Elizabeth Hollander, and Rebekka Voss. I spent several additional months as a senior fellow at the Maimonides Center for Advanced Studies, University of Hamburg, Germany. I am grateful to its director Professor Giuseppe Veltri for his wonderful support and hospitality. During my residency at this latter institution, I organized a colloquium in 2016 on several nineteenth-century converts, including Stanislaus Hoga, who appears in this book. This ultimately resulted in a publication I edited called *Converts of Conviction: Faith and Skepticism in Nineteenth-Century European Jewish Society* (Berlin: De Gruyter, 2017).

In the spring of 2017, I was invited, at the initiative of Professor Andrea Schatz of the Department of Theology and Religious Studies, King's College, London, to give the F. D. Maurice Lectures on Alexander McCaul and his associates. This was the same department at which McCaul taught in the mid-nineteenth century. Needless to say, this was an exciting opportunity, as was a very special tour of what had been Palestine Place and Christ Church, Spitalfields, led by Professor Nadia Valman. What had been a project relying on books and documents was concretized and enlivened in a way I could not have imagined.

During the past five years, I have lectured on aspects of this book before highly stimulating audiences at Princeton University; the Central European University, Budapest; Columbia University; the Goethe University, Frankfurt; the University of Antwerp; the University of Mainz; the Ludwig Maximilian University, Munich; the Jagiellonian University, Cracow; the University of Hamburg; Zentrum für Jüdische Studien Berlin-Brandenburg; the University of North Carolina; the University of Amsterdam; the Ashkenazic Academic Forum, Jerusalem; the Frei Universität, Berlin; the University of Düsseldorf; Oxford University; and the University of Lisbon. My sincere thanks to all my colleagues who invited me and encouraged me in pursuing this project.

Several chapters or parts of chapters of this book are based on essays I have previously published. An earlier version of Chapter 1 appeared as "Towards a Preliminary Portrait of an Evangelical Missionary to the Jews: The Many Faces of Alexander McCaul (1799–1863)," *Jewish Historical Studies: Transactions of the Jewish Historical Society of England* 47 (2015): 48–69. Part of Chapter 2 draws on "Reading Orobio in Nineteenth-Century

England: The Missionary Alexander McCaul's 'Israel Avenged,'" in *Isaac Orobio: The Jewish Argument with Dogma and Doubt*, edited by Carsten Wilke (Berlin: De Gruyter, 2018), 105–13. Chapter 4 is based on "The Intellectual and Spiritual Journey of Stanislaus Hoga: From Judaism to Christianity to Hebrew Christianity," in *Converts of Conviction: Faith and Skepticism in Nineteenth-Century European Jewish Society*, edited by David B. Ruderman (Berlin: De Gruyter, 2017), 41–53. Finally, Chapter 6 draws heavily from "Moses Margoliouth: The Precarious Life of a Scholarly Convert," *Jewish Quarterly Review* 109 (2019): 84–117.

Richard Cohen, Shmuel Feiner, and Iris Idelson-Shein read the entire manuscript of this book and offered thoughtful and challenging comments on every chapter. I am most indebted to them for this extraordinary commitment to me and my work. In addition, Arthur Kiron, Todd Endelman, Ellie Schainker, David Katz, Agnieszka Jagodzińska, Benjamin Nathans, and Carsten Wilke read parts of this book and offered their wonderful expertise, for which I am most grateful. I also want to thank Professor Jagodzińska for sharing the image that I eventually chose for the jacket of this book.

I am indebted to Jerome Singerman, Senior Humanities Editor at the University of Pennsylvania Press, for his engagement with this project, for our collaboration over the years in publishing books of Judaic scholarship, and for his friendship. I offer my sincere gratitude to Erica Ginsburg, managing editor at the University of Pennsylvania Press, who significantly contributed to the preparation of this book. I also want to thank Jennifer Shenk for her skillful copyediting.

My sincere thanks go to the family of Eleanor Meyerhoff Katz and Herb Katz for their support of this book and so much more. They have been wonderful collaborators over the course of much of my career on behalf of Judaic studies. It has been a great privilege to work with them and come to know them.

As always, my wife, Phyllis, has been a constant support and delight. I could not have written one word of this book or any of the others without her loving and devoted partnership. The book coincides with our fiftieth wedding anniversary, which I celebrate with utmost joy and gratitude. The book is dedicated to our dear grandchildren: Jonah, Gabriel, Sydney, Ella, and Caleb. It is my hope that they may notice this book and appreciate it one day, as the work of their loving grandfather, who takes pride in their wonderful lives and accomplishments.